W9-CIR-305
070 042 676

Getting Choice Right

Getting Choice Right

Ensuring Equity and Efficiency in Education Policy

JULIAN R. BETTS AND TOM LOVELESS
EDITORS

BROOKINGS INSTITUTION PRESS
Washington, D.C.

1775 Massachusetts Avenue, N.W., Washington, D.C. 20036
www.brookings.edu

Library of Congress Cataloging-in-Publication data

Getting choice right : ensuring equity and efficiency in education policy / Julian R. Betts and Tom Loveless, editors.
p. cm.
Summary: "Analyzes the potential costs and benefits of school choice and discusses policy mechanisms that would maximize its benefits while mitigating its social costs, specifically in terms of racial and religious issues and the promotion of civic values"—Provided by publisher.
Includes bibliographical references and index.
ISBN-13: 978-0-8157-5332-2 (cloth : alk. paper)
ISBN-10: 0-8157-5332-2 (cloth : alk. paper)
ISBN-13: 978-0-8157-5331-5 (pbk. : alk. paper)
ISBN-10: 0-8157-5331-4 (pbk. : alk. paper)
1. School choice—United States. 2. School choice—Economic aspects—United States. 3. Educational equalization—United States. 4. Education and state—United States. I. Betts, Julian R. II. Loveless, Tom, 1954– .
LB1027.9.G475 2005
379.1'11—dc22 2005027078

9 8 7 6 5 4 3 2 1

The paper used in this publication meets minimum requirements of the American National Standard for Information Sciences—Permanence of Paper for Printed Library Materials: ANSI Z39.48-1992.

Typeset in Adobe Garamond

Composition by Cynthia Stock
Silver Spring, Maryland

Printed by R. R. Donnelley
Harrisonburg, Virginia

Contents

1

School Choice, Equity, and Efficiency

JULIAN R. BETTS AND TOM LOVELESS

In 2001 the Brookings Institution initiated the National Working Commission on Choice in K–12 Education, chaired by Paul Hill. With funding from the Bill and Melinda Gates Foundation and the Annie E. Casey Foundation, the commission worked over several years to study school choice in the United States. This book evolved from the deliberations of that commission. It analyzes the potential costs and benefits of school choice and the mechanisms that policymakers can adopt to maximize the benefits of choice while mitigating its risks.

This approach may seem unusual given that current public debate in the United States is often focused on the more elemental question of whether school choice is "good" or "bad." Although commission members had a wide range of views on school choice, they unanimously agreed that the debate over school choice needed to move beyond the issue of whether parents should be allowed to choose a school for their children. The commission report recognizes the reality that school choice in the United States is here to stay and is likely to grow.[1] In this context, the most important policy question is, How can we implement school choice in a way to maximize the benefits while mitigating the potential costs?

Indeed, the question of school choice is not an "if" or a "when." We have always had school choice in the United States, through the right of parents to send their child to a private school and through the ability of parents to pick a public school for their child by choosing where to live. Clearly, affluent parents have typically been the main beneficiaries of these forms of school choice.

In recent decades new forms of school choice have arisen that have fundamentally changed the education landscape. In many cases these new mechanisms have provided less affluent families with their first taste of school choice. The busing efforts beginning in the 1960s sought to desegregate schools, often under court order. Magnet schools sought to provide specialized schools while at the same time desegregating districts. Many of these programs, or variants, survive today.

More recently, charter schools, which are exempt from much of a state's education code, have sprung up in most states. Another program is open-enrollment programs, which make open seats at a school available to students who live outside the local attendance area. In a handful of cities and states, students are eligible to receive vouchers, which they can use toward tuition at a school of their choice.

Supporters of school choice point to several strong arguments in its favor. First, proponents argue, increased competition among schools for students will force schools to operate more efficiently in order to survive. Second, the newer forms of choice level the playing field in favor of less affluent families. Third, decentralized providers of education services better meet the diverse needs of students than does a monolithic public school system.

Ironically, one of the main benefits of school choice espoused by its proponents—increased variety—is also seen by opponents of choice as one of its greatest weaknesses. Opponents worry that school choice will undermine the notion of the common school, that is, the melting pot of shared educational and cultural experiences supposedly provided by public schools. Others fear that school choice will resegregate schools. A third concern is that choice will hurt students who are left behind in failing schools. These concerns deserve serious study.

The essays in this volume assess the basic mechanics of school choice, with a focus on the question of how, if the nation decides to expand choice, it might do so in a way that will benefit students while reducing the social costs. The first part of the book studies lessons for the design of school choice emanating from the economic theory of markets and from practical experience. The essays describe what policies promote both a vigorous demand for and an adequate supply of education choices. Because opponents of choice have raised many valid concerns about the impact of choice on the distribution of education opportunities, the second part of the book examines some related concerns. These range from the impact on students who are left behind in failing schools, to the impact of choice on racial integration, the complex and sometimes nasty politics of school choice, and the implications of choice for the civic engagement of tomorrow's adult population.

Designing School Choice

How should choice systems be designed so as to squeeze the most benefit from a preset education budget? Economic theory, with careful application to the case of schooling, is informative on this point. Similarly, observation of the real-world operation of the demand and supply sides of the market for education yields policy prescriptions.

The Economic Case

Some of the fundamental arguments in favor of allowing school choice derive from economic models of how markets function. Economic theory, backed by a large number of empirical studies of markets for goods and services, argues that the more competition there is to supply goods or services to a market, the better off consumers will be. Many economists, beginning with the Nobel Laureate Milton Friedman in 1955, argue that the American norm of requiring parents to send their child to the nearest public school is economically inefficient because it prohibits competition among schools.[2]

In chapter 2, Julian Betts provides an overview of the lessons provided by economic theory for the design of school choice. The chapter makes several contributions. It discusses the benefits to consumers from a market that is "perfectly competitive" relative to a market that is served by a single monopoly provider. The theory has direct applications to public education, because a school district that strictly limits a family's choice of school to the family's neighborhood is in effect a monopolist. In contrast, a system that affords families a genuine choice from a menu of public (and perhaps even private) schools would generate competition among schools for students. In the case of perfect competition, in which a large number of schools compete for students, less efficient schools would cease to exist, increasing the effectiveness of each dollar spent on education. Theory predicts that under perfect competition no change could be made to the allocation of education dollars that would improve the welfare of one or more students without decreasing the welfare of one or more other students. In addition, a greater variety of schools would spring up to cater to the heterogeneous needs of different students, providing a rich array of services that a single monopoly provider could not hope to imitate.

Opponents of school choice often question, and even mock, the relevance of the economic theory of markets to school choice. According to this line of thinking, education is not a homogeneous commodity that can be provided by a huge number of suppliers. Further, children are not widgets. And just what, exactly, does it mean that the least efficient "firms" (schools, in our case) should be allowed to go out of business? All of these criticisms hold some merit.

Betts discusses these and several other ways in which school choice is likely to fall short of perfect competition. In each case, he offers policy prescriptions to reduce these problems. In addition, it is crucial to understand that the efficiency benefits of competition do not disappear if a market is not perfectly competitive. As the chapter emphasizes, there is a continuum between the myth of a completely monopolistic district at one extreme and a perfectly competitive school choice system at the other extreme. In general, students and their families will be better off with more, not less, competition.

Although perfect competition can improve the efficiency of the provision of goods or services in a market, society cares about equity as well as efficiency. Indeed, one of the most prevalent concerns about expanding school choice is that it would further widen the gap between "have" and "have-not" families. Again, economic theory provides some important insights. Competitive markets can produce a range of efficient outcomes, both equitable and inequitable. What determines the outcome is the initial allocation of "buying power" among families. This has important practical implications. Betts studies these in some detail and outlines a number of potential policies that could level the playing field. Examples include both lottery systems with geographic or other quotas designed to ensure access to the best schools for the disadvantaged and voucher schemes that give schools a financial incentive to enroll educationally disadvantaged students.

Supply and Demand

All choice systems depend on parents choosing schools. In chapter 3, Laura Hamilton and Kacey Guin analyze the demand side by looking at how families make such choices. The topic is crucial. The effectiveness of choice in allowing good schools to flourish and bad schools to go out of business hinges on parents making sound choices. Moreover, schools serve both public and personal interests. If parental choices are based on personal interests at the expense of public ones, the public benefits that schools provide may diminish.

Hamilton and Guin conclude that the literature is consistent in pinpointing academic quality as the top criterion for why parents say they choose a particular school. The situation is less clear when it comes to studies of how parents act rather than what they say. Several studies show, for example, that the racial composition and socioeconomic status of charter schools appears to matter more when choosing schools than parents let on in surveys of preferences. Parents may be responding to surveys with socially acceptable answers rather than expressing their true reasons for selecting schools. Or they could be using demographic characteristics as proxies for school quality. Having good information appears essential for parents who are choosing schools. Hamilton and Guin call for a series of demonstration programs to provide high-quality information to parents, both to facilitate wise choice making and to allow for more research on the matter.

In addition to policies that empower families to choose, or "demand," nonlocal schools, it is essential that an adequate supply of schools be available to meet this demand. Chapter 4, by Betts, Dan Goldhaber, and Larry Rosenstock, studies the supply side of school choice. The chapter reasons that because parents will want to send their children to a school that is not far away, even a well-developed market for school choice would probably resemble monopolistic competition. In this situation, monopoly-like schools have some power either to set the cost of education holding constant school quality or, more realistically, to set the quality that they will provide for a given revenue per pupil. However, more schools will open up in areas dominated by one or a few schools to the point at which new schools would find it unprofitable to enter. This benefits local students by increasing their number of choices while increasing the quality of schooling that can be obtained for each education dollar spent by society.

The chapter then considers the many factors that are likely to influence the supply of schools. Funding of schools of choice is perhaps the most important form of regulation to consider. In practice, most new choice programs have not received adequate funding. Some of the voucher plans put forth across the nation have called for vouchers that would not come close to paying for tuition at the better private schools, which raises concerns that vouchers might in the end prove a sop to well-heeled families that have already enrolled their children in elite private schools. Charter schools provide a second example of the difficulties imposed by inadequate financing.

Charter schools often have to fund the building of a school campus through nongovernmental sources, because the funding formulas do not take this need into account. Further, in many instances charter schools often receive less funding per average daily attendee than regular public schools. This does not seem to be an oversight so much as an actively made political decision. Indeed, when the National Working Commission on Choice in K–12 Education issued its main report, its call to equalize funding between schools of choice and regular public schools was opposed by one of the main national teachers' unions, the American Federation of Teachers. As *Education Week* reporter Caroline Hendrie wrote: "The notion that alternatives to regular public schools should receive funding on a par with district-managed schools is 'pie in the sky,' said Bella Rosenberg, an assistant to AFT President Sandra Feldman."[3]

The decision to create a new school is a very dynamic process that is based not only on current policy but also on *beliefs* about the future policy and funding environment. In practice, school operators face much uncertainty—legal, regulatory, and financial. Taking examples mainly from the case of charter schools, the chapter points out that potential school operators are less likely to open up a school knowing that in recent years some state legislatures have changed the law governing charter schools with little notice and that states and individual chartering districts have similarly sometimes altered their agreements to support charter schools financially. These uncertainties, plus the added uncertainty that a charter school may not have its charter renewed, make it extremely difficult for charter schools to borrow money to build facilities. This puts the charter school movement at a distinct disadvantage vis-à-vis regular public schools, which typically benefit from public bond issues to cover capital expenses.

The chapter concludes with recommendations for policy reforms that could enhance the supply of new schools in the face of these many uncertainties.

Inside the Black Box

In chapter 5, Frederick M. Hess and Tom Loveless examine the operation of schools under choice. The authors liken school choice to a black box, referring to the failure of both critics and supporters to specify the mechanisms producing choice's purported effects on student achievement—whether one believes the outcomes of choice are positive or negative. Choice is not an educational program in the sense of promulgating a new approach to instruction—a particular way of teaching reading or math, for example. Schools of choice may be all over the map in their handling of curriculum and instruction. Indeed, supporters claim heterogeneity as a benefit of choice—that choice regimes would stimulate diverse approaches to important aspects of schooling in order to satisfy diverse consumer preferences.

Surely, Hess and Loveless argue, some of these approaches will prove to be more effective than others. If that is true, then the effects of choice may be confounded with the success or failure of particular practices at the schools parents choose—that is, the practice, not the choice itself, may be producing the effect. The key to replicating successful systems of choice or to importing lessons from choice schools into traditional public schools, then, rests on knowing precisely what it is inside the black box that is producing the benefits. Simply making a choice does not increase student learning. Hess and Loveless analyze how in choice schools school structure, student population, and classroom practices affect outcomes.

School Choice and Social Inequality

Given that competition can lead to all sorts of "efficient" outcomes, which vary dramatically in terms of the distribution of outcomes for students, it is important to be concerned about social equity. The second section of the book studies the impact that a widespread school choice program might have on nonchoosers, offers new thoughts and evidence on the impact of school choice on racial integration, examines the complex politics surrounding school choice, and closes with an analysis of whether the decentralization of decisions about how to educate children will reduce social cohesion by reducing young people's commitment to shared civic values.

Leaving Nonchoosers Behind?

In chapter 6, Dan Goldhaber, Kacey Guin, Jeffrey R. Henig, Frederick M. Hess, and Janet A. Weiss discuss whether school choice will academically help or harm students who do not exercise their choice to attend other than a local school. The theoretical issues here are themselves nuanced, but again, the devil is in the details. As the authors state: "We believe that this debate will be far more useful when it focuses on the policy design of the choice system itself."

The theoretical argument that nonchoosers will benefit from school choice has multiple facets. The basic theory of competition suggests that providing consumers with choice will benefit all consumers by forcing less efficient schools to adopt better teaching methods and curricula to prevent loss of students to more efficient schools. In the extreme, this competition for students will also drive the least efficient providers out of business altogether. In practical terms, this means that badly run schools will be shut down or taken over by those who have better ideas on how to teach children.

There are several other sources of potential benefits to nonchoosers. Should choice lead to greater homogeneity among students who choose to stay at underperforming schools, then these schools might be better able to tailor teaching methods to help these students. A separate mechanism for choice to help nonchoosers operates through political channels. The authors speculate that if choice fosters voter confidence that the public school system is spending resources wisely, it could increase support for higher school spending. Such increased spending could benefit nonchoosers and choosers alike.

The authors also delineate reasons why, in theory, expanded school choice could lower educational quality. One concern is that the cost of operating a school that has lost, for example, half its students through choice programs will cost more than half as much to run than if it were operating at full capacity. This is because many costs such as administration, heating, and lighting are relatively fixed. Second, increased regulatory oversight could reduce funding available for the classroom. Both of these arguments suggest that all students, including nonchoosers, could be hurt by these added costs. Some of the authors' other concerns suggest an especially negative impact on nonchoosers. Chief among these is the idea that choice, by inducing outflows of talented students, could hurt the quality of the student peer group at underperforming schools. This could hurt the academic achievement of those students left behind, based on a growing body of evidence suggesting that students learn from one another.

Goldhaber and co-authors provide a menu of policies that administrators can implement to improve the impact of choice on nonchoosers. For instance, schools that lose students should receive timely notice of how many students have opted out and which schools they have chosen. Otherwise, how will failing schools know what other schools to emulate?

In addition, the authors tackle the ethically difficult question of whether to starve an underperforming school of money or to give it additional funds. They reason that the key issue is whether an underperforming school that loses a student should lose the marginal cost of educating that one additional student, or to lose more or less than this amount of funding. To give these schools a chance to reform and adjust, the authors argue for removing less than the marginal cost of educating the student who left "so that the school will actually have slightly more to spend on each remaining student as school administrators face the initial challenge of responding to market signals." However, this would be a rather perverse incentive to provide to the school in the long run. Thus, they argue, eventually the school should be penalized by more than the marginal cost.

School Choice and Racial Integration

Historically, some of the most bitter fights related to school choice occurred in the 1960s and 1970s, when courts ordered busing in many districts as a means to desegregate schools racially. In chapter 7, Brian Gill provides a thoughtful commentary on school choice viewed as a means to increase racial and socioeconomic integration in schools. He argues that policymakers who promote school integration should think carefully about their goals before designing a school choice program. For example, is integration by race the sole objective, or should we also be concerned about gender and socioeconomic integration? Similarly, should integrationists be concerned more about the racial balance *among* schools or *within* schools? If the main goal of integration is to increase social contact among socioeconomic and racial groups, then policymakers must also think about how to reduce segregation across classrooms in a school.

Although Gill's chapter argues that "external factors" such as families' preferences can greatly influence whether school choice helps or hinders integration, there do remain many policy levers that can improve the chances that a school choice program will increase integration. For example, a school voucher program that provides each family with a voucher that covers only a fraction of typical private school costs would probably exacerbate racial and socioeconomic segregation. A partial subsidy such as this would leave less affluent parents unable to afford many local private schools. Instead, the main beneficiaries would be parents who were likely to send their children to private schools without the subsidy. On the other hand, a targeted voucher that provides generous subsidies only to less affluent groups could integrate both the private and public school sectors if student flows into private schools caused the percentage of public school students who are nonwhite to fall and the corresponding percentage in private schools to rise.

Gill lists a number of factors that policymakers should consider in designing a school choice program with integration in mind. These factors include admissions, funding mechanisms, the supply of schools, and the provision of adequate information to all families.

Just as policymakers need to be clear on why they want school choice to increase integration, researchers need to exercise care in measuring the impact of school choice on integration. Gill argues that many past attempts to examine the impact of choice on integration do not answer the right question. For instance, if administrators seek to increase contacts among social groups, researchers should then measure integration at the classroom level rather than the school level. Such analysis has been rare, in part because of inadequate data. Other problems Gill outlines include inappropriate selection of comparison schools against which to compare schools offering choice, and inadequate information on how school choice programs induce flows of students between the private and public school sectors. He gives the example of a new public magnet school that might look less integrated than other public schools but that drew many nonminority students out of private schools, thus serving to integrate both the public and private school sectors.

In chapter 8, Karen E. Ross studies how charter schools in Michigan have altered racial integration in the regular public schools. Michigan is well worth studying because the number of its charter schools has grown rapidly compared to most other states. In addition, black-white segregation is high in Michigan's schools. Ross asks a series of related questions. First, how does the racial mix at charter schools compare to the mix in nearby regular public schools? Second, do charter schools locate in districts in a way designed to attract mainly white students, thereby perhaps exacerbating segregation in the regular public schools? Third, in districts that have attracted charter schools, has racial segregation in the regular public schools increased or decreased over time?

In Michigan's charter schools, 47 percent of students are black, compared to a mere 17 percent in regular public schools in that state. This huge discrepancy can be explained almost completely by the decisions of charter school operators to open schools in predominantly black neighborhoods. Ross proves this by comparing charter school enrollment to the enrollment at regular public schools within a two-mile radius and finding highly comparable racial mixes. Similarly, the chapter shows that charter schools are much more likely to spring up in districts that already have highly segregated schools and that these areas tend to have greater proportions of black and Latino students than districts that do not attract charter schools. Taken together, these findings provide powerful evidence that in Michigan charter operators on the whole aim to serve nonwhite students, which contradicts the theory that charter schools will skim off affluent (and typically white) students.

Finally, the chapter examines trends in racial segregation in public school districts between 1990 and 2000 and asks whether the arrival of charter schools exacerbated or reduced racial segregation in the regular public schools over this period. The results are mixed, and in many cases no significant link appears. In some districts in which charter schools' enrollment share surpasses the median of 7 percent, black and Hispanic isolation appears to have increased over the decade, although white isolation fell somewhat. In spite of elaborate demographic controls in her models, Ross cautions that it is not possible to know the causal mechanism behind these patterns. Put differently, if charter schools had not been created in the 1990s would these districts have become more segregated—at least in terms of black and Hispanic isolation—anyway?

The Politics of School Choice

In chapter 9, Jeff Henig asks why the politics of school choice are so divisive. Henig acknowledges that ideological differences and interest group politics both play roles. But tensions run deeper. Henig draws a distinction between pragmatic and systematic privatization. He explains that proposals for seemingly pragmatic choice run into stern opposition, in part, because opponents fear that modest forms of privatization could unleash forces that ultimately undermine democratic control over schooling. In the first half of the essay, Henig explains why this fear may be overblown. Inherent in American political institutions is the assurance that change will be incremental, subject to countless veto points, and governed by divided power. Moreover, the public school system, as Henig points out, already offers parental choice in the form of magnet schools, charter schools, inter- and intra-district choice, and the like. In 1999 about 14 percent of children in the public school system attended schools that parents had chosen.

So is opposition to choice unreasonable? Not at all. In the middle part of the essay, Henig discusses the idea that "when there is a prospect that the resulting changes may erode, in ways that are not readily reversible, the basic capacity of public institutions to take the measure of and effectively act for the public interest, there are good reasons to take note and take care." In particular, Henig believes that choice could weaken support among three key constituencies that traditionally support spending on public schools: loyally Democratic African Americans and Hispanics, by exploiting political fissures in minority communities; conservative Jewish voters who want to save Jewish private schools; and homeowners, by weakening the link between schools and property value. Henig concludes the essay by holding out pragmatic privatization as having the greatest potential for offering common ground to proponents and opponents of school choice. But with highly mobilized interest groups and ideological rancor governing the contemporary choice debate, it is doubtful, Henig admits, for common ground to be found any time soon.

School Choice and Civic Engagement

One concern about a widespread system of school choice is that balkanization will result, in the end weakening the ability of the K–12 sector to impart desired civic values to the nation's youth. This concern seems particularly relevant in the case of voucher programs that allow students to attend private schools. In the United States, the vast majority of private schools are religious schools. In chapter 10, Patrick J. Wolf examines school choice and the inculcation of civic values. Public schools occupy a unique place in American society as institutions responsible for handing down the legacy of democracy from one generation to the next. Supporters of school choice argue that this reputation is largely a myth and that private schools are equally adept at preparing good citizens. Wolf examines the empirical evidence comparing public and private schools in teaching civic values and lists seven values in order from the most studied to the least studied: political tolerance, voluntarism, political knowledge, social capital, political participation, civic skills, and patriotism.

Wolf finds evidence supporting the argument that schools of choice are just as effective as public schools in teaching civic values. Of the nineteen studies he reviews, only one uncovered negative results for private schools. The bulk of the studies are neutral to positive. Notably, most of the positive studies are of Catholic schools or Latino students. When Wolf removes studies involving Catholic schools or Latinos from the review, the positive effect is less pronounced. The conclusion remains, however, that research does not support the notion that private schooling undermines the teaching of civic values. As Wolf puts it, "The statistical record thus far suggests that private schooling and school choice rarely harms and often enhances the realization of the civic values that are central to a well-functioning democracy."

Closing Thoughts

As so vividly described in the chapter by Jeffrey Henig, the politics of school choice has brought forth some strong claims by both sides about the likely advantages and disadvantages of moving to a more widespread system of school choice. To believe the strongest proponents, school choice will make all but a few special interests, such as teachers' unions, better off. In particular, it will empower parents living in the nation's inner cities to choose a better school for their children.[4] In contrast, opponents of choice voice concerns that widespread choice will increase the variance in school quality, often to the detriment of less affluent families, while resegregating the nation's schools both racially and socioeconomically.

As is so often the case in public policy, the truth is likely to lie somewhere between the claims made by parties on the two extremes of the debate. School choice by itself is not inherently good or bad. Rather, the ability of school choice to improve both efficiency and equity in the nation's schools hinges upon a number of key policy decisions. As the following chapters show, the flow of information to parents, the mechanisms society provides to induce parents to engage in choosing the ideal schools for their children, the regulatory and funding framework that will influence the supply of schools, and the financial and regulatory incentives that will be given to choice schools to encourage racial and socioeconomic integration all play key roles. Should society decide to move further toward a universal system of school choice, it should do so armed with full knowledge of the potential benefits, the potential risks, and the policy options available to mitigate those risks. This book represents one step in that direction.

Notes

1. National Working Commission on Choice in K–12 Education, *School Choice: Doing It the Right Way Makes a Difference,* Brown Center on Education Policy (Brookings, 2003).

2. Milton Friedman, "The Role of Government in Education," in *Economics and the Public Interest,* edited by Robert A. Solo (Rutgers University Press, 1955).

3. Caroline Hendrie, "Panel Says Choice's Benefits Worth Risks," *Education Week,* November 19, 2003 (www.edweek.org/ew/articles/2003/11/19/12choice.h23.html).

4. For an updated statement by Milton Friedman along these lines, see Milton Friedman, "Public Schools: Make Them Private," *Education Economics* 5, no. 3 (1997): 341–44.

2

The Economic Theory of School Choice

JULIAN R. BETTS

In a variety of forms, school choice is making gains in America's K–12 school systems. At one end of the spectrum are open-enrollment programs that allow students to switch from their local school to other public schools in the same district (or in some cases, other districts) subject to space being available. In addition, almost all states now have provisions for charter schools. At the other end of the spectrum are experimental voucher programs in cities such as Milwaukee that provide public subsidies to students to enroll in local private schools.

School choice, especially its more radical variants such as vouchers, has attracted strong reactions, both positive and negative. In light of this public controversy, it makes sense to take a step back from the fray to think through just why school choice might improve education. Because it is clear that school choice is not about to disappear, it also makes sense for all those who care about K–12 education, regardless of their beliefs about the wisdom of school choice, to examine how school choice should be implemented. This chapter seeks to provide some insights on the why and how of school choice. It draws insights from economic theory, which has developed a mathematical model of outcomes in markets under various assumptions about the degree of competition in the given market. This is directly relevant to school choice because the idea of choice programs is to create a competitive market that forces schools to compete for consumers (families and their students).

The first question I address is the theoretical case for why school choice would improve on the traditional system in which students are compelled to attend their local neighborhood school. The second question I address is how to implement school choice. Theory provides insights here because it yields specific warnings about what can go wrong in markets. The chapter devotes considerable attention to what can go wrong with school choice and offers some concrete suggestions for ways to minimize the potential problems. A second implementation issue concerns inequality in outcomes across different students and their families. Again, economic theory provides insights into mechanisms that might reduce some very real concerns that school choice in practice will lead to large variations in the quality of education received by all students.

While the chapter draws frequently from the well of economic theory, the goal of the analysis is to provide some new—and accessible—insights.

The Theoretical Case for School Choice

For the most part, public school students are required to attend their local neighborhood elementary school and the middle and high schools that are in the same feeder pattern. So roughly speaking families choose a school for their children in one of two ways, either by placing them into private schools or by choosing a public school through their residential decisions. For the last three decades only about 10–13 percent of K–12 students in the United States attended private schools, probably in part because the cost poses a barrier to some. Public school choice is also limited in the sense that most families have a limited number of neighborhoods in which they can afford to live. Taking this further, one could argue that the school district can act as a monopoly provider of educational services. What are the relative outcomes between this simplified world, in which families have virtually no choice among public schools for their children, and a world with school choice, in which parents could enroll their children in any of a large number of schools? Economic theory provides an analysis of these two extremes of monopoly or perfect competition. In the former, a single provider dominates the market; in the latter, there is a large number of providers and buyers (families and their students), none of which is sufficiently influential to manipulate the market outcomes.

Perfect Competition

When the market for a specific good or service is composed of a very large number of buyers and sellers, perfect competition is likely to emerge. Perfectly competitive markets have one marvelous property: if the conditions for perfect competition are met, then no buyer or seller could become better off without making at least one other agent worse off. Economists call this Pareto efficiency. The market is economically efficient in the sense that resources are not wasted and there is no way to make individual consumers of the service or product better off without taking something away from another. The key to this outcome is that individual producers and consumers make optimal decisions in a highly decentralized way. To gain insight into how the market's "invisible hand" generates these outcomes, it is important to review the necessary conditions for a perfectly competitive market to exist:

—Both firms and consumers are sufficiently numerous that none can affect the product's price.

—The market is for a homogeneous commodity or service.

—Firms are willing to sell to all consumers equally.

—There is perfect information on price.

—Firms maximize profits, consumers maximize "utility," that is, their private interests.

—There is free entry and exit for both firms and consumers, so that, for example, new schools can start up without any barriers, and schools that are failing can close.

—There are no externalities in production or consumption. (Externalities refer to interactions between market participants that work outside of the normal market mechanism in which prices adjust to equate supply and demand.)[1]

If all of these conditions are in place, then, simply put, consumers as a whole could not do better. Each firm will have to compete so hard for market share that it makes only a normal rate of profit on its physical investments. If firms are making above-normal profits due to high prices, then new firms will be attracted into the industry. The overall supply of the product will then rise, driving prices down to the minimum that firms can afford to charge without going out of business or switching to another more lucrative industry. In addition, firms that are less efficient than other firms will be forced to shut down, as they cannot compete effectively.

It is easy to extend this model to a world in which consumers buy many goods and services in markets with perfect competition. In this case, the relentless forces of competition cause prices for some goods and services to rise and for others to drop, until just the right mix of goods and services is produced for economic efficiency. Again, changes in prices send signals to producers about what consumers want, inducing the entry of firms into booming sectors and the exit of firms from lagging sectors.

This outcome is a sort of gold standard against which to compare markets in the real world. That is all well and fine, but what does it have to do with public schools? At present, not much. We need to imagine a situation in which school administrators have almost complete control over school size and the mix of services that they provide. We also have to imagine a situation in which parents, perhaps through a voucher program, have a much wider array of schools available for their child than at present. We can think of schools as producing multiple services. If there are enough schools to choose from, parents will find the best school for their children, given their needs and interests.

To give a simple example, suppose that schools provide two types of educational service that parents value to varying degrees: math achievement and language achievement. The curve in figure 2-1 labeled production possibilities frontier shows all the combinations of math and language achievement that a school can provide. The frontier has a negative slope, reflecting the idea that if school administrators decide to boost math achievement they will have to take resources out of programs that are directed at teaching students how to read. The production possibilities frontier is also curved, in a concave fashion. This curvature is based on the concept of diminishing returns: it is possible to increase language achievement further to the right at the cost of decreasing math achievement, but as language achievement is repeatedly increased by, say, one point, the school would have to give up more and more math achievement for each one point gain in language achievement.

The other lines in the figure are indifference curves. The points on a given indifference curve show all combinations of math and language achievement that the family would view as equally good outcomes.[2] Families would prefer their child's math and language achievement to be as high as possible. So points on the indifference curve that is further to the northeast in the figure represent a higher degree of family welfare than any point on the lower indifference curve. If families could choose a school anywhere along the production possibilities frontier they would definitely prefer point *A* to point *C*. Furthermore, point *A* is the very best combination of math and language achievement that the family can obtain: there is no higher indifference curve that is on the production possibilities frontier.

Figure 2-1. *Trade-Offs between Math and Language Achievement for a Specific Family*

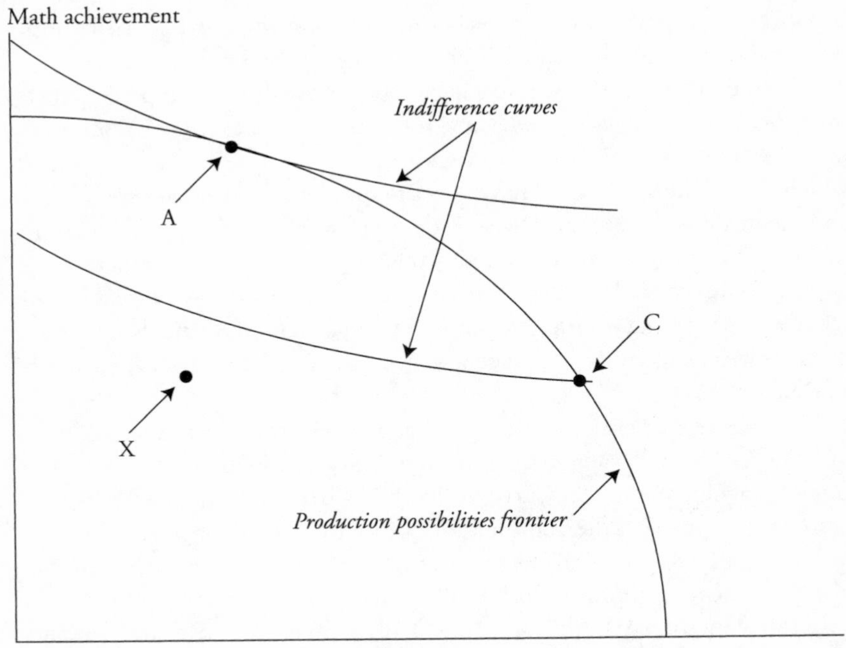

No school would want to provide math and language achievement to the southwest of the production possibilities frontier in the figure, say, at point *X*. (A school might arrive at point *X* if its administrators have goals that do not coincide with what parents care about, thus spending money on something that parents do not value.) If the school does offer a combination of educational achievement given by point *X*, then parents would switch their children to another school that, for the same cost, would provide improved teaching in math or language or both.

School choice, if it worked as described above, could accommodate different tastes among families for the various school services. Suppose that half of families believe that it is extremely important that their children learn technical skills like math, while the other half believe in a broadly based liberal curriculum with a foundation in reading and writing. Figure 2-2 illustrates this, showing the different indifference curves of the two types of family. Schools

Figure 2-2. *Trade-Offs between Math and Language Achievement with Heterogeneous Tastes for Education*

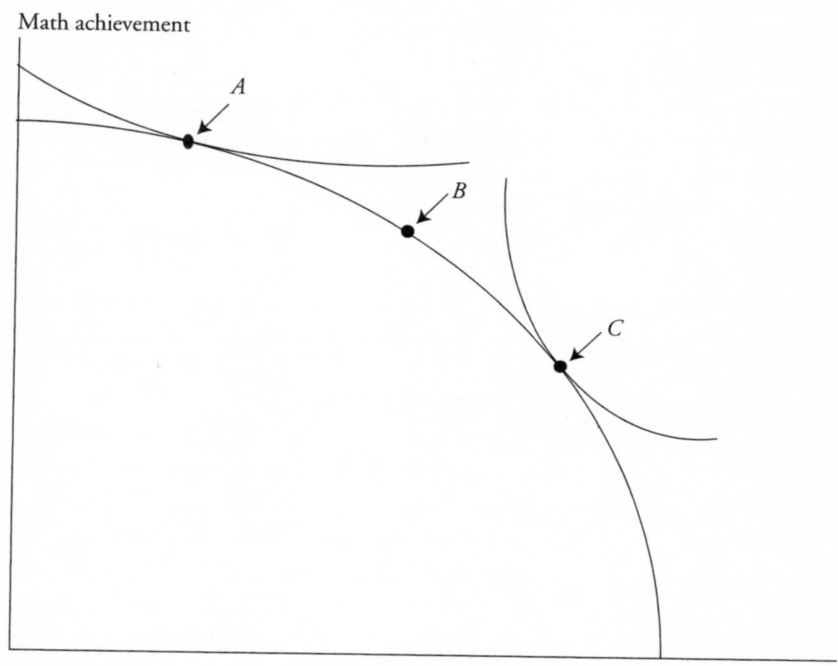

would adjust to these different preferences quickly or would lose all of their students. We would see, in the figure, half of schools operating at point *A* and the other half operating at point *C*. In both cases, schools are being efficient in the sense that either type of school produces the highest level of math achievement that it can without sacrificing language achievement, and vice versa. But the two types of schools differ considerably in their academic focus. Together they jointly serve the needs of the two types of family.

If all schools had to compete for students along the lines described above, then there would be no way to improve the outcomes for one student without hurting outcomes for another student. This is the beauty of perfectly competitive markets. In addition, it is important to note that this first-best outcome is arrived at in a very decentralized way. Thousands of decisions by families within a district—combined with perhaps hundreds of decisions by providers of educational services about whether to set up a school and what sort of services to provide at each school—work through the interaction of supply and demand to create an efficient outcome, in the sense that nobody can be made better off without somebody else becoming worse off.

It is important to note that the first-best result of perfect competition leaves each family as well off as possible in utility terms, without decreasing the welfare of other families. This is not necessarily the same thing as saying that student achievement is maximized. If families care about aspects of education other than achievement in math and reading, then choice will not necessarily maximize achievement. (I return to this point later.)

Monopoly

It is useful to compare the "first-best" case of perfect competition with its polar opposite, monopoly. Monopoly refers to a situation in which there is only one producer of a good or service in a given market. It produces worse outcomes for consumers than does a market with more choice for consumers. Imagine that one producer dominates the market for widgets. As the producer increases production, the overall price of the widget will fall as the increased supply floods the market. While in theory this producer could keep producing more and more units until the price of widgets just equaled the cost of producing one more widget, it will not be profitable to do so. Instead, a monopolist's best course of action is to restrict the amount produced. Reducing output reduces sales volume, but on the other hand it increases prices. The former reduces profits while the latter increases profits. The monopolist will reduce output until these two forces just counterbalance. Consumers suffer compared to a perfectly competitive situation, because not only do they consume less of the product but they pay more.

At first this story about a monopoly widget manufacturer seems to have nothing to do with public education. But upon closer inspection there are close parallels. In the market for widgets, if the monopolist sets the price too high, consumers will not buy any widgets. School is mandatory for young children, but even facing a monopolist school district, parents have the option of "refusing to buy" by sending their children to private school, by home schooling, or by moving to a different locale. So a district that is a local monopolist cannot completely ignore the preferences of local families. But it can afford to do less than would a school in a more competitive setting without losing many of its students. Without the threat of competition, a district will not in general provide the same quantity of resources for a given amount of funding as will a school in a more competitive environment.[3]

The parallel between a monopoly firm and a school district that faces no competition is not faultless. Clearly, public schools and districts do not directly charge parents for the service that they provide. But through the political process, families do choose overall spending per pupil for the district, and the given district then decides how to spend these dollars. Another difference is that districts do not directly control the number of students they serve in the same way that the widget firm sets output levels. But in effect, districts already do decide on the quantity of educational services to provide along many dimensions: the number of teachers at each school, the length of the school day, the intensity of remediation efforts for students who fall behind, and so on. In either case, the lack of competition will remove the incentive to provide the amount of output consistent with making consumers as well off as possible.

Similar arguments apply to the case mentioned earlier in which half of families prefer one type of education while the other half prefer another. Unlike the competitive situation in which schools would be forced to adjust so as to provide exactly the right mix of services for one type of family or the other, a monopolist might find it cheaper to provide a one-size-fits-all set of educational resources. In figure 2-2 this is illustrated by point *B,* in between points *A* and *C,* which are the two types of education strictly preferred by the two types of family. But both types of family would be strictly worse off than in a system with highly responsive and specialized schools that provide an educational mix described by points *A* and *C* respectively. We can see this because at points *A* and *C,* as obtained under perfect competition, both family types are on a higher indifference curve than they would be if their only choice were a "compromise school" operating at point *B.*

There are other costs of organizing education around a monopoly provider. In the perfectly competitive world in which education is not a single service but a complex set of variables, families would move to schools that best matched their children's needs. Thousands of such decentralized decisions by parents prompt the providers of educational services either to respond to families' preferences or to perish. In the case of a school district without competitors, the administration must bear huge information-gathering costs if it desires to provide the best education possible for each student. Even in the unlikely situation in which a district could mimic the perfectly competitive outcome by providing a variety of schools, the cost of creating a bureaucracy that would gather and synthesize all of this information would be daunting.

A related possibility in a monopolistic situation is that the producer's own preferences can lead it to produce less efficiently than it might otherwise. The district would spend money on programs that are of interest to administrators or teachers but that hold no value for families, and the district would produce an outcome to the southwest of the production possibilities frontier, such as at point *X* in figure 2-1. A monopolist district could get away with spending on things that parents do not value, simply because parents have no viable alternative source of schooling. I argued earlier that, in the case of perfect competition, if a school chooses to provide English and math classes at this relatively low level, then parents would switch their children to another school that, for the same cost, would provide better math and language classes. But in the case of monopoly, the families at such schools have little recourse.

Theory and Reality: Lessons for Implementation

This section summarizes some of the most likely deviations between the theory of perfectly competitive school choice and the reality of school choice. The goal here is not to poke holes in the rationale for school choice. On the contrary, the goal is to catalogue some of the obstacles to the first-best outcome of perfect competition and then to offer at least partial policy solutions. Seven assumptions are required for perfect competition to flourish (listed above). We discuss likely deviations from each of these assumptions.

Assumptions One and Two: Numerous Suppliers and Buyers of a Homogeneous Product

Two of the key assumptions required for perfect competition are that the good or service is homogeneous and that there are numerous suppliers and buyers. The assumption of homogeneity in education is clearly incorrect but it is easy to fix in the theoretical model: I already argued that school choice is probably best thought of as a series of markets for different flavors of education. If there are enough schools providing each type of education, then school choice may operate in nearly perfectly competitive conditions within each of these markets. However, because schools in this view operate in a series of closely related markets, the assumption of numerous suppliers of each type of schooling in a city is probably far-fetched. But this misses an important point: competition theory shows that, in a continuum between perfect competition and monopoly, some competition is almost always better for consumers than none, because it increases the quantity or quality of service provided for a given price.

Monopolistic competition is a type of imperfect competition that seems particularly likely in widespread school choice schemes. This situation borrows aspects of both monopoly and perfect competition. The seller gains some market power because consumers are not equally willing to buy from all sellers. For instance, most parents would probably prefer to send their children to a school that is relatively close to their home. This gives local schools some market power over these parents. In the short run the outcome is somewhat similar to a monopoly, with the schools providing lower quantity or quality of services for a given price, without fear of losing all of their students. What about in the long run, after new schools enter the market? Outcomes for students will start to improve due to this competition. However, in the end each neighborhood may have "too many" schools in the sense that each school enrolls too few students to be efficient. Just as grocery stores rarely operate at full capacity, the same could happen to schools in a school choice system with free entry of new schools. It is certainly true that this is inefficient in an economic sense. However, excess capacity at most schools would generate real choice for students. (In contrast, in most school districts that currently offer open enrollment as a form of school choice, there are long waiting lists to get into the best schools.)

Assumption Three: Schools Accept All Students

Earlier I stated that firms must be willing to sell their good or service to any consumer for perfect competition to develop. If firms discriminate in some way against certain types of consumer, then the full benefits of competition will not emerge.

This problem seems particularly likely in any system of school choice that uses test scores to hold schools accountable, as this creates an incentive for schools to accept only the highest achieving students. In addition, many existing private schools prefer students from specific religions. A more radical form of school choice such as educational vouchers would need to take this into account.

In either case, the designers of school choice would need to find ways to minimize the ability of participating schools to limit enrollment based on student traits such as religion and initial test scores. This is not to say that specialized schools should not screen their applicant pools to find students best poised to gain from the offerings of the school. But safeguards need to be found to ensure that school choice does not become school choice only for the most advantaged.

Assumption Four: Perfect Information

To achieve a perfectly competitive outcome, all buyers and sellers must have full information on price. In a richer model with several types of school performing in separate markets (vocational, college prep, and so on), we would also need all market participants to have full information about the quality of schools in each of these separate markets. Lack of information among families will obviously lead them to make imperfect choices for their children. Families need two types of information: information about the choices available to them and information about the academic needs of their children. Both types of information are needed for parents to find a good match for their child. Similarly, if public and private producers of educational services lack full information about the education market, it is likely that pockets of imperfect competition will persist in certain areas, even though it would be in the interests of both local families and education providers to have one or more new schools open up locally.

Assumption Five: The Objectives of Parents and Producers

For perfect competition, consumers must maximize their utility, or welfare, while firms maximize profits. In the case of schooling, parents typically make decisions for their children, so we must assume that parents have their children's long-term interests at heart. The vast majority of parents probably fit this description well, but it does raise the issue of how school choice would affect the small minority of children whose parents are indifferent or even hostile to their children's best interests.

The standard assumption that firms maximize profits applies fully for the small number of schools that are run for profit, such as the Edison schools. But what about schools run by school districts, or charter schools that, while operating fairly independently from school districts, are typically nonprofit? The key here is that in a world with widespread school choice, even nonprofit schools will have to compete with each other for students. Those that fail to produce results in line with parents' expectations will lose students and may ultimately be forced to close. The central point here is simple: in competitive markets consumer sovereignty prevails.

Thus, ultimately, the key question is, What are the goals of parents? If all parents actively seek the best education possible for their children given their children's interests, talents, and needs, then it does not particularly matter whether schools are profit-driven. Even nonprofit schools will have to find ways to satisfy parents in a world with widespread school choice.

Assumption Six: Free Entry and Exit

The assumption of free entry and exit implies that parents are free not only to move their child from one public school to another but also to send their child to a private school or even to homeschool their child. Typically, parents already have these rights, although in some cases, such as open enrollment, district administrators limit the number of opportunities for parents to change their child's school—for instance offering the opportunity for school switching only at the end of the school year or semester.

A more serious issue concerns free entry and exit of sellers—that is, schools. Free entry requires that parties wishing to start a new school face few obstacles. But obstacles, unfortunately, abound: land zoning regulations, for example, or considerable paperwork. This is not to say that paperwork and public scrutiny are always bad things. But the higher the hurdles for potential entrants, the less likely parents will enjoy an abundance of choices.

Free exit of schools is perhaps an even more difficult issue. The logic of perfect competition is that if initially there is imperfect competition, with higher than average profits and lower than average outcomes for consumers, new firms will be enticed to enter. This lowers the price for any level of services provided. Inexorably, the least efficient firms will shut down as they lose clients. Now, translating this to school choice, what will happen when a local school performs so poorly that it loses most of its students? Will it shut down or will government step in to subsidize the school further? Most states have some provision for state takeover of failing schools, but to the best of this author's knowledge there is no evidence that such takeovers produce markedly better schools. An actual closing of a school is rare and would represent a major change in the way we think about public education.

Clearly, any plan for widespread school choice would have to contend with how to deal with failing schools. The genius of competitive markets is that such schools would go out of business. But because even in the most radical of choice schemes schools are likely to be important local providers of education, a choice plan needs to stipulate how local students will be cared for if their school shuts down.

Assumption Seven: Externalities

Perfect competition will not result if there are externalities in production or consumption. Production externalities seem particularly likely in education, in the sense that one student's rate of learning is likely to depend on the characteristics of other students in the classroom. There is a large and increasingly convincing literature that points to the importance of classroom and grade level peers on student achievement.[4]

If it is indeed true that a student learns more quickly if there are many highly achieving students in the classroom, the societal ideal may be to mix high and low achievers. It all depends on two things. First, the extent to which society cares about the *distribution* of student achievement as opposed to average achievement will dictate whether it is socially best to mix low and high achievers in the classroom. Second, there are important and unsettled questions about whether moving from a system of achievement grouping to completely mixed-achievement classrooms would hurt the high-achieving students more than it would help the low-achieving students.

The issue of peer groups has obvious implications for school choice. If all parents want to surround their child with high-achieving peers in the classroom, then the most elite schools in a choice system will be flooded with applications, and if these schools serve parents' wishes, they will probably skim the highest-achieving students from the application pools. Ultimately, this would either recreate or perhaps exacerbate the large gaps in achievement seen among public schools today.

Potential Solutions

Above are listed several challenges to the notion that school choice will yield the first-best outcomes promised by the theory of perfect competition. None of these problems necessarily renders the idea of school choice unworkable. However, each challenge deserves a careful response by current and future architects of school choice. I here suggest some partial solutions to these possible problems.

Imperfect Competition without Free Entry and Exit

With parental and student tastes for education as varied as they apparently are, I argue above that it may be best to think of school choice as operating in several markets for various types of schooling. This heterogeneity, compounded by barriers to free entry by potential school providers, suggests that it is unlikely that perfect competition will ever be attained in the market for schooling. As noted earlier, imperfect competition is better than no competition at all. But policymakers need to design school choice in a way to maximize the extent of competition among schools for students. Obviously, this goal is intricately linked to the goal of creating low-cost entry and exit for school providers. Some suggestions:

—School districts could consider leasing out existing school buildings to other providers of education. This would reduce the large fixed costs of constructing new school buildings and of satisfying local zoning ordinances, both of which currently create barriers to entry. The leasing of school sites to independent providers of educational services would also go a long way toward solving the political issue of whether regulators will ultimately have the nerve to close failing schools. Under a leasing system, closing a failing school means replacing the management of a school with another management under a new lease. The school need not physically shut down. Edison and other private providers of educational services have in some cases taken over existing schools in a similar way.

—Large schools, especially the largest high schools, could be split into parts, creating two or more schools, with perhaps 500–1,000 students in each school. The idea here is for competing schools to share the costs of building upkeep, food, and transportation, while operating under the same roof. The Gates Foundation has embraced a similar approach by subsidizing the conversion of large low-performing schools into multiple "learning communities" on a single campus.

—The paperwork required to open a new school should be the minimum needed to provide sufficient public scrutiny. This suggestion stems from the simple observation that bureaucracy can create formidable barriers to entry for new schools.

—Any district that grants a school charter should clearly guarantee the amount of funding that the school will receive for busing its students. Further, state funding mechanisms should allow for choice schools to receive above-average busing support. The idea here is that parents can send their students to a given school if there exists a means of public transport to get the student from home to the school. Obviously, American cities vary in size and in the density of their public transit networks. In many cities, though, especially those that lack a subway system, it would prove very difficult for a student to attend a distant school without adequate funding for school busing.

Schools Accept All Students

The two central issues here have to do with whether schools will avoid accepting students who lag behind academically and, in the case of private school voucher schemes, whether private schools will exclude students based on student characteristics such as religion and gender.

There is a straightforward solution to the latter problem, even though it might reduce the number of private schools willing to participate in a voucher program: any school choice system, and particularly one that includes vouchers allowing students to attend private schools, must explicitly indicate that schools cannot select students on the basis of gender, race, sexual orientation, or religious belief.

But what about the problem of schools skimming off the cream? As mentioned in the last section, it is probably unwise to insist that every school participating in a choice system must accept every student who applies. The diversity of charter schools already in existence suggests that one benefit of choice is the variety of scholastic emphases. In this case it probably is reasonable for specialized schools to screen student applicants to ensure that students' interests and talents are aligned with the goals of the school. For instance, a school devoted to the performing arts probably should be able to screen student applicants for talent and interest in this direction. Below are some suggestions that might strike the right balance between granting schools flexibility while preventing their skimming off the most highly achieving students.

—While some schools participating in a choice system may screen student applicants for academic achievement, mechanisms such as quotas on the number of students who can be accepted from the most affluent neighborhoods, or school funding formulas that reward schools for drawing from a wide distribution of academic performance, can ensure that no school accepts only the very top students.

—If a school is oversubscribed, then the school should be required to conduct a lottery in a public setting to determine which new students enter the school. While the school should have the right to screen applicants for interests, motivation, and academic achievement, the lottery should include a minimum percentage of applicants. For example, if a school receives A applications for S spaces, where $A > S$, then setting the minimum lottery pool size to $S + (A - S)/2$ would ensure that at least half of the excess number of candidates would be included in the lottery. However, this stipulation alone could create an incentive for schools to recruit exactly the set of students that they want to enroll ($S = A$), removing all chance from the lottery. So a second stipulation could be that a school can accept no more than, for example, 80 percent of applicants (that is, $S \leq 0.8A$).

Such lottery mechanisms have other advantages. First they put the onus on schools to recruit widely if they are to meet their enrollment targets. Second, they ensure that schools' admission standards are not rigid but instead fluctuate with student demand, but in a controlled way. This in a sense mimics the manner in which the price of a good or service adjusts in a regular market to equate the quantity demanded with the quantity supplied. As the reputation of a school rises, the number of applicants will rise, but such schools cannot simply skim off the very best candidates, because the size of the lottery pool will rise with the number of applications.

—A new school should be exempted from the requirement to have a lottery ($A > S$) for a short period of time, perhaps one or two years, until it has become well enough established to fill at least a minimum number of slots.

Perfect Information

Obviously, much can be done about providing information:

—Assuming that the school district remains the focal point of school choice, then each district should distribute a pamphlet detailing the characteristics of all schools available under each component of choice (open enrollment, traditional busing, magnets, charters, and any private schools participating in a vouchers program). The information should include the academic focus of the school, admissions procedures, information on transportation options, and summaries of the teachers' qualifications. This information should also be available on the web.

—As Laura Hamilton and Kacey Guin argue in chapter 3 in this volume, school choice will only succeed insofar as parents can obtain detailed information on how successfully schools are meeting state standards. Accessible and up-to-date information on levels and gains in student performance on state-mandated tests is crucial in this regard.

—Private schools participating in a school voucher program should administer the same tests given to students in regular public schools, to provide parents with a valid comparison of student outcomes.

—A second role of testing is to provide teachers and parents with information on each student's academic strengths and weaknesses. In reality, state testing systems vary markedly in their diagnostic power. States should consider adopting tests that give parents and teachers not only data on overall achievement in subjects such as math and reading, but also specific information on areas within these subjects in which the student needs to concentrate. This sort of information will increase the probability that parents can find a school well matched to their child's needs.

Anecdotal information based on conversations with charter school administrators suggests that sometimes regular public schools do not welcome requests for meetings between charter school representatives and the public school's parents or students. This is particularly true when the charter school is recruiting students from a grade that is not the "exit" grade at the public school, because administrators at the latter school view this as a threat. This insight leads to the following suggestion:

—Each public school should institute and publicize a systematic method for disseminating information to parents about choice schools available to their children. Examples might include an annual choice fair or a regular series of mailings.

The Objectives of Parents and Producers

The most worrying issue here is the minority of parents who are indifferent to their children's academic achievement. Chapter 6 in this volume, by Dan Goldhaber and co-authors, carefully assesses the implications of expanded choice for students who are nonchoosers. However, I do offer two suggestions in this regard:

—In schools that are not meeting state academic standards, districts should actively seek out parents to alert them to the choice options available to their children. Ideally, an advocate outside the given school should be assigned to the school to communicate these choice options to parents. It is unlikely that this alone will overcome the problem of parents who are indifferent or otherwise unable to seek out the best school for their children, but it could help.

In addition, districts might want to identify parents who are least engaged in their children's education and focus these outreach activities on those families. Here is one possible mechanism:

—Toward the end of each school year parents should be asked to fill out a school choice form that asks parents to make an explicit decision about whether to leave their child in the same school next year. Parents who fail to return the form could be selected for follow-up by the school choice advocate described above.[5] Notably, the federal No Child Left Behind (NCLB) law calls for schools deemed as underperforming to notify their students that they can opt to be bused to another school. This represents a first step in the direction being espoused here.

Externalities

If peer group effects exist, as a growing body of evidence suggests, then there is no easy solution to the issue of how a school choice system will redistribute the most highly achieving students across schools in a district. While it is certainly possible that grouping of students by achievement across schools could become more accentuated in a choice system, some of the suggestions listed earlier, such as admission lotteries, can mute the tendency for this to happen.

Unequal Educational Quality

As mentioned earlier, competition produces a Pareto efficient outcome, which is a situation in which no person can be made better off without making at least one other person worse off. No resource goes wasted. This result is known to economists as the first theorem of welfare economics. While this is a salutary outcome, society typically places value not only on the total level of production but also on its distribution among consumers. It is extremely unlikely that, for instance, a school voucher program would lead to identical educational outcomes for all students. Indeed, many opponents of school choice fear that it would aggravate the existing achievement gap between various racial groups and between students who live in affluent neighborhoods and those who live in less affluent neighborhoods. The biggest reason for unequal outcomes under a choice regime is that relatively affluent families will be able to "top up" the educational voucher provided by the government, enabling their children to attend more elite private schools than will relatively disadvantaged families. In addition, families with relatively high socioeconomic status also are likely to have better information about the quality of schools than other families, which may further skew the quality of education. This problem will also afflict more conservative versions of school choice, such as charter school and open-enrollment programs.

These realizations lead to an important question: Is there any reason to think that an equitable education for all could result from the creation of a competitive market through school choice? Again, economic theory provides a distinct answer. The second theorem of welfare economics states that, subject to some technical conditions, *any* Pareto efficient outcome can result from perfect competition. What is required to shift the market from one Pareto efficient outcome to another is to change the distribution of buying power among consumers. In other words, the outcome of school choice can be quite inequitable or highly equitable. What determine the outcome are the relative amounts of resources put in the hands of each family initially.

One way to see this point is to examine a variant of the production possibilities frontier shown in figure 2-1. Figure 2-3 shows a production possibilities frontier for average student achievement for students living in two different neighborhoods in a city. Suppose that neighborhood 1 is relatively disadvantaged compared to neighborhood 2. Point *A* shows the outcome in

Figure 2-3. *Trade-Offs between Average Achievement of Students Living in Neighborhoods 1 and 2, with and without Choice*

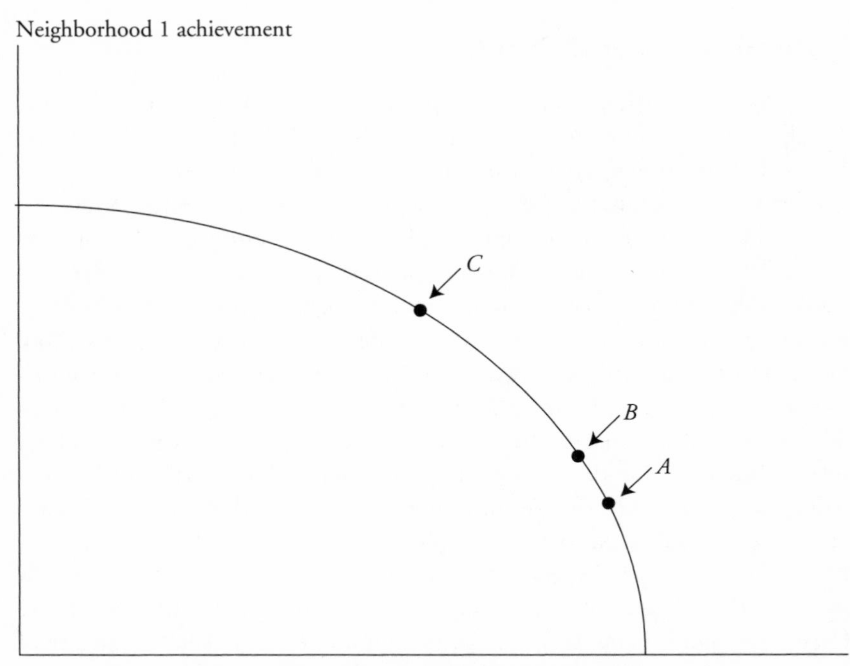

the status quo with all students attending local schools. Average achievement among students from neighborhood 1 is lower than that for students from neighborhood 2 because of the direct impact of poverty on learning opportunities, the impact of peers' achievement on learning, and the sorting of teachers between schools in the two areas.

Now, suppose that a fixed quota of seats in schools in neighborhood 2 is made available on a lottery basis to students from neighborhood 1. Through increases in peer group achievement and teacher quality, achievement of students from neighborhood 1 who attend schools in neighborhood 2 may rise. Overall, we might move from point *A* on the production possibilities frontier to point *B:* students from neighborhood 1 become much better off on average, while students from neighborhood 2 become only slightly worse off.[6]

Perhaps point *B* is not satisfactory to society because students from neighborhood 1 are still learning far less than students from neighborhood 2.

What the second theorem of welfare economics tells us is that we could do even better, perhaps arriving at point *C,* by finding a way to reallocate "buying power" toward the families living in neighborhood 1.

Finding an exact mechanism for this reallocation of resources will prove difficult. A simple but ham-fisted way to help more students from neighborhood 1 is to set quotas for students from each neighborhood who will attend a school. For instance, instead of one lottery for admissions to a choice school in neighborhood 2, there could be two lotteries, with *x* percent of admissions assigned to neighborhood 1 applicants and the rest of admissions assigned to students from neighborhood 2. In practice this could become specific, using even zip codes to define the separate lottery pools.

Other mechanisms of achieving a mix of students in each school would be to take a leaf from the recent annals of U.S. deregulation of the airwaves and environmental regulation. In both cases, auction mechanisms have been used by the U.S. government to allocate scarce resources (for instance, sections of the radio frequency and rights for factories to emit specific types of pollutants). At first glance these examples seem far afield from the issue of school choice. But imagine a system in which each school is granted rights to enroll a fixed percentage of students with very high achievement. These rights would be individually tradable among schools. How would this work in practice? Let's begin with a summary of a hypothetical status quo before the choice system is introduced.

Suppose, as we have seen in so many urban school districts, that high-achieving students typically come from the most affluent areas of the city and attend highly ranked schools in their local neighborhoods, while inner-city schools have far fewer highly achieving students. At the same time, the pattern seen repeatedly is that the most highly educated and experienced teachers tend to migrate to the suburban schools in the most affluent areas over time. In both of these ways, inner-city students get the short end of the stick. Now imagine that at the start of the new school year a tradable market in enrollment rights is created. Some of the affluent schools find themselves with far too few rights to claim highly achieving students. Inner-city schools find themselves with a surplus of these rights. For example, suppose that the district average of high-achieving students is 50 percent and that one particular high school has 1,000 students, of whom 600 are high achieving and 400 are low achieving. It has been granted 500 permits but needs 600. The school could avoid buying any additional permits by accepting 200 new low-achieving students who have applied from other schools to bring it to the district average of a 50-50 split. Alternatively, the school could buy 100 permits on the open market from one or more schools at which more than 50 percent of students were low achieving.

The beauty of this idea is that when an inner-city school sells a right to enroll a high-achieving student it banks the money paid by the urban school. Through competition among schools with high percentages of high-achieving students, the price of each right would rise to the point at which the suburban schools are indifferent between enrolling one additional high-achieving student and buying one more right. At one extreme, then, there could be no exchange of students whatsoever. Instead, there would be an exchange of funds from schools with high-achieving students to less fortunate schools. At the other extreme, there could be no trading in rights, with high-achieving schools recruiting low-achieving students from other schools. In reality we would expect some of both: some students would leave low-scoring schools to attend high-scoring schools, and the high-scoring schools would also provide financial compensation to the low-scoring schools for refusing to enroll a fully proportionate share of low-achieving students.

The inner-city schools would get every dollar received from the purchase of their rights. They could spend this fund on any number of academic aids, such as supplemental reading materials, after-school classes, and instructional aides. The improved resources at the inner-city schools would, we would hope, go some way toward removing the gap in performance between inner-city and suburban schools. In turn, this might induce fewer students to leave inner-city schools and could even induce some students to leave their suburban schools for better-funded urban schools. In addition, it might attract some of the most highly experienced and educated teachers in the district back to inner-city schools from the suburban schools to which they gravitated as they gained seniority. In practice, what would likely result is that most suburban schools would opt to accept more low-achieving students from elsewhere while sacrificing some funding to pay for the right to continue to enroll an above-average percentage of high-achieving students.

There is a potentially fatal flaw in this proposal for tradable enrollment rights. Suppose that a superb school in an urban area wants to thwart a district's choice program so as to "keep the school local." It could instruct its students intentionally to perform poorly on the test used to label students as high achieving or low achieving. Then it would not come close to filling its quota of high-achieving students. In an extreme example, instead of having to buy additional enrollment rights it could fraudulently obtain surplus rights by qualifying as an underperforming school and then selling its surplus rights to other schools. So it would keep its high-achieving students and unethically make a profit at the same time!

Two solutions to this form of cheating are evident. First, if these test scores matter to students and school administrators for other reasons, then it becomes less likely that administrators will encourage students to perform poorly and even less likely that individual students will play along. For example, in California, as in many other states, high school students will soon have to pass a high school exit examination in order to graduate from high school. Neither administrators nor students will want bad outcomes on this test. Similarly, some states' accountability systems and the NCLB program impose sanctions on schools that underperform. In some cases, states have also created financial carrots for teachers and administrators to reward high performance or gains in performance on the state test. Typically, these sanctions and rewards are quite weak, but they could mitigate the temptation for school administrators and teachers to discourage student effort on the state test. Furthermore, in California strong individual student performance in grades 9 through 11 up to 2002 earned students college scholarships, providing a direct incentive to at least some students to take the state tests seriously.[7] In a similar vein, Georgia offers its HOPE scholarships to high school graduates who maintained a grade point average of at least 3.0, or B, in core subjects in high school.

Financial incentives may not be enough to prevent schools from attempting to mislabel students as low achieving. A more bulletproof solution technically is to assign tradable enrollment rights using some characteristic of students that is less manipulable. For instance, each school could receive permits to enroll the district average percentage of students who are not eligible for lunch assistance. Those schools with almost no students eligible for lunch assistance would have to bus disadvantaged students in, pay inner-city schools for their excess permits, or a combination of both. Other alternatives include using parental education or even student race as a proxy for achievement. While these student characteristics are less susceptible to manipulation, it is clearly much more politically intractable to allow schools to sell enrollment rights for "rich students" or even more explosively, students of a given race. For these reasons, classifying students by their achievement levels, on tests that matter, may prove a more realistic if still imperfect solution.

A closely related concern is that even if schools do not cheat by encouraging students to perform poorly on tests the first year, they still have an incentive to encourage students not to improve much over time. After all, a school that initially has mediocre test scores and that then works hard to improve student achievement would suddenly have to buy permits to keep its students whose scores had improved. This is a rather perverse incentive. One solution that would work well for high schools and middle schools is that the district would categorize students as high achieving or low achieving based on a battery of test scores in the students' final year in the feeder school before he or she graduated to middle or high school. Solutions for elementary schools are less obvious. Here, perhaps pretests of cognitive development given by the district when the students begin elementary school would reduce a school's opportunity to manipulate skills downward.

A final concern with this market for enrollment rights is that the sellers of rights (the schools with below-average percentages of high-achieving students) may have an incentive to collude, just as energy producers apparently conspired in 2000 to restrict natural gas and electricity supplies to California, thereby driving prices sky-high. Drawing a lesson from this attempt at energy deregulation gone awry, the school district could set a cap on the maximum price for which a single enrollment right could sell. One way to do this is to tell high-achieving schools that they can either buy the required number of permits on the open market or pay a fine of, say, $500 for each high-achieving student lacking a permit. This penalty would guarantee that no school would be willing to pay more than $500 for an enrollment right. The proceeds from any penalties paid could be spread across all schools equally or used to subsidize the busing programs that school choice would require. An advantage of the tradable permits proposal over the quotas idea is that the former would shift money from schools with a larger share of high-achieving students to schools with fewer high-achieving students. This transfer of cash would mitigate the concerns many have that choice will hurt students who continue to attend failing schools.

Both of these proposals, quotas combined with lotteries and an interschool market, may appear to some readers to be monstrously radical notions that bear some resemblance to Jonathan Swift's "A Modest Proposal," without Swift's tongue-in-cheek delivery. But in the case of both quotas and markets for tradable enrollment rights the goal is the same: to improve outcomes for the least advantaged students in a school district through a choice mechanism. Moreover, flavors of at least the first proposal already exist. The NCLB legislation calls for schools that states identify as failing for two consecutive years to allow some of their students to be bused at public expense to better schools. In this plan, the low-achieving students have the first right to transfer out of their school. Similarly, lotteries have become a common way to admit students to charter schools, and in California state law requires this in cases where charter schools are oversubscribed.

Concluding Remarks

This chapter lays out the theoretical justification for school choice by tracing the logic behind the economic model of perfect competition and explaining why competition leads to a first-best efficient outcome. It then assesses numerous ways in which school choice systems might violate the assumptions needed for perfect competition to work. It will take real-world policy experiments to understand whether these potential problems are mere flies in the ointment or quite severe barriers to school choice programs. Each of these potential obstacles to school choice is addressed and steps are offered that policymakers might take to mitigate these problems.

It seems apparent that it will not be possible to remove all of the inherent tensions in school choice. For instance, school choice will probably create greater heterogeneity in teaching styles and curriculum than currently exists, and this balkanization of the "market" for education stands in direct opposition to the idea that school choice will improve schools through large numbers of schools competing to produce a homogeneous service. There is also a tension between the goal of increasing the number and range of schools available to each student and the goal of reducing the large achievement gap between disadvantaged and more affluent students and among racial and ethnic groups. However, as the penultimate section indicates, with a few technical restrictions competitive forces can produce any Pareto efficient outcome policymakers seek, whether equal or unequal, depending on the initial distribution of buying power among consumers. Therefore, those who are concerned that choice will widen existing inequalities in outcomes should favor choice programs that level the playing field in favor of the poor. Two ways of achieving this in some part are either to set geographic or other quotas for each school's student body or to use more sophisticated market mechanisms that force schools in more affluent areas to compensate schools in less affluent areas for the right to enroll above-average shares of high-achieving students.

Neither of these tensions can be resolved completely, but careful implementation, perhaps using some of the suggestions outlined here, might alleviate these and other negative consequences that could accompany a system of school choice.

Finally, it seems clear from the above analysis that unregulated school choice is not consistent with good public policy. We have consumer protection laws and government oversight in all sorts of markets; the market for schools should not be an exception to this rule.

Notes

This chapter is based on a paper prepared for the National Working Commission on Choice in K–12 Education, of which Betts was a member. He thanks fellow commission members for helpful comments on a preliminary draft.

1. The textbook example of a negative externality is a firm that pollutes water, worsening outcomes for both firms and consumers who are located downstream.

2. These curves are U shaped, indicating that if a child's achievement in one domain is very low, the family would not be willing to see the child's achievement in that domain fall any further unless achievement in the other domain rose by a very large amount to compensate.

3. In addition, in some important senses, teachers' unions affect districts' spending decisions. For instance, see Julian R. Betts, Kim Rueben, and Anne Danenberg, *Equal Resources, Equal Outcomes? The Distribution of School Resources and Student Achievement in California* (San Francisco: Public Policy Institute of California, 2000). These authors find examples of teachers' collective bargaining agreements in major California school districts that set limits on class size, that restrict how teachers are allocated across schools, and of course that set teachers' pay. As a co-monopolist, teachers' unions have distinct incentives to place restrictions on both the price and quantity of teachers, which on the whole will increase the cost of education beyond what would be seen in a fully competitive system with many independent producers.

4. See for instance Caroline Hoxby, "Peer Effects in the Classroom: Learning from Gender and Race Variation," Working Paper 7867 (Cambridge, Mass.: National Bureau of Economic Research, 2000); Eric A. Hanushek and others, "Does Peer Ability Affect Student Achievement?" Working Paper 8502 (Cambridge, Mass.: National Bureau of Economic Research, 2001); Julian R. Betts, Andrew Zau, and Lorien Rice, *Determinants of Student Achievement: New Evidence from San Diego* (San Francisco: Public Policy Institute of California, 2003).

5. I thank Rick Hess for this suggestion.

6. This simple example assumes something like a zero-sum game, in which students in more affluent areas can only lose from school choice. This is certainly a possibility that policymakers must consider when designing school choice systems that must meet a political litmus test. What is missing from this example is the possibility that school choice could enhance the quality of all schools in all neighborhoods, through the competitive effects discussed earlier.

7. Recent experience in California provides a cautionary tale on these strong forms of accountability that contain financial or other tangible rewards and sanctions. The high school class graduating in 2004 was supposed to be the first subject to the California High School Exit Exam requirement, but the requirement was waived after legislators learned

that a large minority of students in the class of 2004 had not passed the test by spring 2003. Instead, the state decided that the class of 2006 will be the first class required to pass this test to graduate from high school. Similarly, although in 1999 and 2000 California passed legislation to introduce financial bonuses for schools as well as a generous pay incentive for both teachers and administrators at schools that either had high test scores or large improvements in test scores, financial cutbacks forced the abandonment of these programs after a single year of operation. Further, the scholarship program was discontinued after 2002.

3

Understanding How Families Choose Schools

Laura S. Hamilton and Kacey Guin

Although choice systems take a variety of forms, the effectiveness of any of them depends in large part on the responses of the families who are offered choice.[1] To the extent that a choice system encourages families to choose schools that promote academic achievement and to avoid those that do not, the system should create incentives for all schools to focus on the goal of raising student achievement.

Some skeptics of choice worry that many families, particularly those from disadvantaged backgrounds, will either fail to make choices or will emphasize nonacademic criteria when they do make choices.[2] Others worry that families will not have the information needed to accurately assess what schools have to offer. And still others fear that differing educational priorities will lead parents to self-segregate by race, ethnicity, income, and religion in ways that might be socially undesirable. This chapter explores what is currently known about how families choose schools and discusses strategies for understanding choosers' behavior as new choice systems are implemented.

Choice systems potentially give parents the opportunity to find a school that matches their own preferences in education. Researchers list several conditions that must be in place for parents to make good choices.[3] Parents must:

—Have preferences about education and schooling and gather information about the schools available to their children.

—Make trade-offs between the attributes of these schools.

—Choose the school that best fits their preferences.[4]

In addition, once a school is selected, parents must monitor its progress and seek a new school if they decide their original choice was not correct. To the extent that these conditions are met, they should eventually lead to a supply of schools whose diversity reflects the diversity of parental preferences and should create incentives for existing schools to improve on the dimensions that parents value most.

It is important to recognize that these conditions do not guarantee that choices will reflect broader public goals such as improved student learning and citizenship; they only ensure that parents' choices will match parental preferences, whatever those preferences may be. Schools provide a number of public and private benefits, and the success of any choice system must ultimately be evaluated on the basis of its responsiveness to the needs of both families and society.[5] If families value academic achievement, civic knowledge, and other outcomes that are believed to be important for maintaining an economically productive, democratic society, then choice should lead to a school system that is effective at serving individual students and society at large. To the extent that families value outcomes that are not consistent with the needs of the broader society, choice may ultimately meet the demands of some families without providing the public benefits that are expected of schools.

The next section briefly summarizes what we currently know about how parents choose and whether different types of parents value different school attributes. As the discussion reveals, there are a number of unanswered questions that need to be explored as new choice systems are implemented. In the final section of this chapter we discuss some approaches for gathering this information and provide recommendations for designing systems that promote good decisions on the part of parents.

How Parents Choose

Several studies have examined the factors that influence parents' choices among schools. Some of this work relies on surveys that ask parents to describe the criteria they use when choosing a school, whereas other studies examine actual choice behavior. The following review of this literature is not exhaustive but is intended to summarize the major findings and to highlight areas about which the literature is inconclusive.[6]

What Parents Say

When asked what factors contribute to their decisions about where to send their children to school, most parents rank educational quality at or near the top. When families that use vouchers are asked about the reasons for that decision, academic quality is typically cited as the most important reason, though religion and cultural values often rank highly as well.[7] Results from a survey of charter school choosers indicate that educational quality and small class size were among the top factors cited by parents of all racial and income groups.[8] A study that examined an interdistrict choice program in Massachusetts cites high standards and curriculum as top reasons given by both parents and students for choosing a school.[9] Other studies of charter schools and magnet schools provide additional evidence of the importance of academic quality in parental decisionmaking.[10] Moreover, several of the studies cited above, along with a 1998 Public Agenda survey, find that in contrast to some choice critics' concerns, low-income and minority parents appear to value academic quality as much as high-income and nonminority parents.[11]

Other work, however, indicates that parental preferences may vary as a function of racial, ethnic, and socioeconomic background. Mark Schneider and colleagues have done extensive work on intradistrict school choice in both urban and suburban school districts, and their work suggests that the preferences of parents differ in several ways depending on their racial, ethnic, and socioeconomic status.[12] In particular, survey results indicate that low-socioeconomic-status (SES) and minority parents are more concerned with safety and test scores than are high-SES and white parents.[13] The findings related to test scores build on previous research that has found that racial minorities and parents from low socioeconomic groups are more concerned with their children learning the "basics," particularly math and reading skills, than white, middle-class parents.[14] Learning the basics is assumed by many minority and low-income parents as a necessary step to propel their children through important "gate-keeping points" toward higher education and economic success,[15] and this assumption may reflect accurate perceptions of what their children need most urgently. Based on these findings, researchers argue that racial and social stratification may occur because minority and low-income parents "stress a different set of values in education and choose schools that reflect the fundamental (and different) dimensions of education they view as important."[16]

These studies provide evidence in support of one of the key assumptions of the choice model: that parents will choose on the basis of educational quality. However, the precise meaning of educational quality differs across studies and, as indicated by some of the research findings, is likely to differ across racial-ethnic and socioeconomic groups. In addition, parents' definitions of educational quality may not refer exclusively to test scores but instead may involve broader notions of factors that contribute to student achievement. For example, one study found that, overall, parents are almost three times as likely to value teacher quality over high test scores within a school.[17] Similarly, parents participating in focus groups as part of a choice program in Washington, D.C., were highly concerned about the academic environments of the schools their children attended but less concerned about academic outcomes such as test scores.[18] When parents actually make choices, however, they must rely on the information that is available to them, and most parents will probably have better information on test scores than on teacher quality. This may be one reason why, as we discuss in the next section, survey reports of parents' stated preferences may produce information that is inconsistent with how parents actually behave when confronted with choices.

What Parents Do

The studies cited above suggest a large degree of consistency in what parents say they value most. Studies of intra- and inter-district choice, as well as of charter schools and vouchers, all report parents citing measures of academic quality as a primary reason for choosing their child's school. Because some answers may be seen as more or less socially desirable than others, there is some risk that parental reports of their decisionmaking criteria might be misleading. Parents may, for various reasons, be unlikely to report that they factor race or their own personal convenience into their school selection criteria. For example, studies comparing public opinion polls to actual voting behavior have found that more respondents are likely to *say* they will vote for African American candidates than actually do so once they are in the booth.[19]

Reinforcing this concern about the validity of self-reported data is the fact that some analyses of actual school choice behavior point to different results than those obtained through surveys, particularly with respect to parents' reported emphasis on race, ethnicity, and socioeconomic status. In one study, parents participating in a public school choice program in Minneapolis preferred schools that were in close proximity to their homes and where their children would be in the racial majority.[20] Additionally, the socioeconomic status of school peers was an important predictor of the school chosen. This evidence is consistent with findings on enrollment patterns for a magnet school program in Montgomery County, Maryland, where parents selected schools that closely mirrored their own racial and socioeconomic status.[21] Research on the open-enrollment program in Massachusetts, in which 95 percent of participating students were white, found that parents were most likely to move their children to districts with higher median incomes, adult population education levels, and per pupil spending.[22]

An examination of a high school intradistrict choice program found that the majority of white families in the program appeared to make school choice decisions using a two-step process.[23] First, they eliminated predominately African American high schools from their school options. Only then did they begin to apply other criteria such as academic quality or school safety in the decisionmaking process. The authors note that the exclusion of predominately African American schools often resulted in families selecting schools with lower academic quality and safety records than would have been selected if these exclusions had not been made. African American families in the study did not follow this same two-step pattern; race was not a factor in their school choice decisions. School poverty rates, however, did have a modest impact on the schools selected by African Americans families.

An analysis of parents' use of an Internet database to gather information on schools found that parents were very concerned with school demographics.[24] Not only was "student body" one of the first school attributes searched but also, as the searches became more sophisticated, the percentage of African Americans in the schools searched decreased. These findings contradict the previously cited survey-based research, which suggests that racial composition rarely plays a role in parents' choice of school.

This contradiction has even been observed within a single study. An analysis of over 1,000 charter school households in Texas found that the only statistically significant difference among stated preferences of African American, Hispanic, and white households was that African Americans were more likely to cite moral values as the most important criterion in their decisionmaking process.[25] Racial composition of a school's population was ranked last among the six preferences for all three groups. An analysis of schools chosen by these families, however, found that household race was one of the best predictors of the racial composition of the charter schools selected. Additionally, citing test scores as a top preference had no effect on the probability of selecting a higher performing charter school. This finding indicates that households' stated preferences are likely to be different from their behavior. A similar mismatch between stated preferences and behavior was observed among parents choosing schools in Chile.[26]

The reasons for these discrepancies in preference and behavior are not known. Parents may lack the information needed to make choices along academic or teacher quality lines and may use race, ethnicity, and average student socioeconomic status as proxies for school quality. For example, the average student socioeconomic status is perceived by parents (in many cases justifiably) to be related to a number of other factors, including the level of resources, the quality of classroom work, the level of parental involvement, and the quality of teachers, all of which are associated with high-quality schools.[27] Several studies reveal that schools with high levels of poverty and large numbers of minorities have, on average, lower levels of resources and less qualified teachers than schools with small numbers of poor and minority students.[28] With regard to expenditures, a study of several urban districts demonstrates that schools with greater numbers of low-income students often receive fewer dollars than other schools within the same district.[29] Because student demographic information is typically more widely available than information on some of these other factors, it is possible that parents will emphasize these demographic variables as an informational shortcut in their decisionmaking, in order to maximize their chances of choosing a school with high levels of resources. What we do not currently know is whether parental choice would better reflect parents' weighted sets of preferences if in fact parents had good information on each of the attributes of interest. Of course, parents may also be concealing their true preferences, giving the socially appropriate response when asked.

Research also demonstrates that regardless of what attributes of schools parents value, the propensity to engage in choice varies as a function of parental education, which in turn is related to racial, ethnic, and socioeconomic background. Several studies reveal that participants in choice programs tend to have higher levels of education than those families who are offered choice but who decline to choose—and that in some cases the difference may be attributable to different levels of access to information about schools.[30]

There is some qualitative research that suggests possible reasons for some of the choice behavior described above. A study on interdistrict choice in the St. Louis area indicates that choices made by inner-city African American students and their parents are likely to differ based on cultural norms and educational expectations.[31] Some students chose to remain in the inner-city, all-black schools, which they found culturally familiar, even when they viewed the predominately white, suburban schools to be academically superior.

Other students and their parents consciously selected suburban schools in hopes of obtaining a higher quality education and greater life opportunities. However, even these academically motivated families often failed to gather information on the suburban schools available to them and chose from among those schools in a somewhat arbitrary manner. These results indicate that, even when school choices are made available, some students and parents may value cultural familiarity over academic quality, a finding that is consistent with other research.[32]

Moreover, these findings are not limited to low-income families. Interviews with the parents of eighty-eight students in public and private schools, including both high- and low-income families, found that while income and access to information predicted some choice behavior, a number of other factors were also important.[33] These included the family's religious beliefs, the characteristics of the public schools available in the family's neighborhood, and the parents' past educational experiences in public and private schools.

If these studies accurately represent the decision processes in which choosers engage, they point to some possible negative consequences of allowing widespread parent choice. In particular, emphasis on the racial and ethnic composition of schools may lead to increased levels of segregation among schools, a fear that is frequently expressed by critics of choice programs. Of course, the level of segregation resulting from a choice program would need to be compared with the segregation that occurs as a result of neighborhood assignment, so even if choice leads some parents to emphasize race and ethnicity, it is not clear that segregation will be exacerbated. Still, these studies suggest that designers of choice programs need to account for the possibility that choice will lead to segregated schools. We return to this topic in the discussion of demonstration programs near the end of this chapter.

Using Information

A critical factor influencing parental choice behavior is the quality of information available to parents on schools operating within the choice system. As discussed earlier, choices are likely to be influenced by the weighted set of preferences that each parent has regarding desired attributes of schools. Presumably these weights will influence how parents choose but only to the extent that valid and accessible information is available on each attribute. Public information systems vary across districts and schools, but none of them is likely to address all of the attributes that parents believe are important. Furthermore, it is likely that parents will vary in the extent to which they will seek additional information beyond what is made easily accessible to them. Some parents may rely exclusively on public reporting systems, whereas others may use their personal networks to gather opinions and inside information on schools, and some may even visit and observe in schools before making a choice. Indeed, social networks, including extended family and friends, are a primary source of information about schools for many parents.[34]

A study commissioned by *Education Week* explores the information needs of parents and other taxpayers through focus groups.[35] Both parents and taxpayers expressed the desire for school-level reports that provide a mix of quantitative and qualitative information, particularly on topics related to school safety, teacher qualifications, and academic achievement. In addition, respondents want a succinct format for reporting the information and comparative data on all schools in the district or state. Consistent with some of the results reported earlier, participants in these focus groups rank demographic information as being the least valuable type of information—though as the earlier discussion suggests, these responses may not reflect true preferences and should be interpreted cautiously. This study also indicates that parents and other taxpayers have concerns about the validity and appropriateness of using standardized test scores to evaluate schools; many respondents worried that the tests may not measure all students' abilities equally well and that educators may "teach to the test" in a way that raises scores without improving students' knowledge and skills.[36]

Sources used to obtain information may vary by parent characteristics. Research on intradistrict choice finds that race and level of education appear to affect the type of information parents find useful when selecting a school.[37] Parents with higher levels of education rely more on social or informal forms of information. Parents with lower levels of education, as well as African American and Hispanic parents, tend to have less-informative social networks and are more likely to rely on formal sources of information, such as the media. Researchers also argue that less-informed parents may use basic visual cues, such as school cleanliness, as a shortcut to identifying quality schools.[38] To the extent that different types of parents rely on different forms of information, there is a risk that choice may lead to stratification by parent education level, particularly if the information available to less-educated parents is of poor quality or irrelevant to the outcomes in which they are truly interested. At the same time, research suggests that choice creates incentives for parents to gather information that may eventually reduce inequities if efforts are made to ensure easy access to the information.[39]

It is important to recognize that most of the work on parents' use of information was conducted before school report cards and other school-level information systems became widely available, as they are today. The relative importance parents place on formal and informal sources of information may be different in states and districts where accurate, comprehensive data on schools are broadly disseminated. As we discuss later, the design of information systems is likely to have a significant impact on how choice policies work in practice, and any information system used for choice purposes will have to take into consideration the kinds of information currently mandated under state and federal education law. At the same time, if those mandates apply only to public schools within a choice system that also includes private schools, some provisions will need to be made to address the discrepancies in available information across schools.

Who Must Make Good Choices?

The discussion so far emphasizes the importance of effective choice behavior on the part of parents and raises concerns about differences among parents in propensity to make good choices and in access to good information. However, some scholars argue that in order for school choice to produce competitive benefits, not all parents need to make informed choices.[40] Competition can be generated through a small subset of well-informed parents who exert pressure on all schools to improve and to promote the outcomes those parents value. Such marginal consumers engage in choice behavior that creates incentives for schools to improve for all students. They also tend to be more involved in their children's schools, which may further increase the pressure schools face to respond to their wishes.[41] For example, in a study of choice among low-income families in New York City, although the majority of parents were relatively uninformed about the quality of schools in their neighborhoods, the small percentage of well-informed parents appeared to lead to improvements in the quality of education at all schools affected by the choice system.[42]

There are questions about whether the choice behavior of marginal consumers will always lead to improved outcomes for all consumers, or whether these parents' choices will result in better outcomes only for their own children. For example, it is conceivable that schools would accommodate marginal consumers by establishing distinct tracks, programs, or classroom assignments that meet their particular desires but that do not provide spillover benefits to those in the more conventional classroom settings in the same school. Also, scholars of choice often fail to recognize that information must flow two ways—not only do parents need good information in order to choose schools, but schools need information about parent preferences and reasons for choosing in order to respond effectively to choice.[43] The problem of differences across families in access to, and use of, information on schools is likely to persist even as that information becomes more widely available, particularly if low-income or poorly educated parents are unable to communicate or act on their preferences as well as more affluent parents. At the same time, the existing research on marginal consumers should mitigate some concerns about the possible negative effects of choice when some parents are not well informed about their choices.

Understanding What Parents Should *Value*

Much of the writing on how families choose seems to be based on an assumption that the academic performance of the school, as measured by test scores, should be of paramount importance and that parents who do not emphasize this are ill informed or irrational. For example, parents often give more weight to factors such as distance from home and availability of day care than they do to test scores; such factors are generally considered ancillary or irrelevant to educational quality.[44] Critics worry that emphasis on nonacademic criteria will create incentives for schools to deemphasize student learning. Although this concern is well-founded, the assertion that parents should only make choices on the basis of academic quality fails to recognize the diversity of contexts in which families are making decisions. An after-school program may be essential if parents wish to avoid having their child spend the after-school hours staying at home watching television or playing outside in crime-ridden neighborhoods; in such cases it may be quite rational for parents to prioritize those programs when selecting schools. Similarly, distance may be a critical criterion for parents who lack access to transportation.

Even parents who value academic outcomes above other considerations are likely to incorporate information other than test scores into their decisions, especially if they have concerns about the validity or comprehensiveness of the tests. Many parents believe that peer effects (the average ability level of the child's schoolmates) and resources (for example, class size) are important determinants of student outcomes and, therefore, are likely to emphasize these factors if they have information on them. Of course, if the primary goal of the choice system is to maximize test scores, it is critical that parents emphasize achievement data or factors that are known to contribute to high test scores. Most parents, however, expect schools to do more than raise test scores, and it is important to understand how parents balance the various outcomes as well as processes when they select schools. The tendency to deemphasize test scores may be especially acute in the high-scoring, suburban neighborhoods that have been the locus of much of the backlash against high-stakes testing. For parents whose children have demonstrated high levels of accomplishment in tested subjects (typically reading and mathematics), a school that has proven successful at raising reading scores of incoming students may be less appealing than one that offers enriched instruction and evidence of accomplishment in science, social studies, and the arts. For parents of lower achieving students, however, evidence that a school has contributed to improving students' performance on mathematics and reading tests may be the most important criterion.

Finally, parents may recognize that the test-score information that is available to them does not tell them what they want to know about the likely effects of a particular school on their own child's future achievement. Specifically, most published school report cards lack information on student achievement growth, making it impossible to determine whether the school actually produces high achievement or whether it simply attracts high-achieving students. Recent developments in value-added modeling are helping researchers and policymakers disentangle the effects of schools or teachers from student background characteristics, but few states or districts use such methods in their reporting.[45] Even when this information is available, it is not clear that most users are capable of understanding what it means or evaluating its limitations. In short, the information parents need to evaluate schools' *effects* on student achievement is almost never available, so it is not surprising that even well-informed parents turn to information other than test scores to make decisions.

Demonstration Programs

Although the studies discussed above shed some light on how parents choose schools, one of the only truly unambiguous findings is that, when asked, most parents will say that they value academic quality above other attributes of schools. As with most outcomes of choice programs, the literature on how parents choose has produced mixed results, and leaves many important questions unanswered.

To date, most studies have been limited to small-scale choice programs operating within fairly constrained contexts. For example, while the voucher studies conducted by Paul Peterson and colleagues provide valuable evidence regarding choice behavior among low-income parents in large urban centers, these findings may not generalize to programs that serve parents from other demographic groups or to choice programs that offer a wider range of options.[46] One way to overcome this limitation is through the implementation of demonstration programs to enhance our understanding of the effects of various school choice policies. These programs would be designed to address a number of research questions, including questions about how families make choices and, as a result, what kinds of incentives are created for schools. They would also help point the way toward design options that have been shown to promote effective choice behavior. We use the term "demonstration programs" rather than simply "research" because it is important that questions about choice be addressed in the context of actual choice programs that are designed in a way that facilitates exploration of specific questions. In other words, rather than conducting research on a program that is implemented without regard to specific research questions that can be answered, a demonstration program would be designed with specific studies in mind.

In discussing these demonstration programs, it is important to note that most studies fail to investigate all of the factors that parents typically consider when choosing a school. Although some efforts to survey parents about their preferences have offered parents the opportunity to mention such attributes as school safety and curriculum, studies of actual choice behavior have focused on easier-to-measure attributes such as test scores and racial and ethnic composition, avoiding the extremely difficult task of considering the broad set of attributes that may influence parental decisions. This lack of evidence concerning the relative emphasis placed on the variety of attributes that parents consider limits our ability to understand all of the influences on their decisions.

Additionally, it is important to consider the kind of data that parents are likely to encounter as a result of the increased trend toward public reporting of achievement test scores and other information. For example, the No Child Left Behind (NCLB) legislation requires schools to report test scores for racial, ethnic, and socioeconomic subgroups and to provide limited information on teacher quality. As parents become accustomed to having this type of data readily available, their propensity to use this information will almost certainly increase, though there may continue to be differences in access to information across groups.

Here we raise some questions that could be addressed in future research and discuss some specific features that might be included in a demonstration program and that would enhance our understanding of how parents make choices:

—Does the correspondence between parents' stated preferences and their actual choice behavior improve when better information on dimensions of interest is available?

—How does choice behavior differ as a function of location and parental employment?

—How is parental choice influenced by the supply of schools, and how do parental preferences affect supply?

—How are the responses of schools and choosers shaped by the design of information systems?

Parents' Stated Preferences and Their Behavior

The state report cards that have been produced as a result of the NCLB legislation have made certain types of information available in a form that allows users to evaluate a school's overall achievement as well as changes in achievement over time for the school as a whole and for specific subgroups. Some states and districts are taking additional steps to make sure information is presented in a form that is useful for parents. For example, some have contracted with vendors that repackage test score data in ways that allow parents to compare demographically similar schools or to view profiles of achievement on specific areas of skill or knowledge. There are also a number of public and private initiatives that are designed to facilitate better information use and that have resulted in web sites such as schoolmatters.com and greatschools.net. In addition, several states are exploring the use of value-added models or other methods for measuring individual student growth, though few have yet incorporated this information into their published report cards. A careful investigation of the ways in which parents use this information, and of which parents are most likely to use it, will shed light on whether these efforts are worthwhile and whether they are likely to improve school choice behavior.

At the same time, the NCLB law by itself does not improve the quality of information on other dimensions. There are provisions for reporting data on school safety and teacher quality, but the information that states will report may not address the specific concerns that parents have about these factors. Consider parents' frequently reported emphasis on "high standards." Although test scores may be interpreted as evidence of the kinds of standards a school promotes, by themselves they probably do not fully address what parents want to know.

A demonstration program should explore the utility of providing additional information on the factors that parents have cited as important and should examine how the provision of this information influences choice behavior. Studying these issues would require examining the variation in the information available to different families (by manipulating the information systematically, if possible) and tracking parents' use of that information as well as their eventual choices. While surveys or focus groups may help illuminate what features of the information system are most likely to be useful, the research cited earlier suggests that relying exclusively on parents' self-reports is likely to produce somewhat misleading conclusions.

The increasing availability of the Internet provides an opportunity not only to disseminate information in a timely way but also to track parents' behavior as they access the information. Problems of unequal access to the Internet would need to be addressed, perhaps through the provision of equipment, connections, and training for low-income study participants.

Parental Behavior as a Function of Location and Parental Employment

Much of the research to date has examined differences in choice behavior among parents from different racial, ethnic, and socioeconomic groups as well as among parents with differing levels of education. This research should be expanded to consider other factors that are likely to affect the choices parents make: emphasis on nonacademic factors such as distance from home or the presence of an after-school program, for example, may be influenced by parents' personal constraints such as work schedules or access to public transportation. If such constraints promote choices of academically inferior schools, or if parents' emphasis on nonacademic factors causes schools to focus on these factors rather than on educational quality, the goals of choice advocates may not be realized.

This question could be explored using existing choice programs and data collection approaches similar to those used in earlier studies. To understand the causal links between family circumstance and choice behavior, however, it would be preferable to design a study that systematically varied options for parents in different circumstances. If that is not feasible, a longitudinal study tracking parent choice behavior as new options become available, combined with information gathered directly from parents, could shed some light on ways in which work, neighborhood, and other factors affect how parents choose.

Parental Preferences and Education Availability

Much of the existing research fails to consider interplay between demand and supply. Parental choice is obviously constrained by the options available to them, and in many cases the options are quite limited. For example, the NCLB legislation has resulted in an increased number of families being offered choice among public schools in their districts, but many states and districts face significant shortages of available slots, and the shortfalls are likely to grow as an increasing number of schools are labeled as needing improvement and are forced to offer choice. Even programs that offer private school vouchers may be subject to shortages, particularly if the dollar amount of the voucher is too small to be attractive to many private schools, or if parents are forced to pay part of the cost of private school attendance.

To understand how a large-scale choice program will work in the long run, both in promoting improved student outcomes and in generating a new supply of schools, it will be necessary to launch a demonstration project that offers relatively unconstrained choice and that makes it relatively easy for new providers to open schools. The National Working Commission on Choice in K–12 Education report discusses the importance of the supply response, and clearly the interplay between what parents demand and how schools and providers respond will be critical to the success of any large-scale choice program.[47]

A related issue that is rarely addressed in research is how parents communicate their preferences to the suppliers of education and what actions on the part of parents contribute to improved supply. In a system that promotes relatively easy entry into the market, providers are likely to take cues from parents as they design their schools and instructional programs. And existing schools will use information from parents to make changes designed to attract new students and discourage exit. How do parents communicate what they want to schools, and do school personnel pay attention? Are some parents better able to communicate their preferences than others? What are the specific behaviors in which parents engage to get their message across? All of these questions are relevant to the issue of supply response.

Information and the Responses of Schools and Choosers

Information sends cues not only to choosers but also to schools. High-stakes testing programs that impose rewards or sanctions on schools or teachers often lead to significant changes in teachers' practices, and sometimes the mere publication of scores is sufficient to induce change in behavior.[48] If school personnel believe it is important to attract new families, and if they believe that families are using existing information systems to make decisions, they are likely to alter their behavior to improve their standing on whatever information systems are most commonly used. To the extent that there is no formal information provision mechanism, the responses of school personnel will probably vary depending on their own beliefs about what parents value or on direct feedback from parents. However, as report cards and other reporting systems become more common and standardized across schools and districts, providers are likely to strive to make themselves look better on those measures. As a result, the specific measures used in the reporting system may influence providers' behavior. For example, the decision to publish information on student-teacher ratios may ultimately affect the emphasis school personnel place on efforts to lower class size. Similarly, a system that reports only school averages might induce different behaviors than one that also reports information based on student achievement growth. This is largely speculation, of course; some of the demonstration programs described above could be designed to collect systematic data on how schools respond to information systems.

Similarly, the design of the information system may affect parents' choice behavior by focusing their attention on specific attributes of schools or by sending an implicit message that certain characteristics of schools are considered more important than others. Research is needed to understand how parents respond to these systems, whether some parents are more likely than others to shift their criteria in response to the way information is provided, and whether uniformity of reporting increases uniformity of decisionmaking.

Additional Research Questions

A number of other questions that the earlier literature reviews and discussions have raised could be addressed through demonstration programs. These include questions about the role of marginal consumers (for example, who they are, how they affect outcomes, and in what way their role depends on how the system is designed) and questions about the factors that affect parent and student behavior after a choice is made (for example, what determines whether the student will remain in the chosen school or will return to the original school and how decisions to remain or leave are related to parent involvement in the child's school).[49] Certainly an almost unlimited number of additional questions could be raised. Although research gives us some guidance as well as reason to be cautiously optimistic about the effects of parental choice, as policymakers move forward to implement choice schemes they should try to design the programs in a way that allows researchers to attempt to answer some of the questions raised in this section; this will, in turn, lead to improved program design and more desirable outcomes.

Promoting Good Choices

Even as policymakers and researchers move forward with the demonstration programs discussed in this chapter, others will be looking for guidance as they implement various forms of choice before the results of these programs become available. We should therefore use what we know about choice behavior to make recommendations for design options that will improve decisionmaking in existing choice systems. In this section we provide some guidelines that policymakers can follow to promote good choice behavior. This list is not complete, but it addresses some of the important factors that affect the ways in which families make choices.

—Improve information systems by making them more widely available, easier to understand, and more comprehensive. The increasing availability of the Internet provides an opportunity to improve the way information is disseminated, though it will continue to be necessary to rely on other means as well for those parents who lack easy Internet access. Information on school performance should be presented in a format that is easily understood and that addresses the variety of attributes that parents say matter to them (in particular, most parents believe school quality involves more than test scores and would like information on other aspects of quality). Several organizations have developed web-based tools to provide information to parents and others; these include the Grow Network, Standard and Poor's School Evaluation Services, and Just for the Kids. These provide good models for states or others who wish to develop their own systems, but it is important to obtain input and feedback from parents to ensure that local needs are met.

—Subject private schools participating in choice programs to the test administration and reporting provisions that public schools must meet. As a result of NCLB, parents in all fifty states are able to obtain comparative information on their public schools. Private schools, however, are not required to test their students or to publish results, which prevents parents from having accurate information on how they are performing academically. In addition, the ambitious targets imposed by NCLB have resulted in large numbers of public schools being labeled as "needing improvement," whereas no such negative label will be attached to private schools. To ensure fair comparisons and good decisionmaking, choice programs that include private schools should subject participating private schools to the same testing and reporting requirements that public schools must meet. Some private schools will undoubtedly resist, but permitting one set of schools to avoid the spotlight that the federal legislation shines on public school performance will lead to a system that is perceived to be unbalanced and unfair and that may lead to wildly different behavior on the part of the public and private sectors.

—Create incentives for parents to seek out and use information. These include offering a large number of choices and limiting any regulations that restrict a child's ability to attend the school of their parents' choice (for example, strict racial and ethnic quotas). No matter how accessible the information is, parents are unlikely to use it if they believe their choices are highly constrained. To encourage parents to gather information and to choose a school that reflects their preferences, choice systems must be designed in a way that offers real choice. This does not mean that the system must be completely unconstrained, only that constraints must not restrict parents to only a few options.

—Create a mechanism for feedback from the demand side to the supply side. As we discuss earlier, schools are likely to respond to parental preferences if they feel pressure to attract new students and if they understand what parents actually want. "Sending schools" (those that students leave to attend schools of choice) may not be aware of why students or parents have decided to leave, and therefore they may not know how or what they should be improving.[50] A formal mechanism that asks parents to articulate reasons for their decisions could enhance the decisionmaking process as well as the quality of the supply-side response.

Some of these recommendations are easier to implement than others, and none of them has been tried in a large-scale choice system, so it is difficult to predict exactly what outcomes would result from their implementation. Still, based on what we know about parental choice, we believe these steps will improve decisionmaking and will ultimately result in an increase in the extent to which parents influence what schools do.

Notes

1. Throughout this chapter we refer to parents or families as choosers, but it is important to keep in mind that students also influence choices, particularly as they reach the secondary grades.

2. See discussion in Terry M. Moe, *Private Vouchers* (Stanford, Calif.: Hoover Institution Press, 1995).

3. Mark Schneider, Paul Teske, and Melissa Marschall, *Choosing Schools: Consumer Choice and the Quality of American Schools* (Princeton University Press, 2000).

4. Ibid., p. 87.

5. Henry M. Levin, "A Comprehensive Framework for Evaluating Educational Vouchers," *Educational Evaluation and Policy Analysis* 24 (2002): 159–74.

6. For a more complete review of literature on parental decisionmaking see Paul Teske and Mark Schneider, "What Research Can Tell Policy Makers about School Choice," *Journal of Policy Analysis and Management* 20, no. 4 (2001): 609–31.

7. Jay P. Greene, Paul E. Peterson, and Jiangtao Du, "School Choice in Milwaukee: A Randomized Experiment," in *Learning from School Choice,* edited by Paul E. Peterson and Brian Hassel (Brookings, 1998); Paul E. Peterson and David E. Campbell, "An Evaluation of the Children's Scholarship Fund," PEPG/01-03 (Program on Education Policy and Governance, Harvard University, 2001); John F. Witte, *The Market Approach to Education: An Analysis of America's First Voucher Program* (Princeton University Press, 2000); Valerie Martinez and others, "The Consequences of School Choices: Who Leaves and Who Stays in the Inner City," *Social Science Quarterly* 76 (1995): 485–501.

8. Brett Kleitz and others, "Choice, Charter Schools, and Household Preferences," *Social Science Quarterly* 83, no. 3 (2000): 846–54

9. David J. Armor and Brett M. Peiser, "Interdistict Choice in Massachusetts," in *Learning from School Choice,* edited by Peterson and Hassel.

10. Ellen Goldring, "Parent Involvement and School Choice: Israel and the U.S.," in *Diversity in Schooling: Perspectives and Prospects,* edited by Ron Glatter, Philip Woods, and Carl Bagley (London: Routledge, 1997); Gregg Vanourek and others, "Charter Schools as Seen by Students, Teachers, and Parents," in *Learning from School Choice,* edited by Peterson and Hassel.

11. Steve Farkas and Jean Johnson, with Stephen Immerwahr and Joanna McHugh, "Time to Move On: African American and White Parents Set an Agenda for Schools" (New York: Public Agenda, 1998); Martinez and others, "The Consequences of School Choices."

12. Schneider, Teske, and Marschall, *Choosing Schools.*

13. Ibid. p. 107. An emphasis on safety among low-income families is consistent with surveys that indicate a high level of violence in many of these families' neighborhood schools. See William G. Howell and Paul E. Peterson, with Patrick J. Wolf and David E. Campbell, *The Education Gap: Vouchers and Urban Schools* (Brookings, 2002).

14. Mark Schneider and others, "School Choice and Culture Wars in the Classroom: What Different Parents Seek from Education," *Social Science Quarterly* 79, no. 3 (1998): 489–501.

15. Ibid., p. 498.

16. Ibid., p. 499.

17. Schneider, Teske, and Marschall, *Choosing Schools.*

18. Thomas Stewart, Patrick J. Wolf, and Stephen Q. Cornman, "Parent and Student Voices on the First Year of the D.C. Opportunity Scholarship Program," SCDP 05/01 (School Choice Demonstration Project, Georgetown University, 2005), available at www.georgetown.educ/research/scdp/.

19. Harlan Hahn, David Klingman, and Harry Pachon, "Cleavages, Coalitions, and the Black Candidate: The Los Angeles Mayoralty Elections of 1969 and 1973," *Western Political Quarterly* 29 (1976): 507–20.

20. Steven Glazerman, "A Conditional Logit Model of Elementary School Choice: What Do Parents Value?" (Harris School of Public Policy, University of Chicago, 1997).

21. Jeffrey Henig, "Choice in Public Schools: An Analysis of Transfer Requests among Magnet Schools," *Social Science Quarterly* 71, no. 1 (1990): 69–85.

22. Richard Fossey, "Open Enrollment in Massachusetts: Why Families Choose," *Educational Evaluation and Policy Analysis* 16, no. 3 (1994): 320–34.

23. Salvatore Saporito and Annette Lareau, "School Selection as a Process: The Multiple Dimensions of Race in Framing Educational Choice," *Social Problems* 46, no. 3 (1999): 418–39.

24. Mark Schneider and Jack Buckley, "What Do Parents Want from Schools? Evidence from the Internet," *Educational Evaluation and Policy Analysis* 24, no. 2 (2002): 113–44.

25. Gregory R. Weiher and Kent L. Tedin, "Does Choice Lead to Racially Distinctive Schools? Charter Schools and Household Preferences," *Journal of Policy Analysis and Management* 21, no. 1 (2002): 79–92.

26. Gregory Elacqua, *School Choice in Chile: An Analysis of Parental Preferences and Search Behavior* (National Center for the Study of Privatization in Education, Teachers College, Columbia University, 2004).

27. Helen F. Ladd, "School Vouchers: A Critical View," *Journal of Economic Perspectives* 16, no. 4 (2002): 3–24.

28. See National Center for Education Statistics, "The Condition of Education" (U.S. Department of Education, 2003); Hamilton Lankford, Susanna Loeb, and James Wyckoff, "Teacher Sorting and the Plight of Urban Schools: A Descriptive Analysis," *Educational Evaluation and Policy Analysis* 24, no. 1 (2002): 37–62; *Education Week,* "'If I Can't Learn from You . . .': Ensuring a Highly Qualified Teacher for Every Classroom," Quality Counts 2003 Report (Washington, 2003).

29. Maguerite Roza and Karen Hawley Miles, "A New Look at Inequities in School Funding: A Presentation on the Resource Variations within Districts" (Seattle: Center on Reinventing Public Education, 2002).

30. R. Gary Bridge and Julie Blackman, "A Study of Alternatives in American Education: Family Choice in Schooling" (Santa Monica, Calif.: RAND, 1978); Valerie E. Lee, Robert Croninger, and Julia Smith, "Equity and Choice in Detroit," in *Who Chooses? Who Loses?* edited by Bruce Fuller, Richard Elmore, and Gary Orfield (Teachers College Press, 1996); John F. Witte, "First-Year Report: Milwaukee Parental Choice Program" (University of Wisconsin, Department of Political Science, and the Robert La Follette Institute of Public Affairs, 1991); Richard L. Nault and Susan Uchitelle, "School Choice in the Public Sector: A Case Study of Parental Decision Making," in *Family Choice in Schooling: Issues and Dilemmas,* edited by Michael E. Manley-Casimir (Lexington, Mass.: Lexington Books, 1982).

31. Amy Stuart Wells, "African-American Students' View on School Choice," in *Who Chooses? Who Loses?* edited by Fuller, Elmore, and Orfield.

32. Jeffrey Henig, "Choice in Public Schools"; John Maddaus, "Parental Choice of Schools: What Parents Think and Do," in *Review of Education Research,* edited by Courtney B. Cazden (Washington: American Educational Research Association, 1990).

33. Robert C. Bulman, "School-Choice Stories: Unraveling the Dynamics of High School Selection" (University of California, Department of Sociology, 1999).

34. Janet R. Beales and Maureen Wahl, "Private Vouchers in Milwaukee: The Pave Program," in *Private Vouchers,* edited by Terry M. Moe (Stanford, Calif.: Hoover Institution Press, 1995); Schneider, Teske, and Marschall, *Choosing Schools.*

35. Education Week, "Accountability for Public Schools: Developing School Report Cards" (Washington, 1998).

36. Laura S. Hamilton, "Assessment as a Policy Tool," in *Review of Research in Education,* vol. 27, edited by Robert Floden (Washington: American Educational Research Association, 2003).

37. Schneider, Teske, and Marschall, *Choosing Schools.*

38. Mark Schneider and others, "Shopping for Schools: In the Land of the Blind the One-Eyed Parent May Be Enough," *American Journal of Political Science* 42 (1998): 769–93.

39. Schneider, Teske, and Marschall, *Choosing Schools.*

40. Ibid.; Paul Teske and others, "Establishing the Micro Foundations of a Macro Theory: Information, Movers, and the Competitive Local Market for Public Goods," *American Political Science Review* 87 (1993): 702–13.

41. Schneider, Teske, and Marschall, *Choosing Schools.*

42. Schneider and others, "Shopping for Schools."

43. Paul F. Manna, "The Signals Parents Send When They Choose Their Children's Schools," *Education Policy* 16, no. 3 (2002): 425–47.

44. Schneider and Buckley, "What Do Parents Want from Schools?" p. 134.

45. Daniel F. McCaffrey and others, *Evaluating Value-Added Models for Teacher Accountability* (Santa Monica, Calif.: RAND, 2003).

46. For example, Daniel P. Mayer and others, "School Choice in New York City after Three Years: An Evaluation of the School Choice Scholarships Program" (Washington: Mathematica Policy Research, 2002); Peterson and Campbell, "An Evaluation of the Children's Scholarship Fund"; Martin West, Paul E. Peterson, and David E. Campbell, "School Choice in Dayton, Ohio, after Two Years," PEPG/01-04 (Harvard University, Program on Educational Policy and Governance, 2001); Patrick J. Wolf, Paul E. Peterson, and Martin R. West, "Results of a School Voucher Experiment: The Case of Washington D.C. after Two Years," PEPG/01-05 (Harvard University, Program on Education Policy and Governance, 2001).

47. National Working Commission on Choice in K–12 Education, *School Choice: Doing It the Right Way Makes a Difference* (Brown Center on Education Policy, Brookings, 2003).

48. Hamilton, "Assessment as a Policy Tool"; Brian M. Stecher, "Consequences of Large-Scale, High-Stakes Testing on School and Classroom Practices," in *Making Sense of Test-Based Accountability in Education,* edited by Laura S. Hamilton, Brian M. Stecher, and Stephen P. Klein (Santa Monica, Calif: RAND, 2002). Similarly, the publication of health care report cards has been shown to influence what health care organizations do, particularly when those organizations operate in competitive markets. Daniel R. Longo and Allen J. Daugird, "Measuring Quality of Care: Reforming the Health Care System," *American Journal of Medical Quality* 9, no. 3 (1994): 104–15; Martin N. Marshall and others, "The Public Release of Performance Data: What Do We Expect to Gain? A Review of the Evidence," *Journal of the American Medical Association* 283 (2000): 1866–874.

49. See Wells, "African-American Students' View on School Choice."

50. Manna, "The Signals Parents Send When They Choose Their Children's Schools."

4

The Supply Side of School Choice

JULIAN R. BETTS, DAN GOLDHABER,
AND LARRY ROSENSTOCK

A supply-side response to a school choice program is an essential part of the theory that greater choice will lead to positive systemic changes in K–12 education. The number and type of schools that open or expand will determine both whether students wishing to exercise choice have viable options as well as the extent to which all schools face competitive pressures. Thus understanding the influences on the supply of schools (more precisely, the supply of educational slots) is crucial to identifying the likely impacts of various choice programs.

A basic assumption of any school choice system is that, under such a system, K–12 education would function more like a market. In theory, suppliers should therefore enter the market to meet any increase in demand. However, as described in this chapter, even if the market analogy proves to be apt, the specific provisions of choice programs combined with community context factors are likely to have a major influence on any supply response.

We begin by presenting a simple theoretical model that describes the various factors influencing the supply of schools. In the following two sections we discuss the implications of our theoretical model for the real world of K–12 education and review some of the existing research on the determinants of school supply. This body of research is useful but does not alone give a full picture of how the supply of educational slots might expand in a widespread choice system. Therefore, in the following section we bring together observations from a variety of sources on barriers that currently prevent more schools of choice in California from opening their doors and keeping them open. In the final section we offer some conclusions and public policy recommendations.

The Theoretical Model

Because the theory of a supply-side response to the introduction of choice is grounded in the market analogy, it is useful to explore the assumptions of school supply in a market context. In the private sector, the motivating factor determining supply-side decisions is profit. Though many schools wishing to enter the K–12 education market may be motivated by profit, it is likely that many will not.[1] Nonetheless, it is still helpful to use the market framework when analyzing the supply decisions of schools, because the effects of changes in conditions are likely, all else equal, to have the same effect on the probability of entering the market for a nonprofit organization as they would for a profit-maximizing organization. In a typical nonprofit school scenario, for example, "excess profits" translate into the school's being able to pay higher salaries to teachers and administrators, to have annual budget surpluses and a positive fund balance, and even to accumulate an endowment. All of these features would serve to stimulate other school operators to enter the market, just as profits would in a traditional market scenario.

If we imagine a comprehensive choice system whereby educational consumers have the freedom to choose among many schools, each school would be relatively small compared to the market as a whole. While different assumptions of market structure would change the estimates of the number of entrants into the market, the direction of supply effects (that is, supply increases or decreases) will be consistent regardless of the assumed structure.[2] Thus we begin by examining the supply decision under the idealized conditions of a perfectly competitive market. While idealized, this serves to outline the way in which competition can enhance the provision of services. We discuss the implications of relaxing the assumption of perfect competition below.

According to economic theory, several important features characterize a perfectly competitive market. From the perspective of the schools, a competitive market is one in which there are many schools offering an undifferentiated product and in which market entry or exit does not substantively affect the market as a whole, due to the relatively small size of each individual

school. In addition, schools are price takers in the sense that they face an infinite demand for their product at a given price, but if they raise their price (tuition), all students would opt to attend a different school. Finally, this market structure assumes a free flow of information to all students about the quality of all the schools in the market.

Like any market, at least in theory, we would expect the demand for schooling to increase as the price of schooling falls. Thus were we to graph various prices (per pupil spending) against market demand, the slope of the line representing this demand would be negative. Conversely, the theoretical line representing the relationship between price and the supply of schooling (number of enrollment slots) is expected to be upward sloping, since existing school suppliers would likely supply more schooling if they could get a higher price for it, and we would expect more educational entrepreneurs to enter the education market if prices were higher.

Figure 4-1 shows these hypothetical relationships. The left-hand part of the figure shows how the overall demand for and supply of enrollment in schools of choice interact to determine an overall payment per pupil for schools of choice. The right-hand part of the figure shows how administrators at an individual school of choice would respond to this market price by setting overall enrollment at the school. In the left-hand graph, the market supply curve reflects the total number of slots that all schools together are willing to provide for a given level of funding. The unique price or funding level at which the quantities demanded and supplied are equal determines the overall price in the market.

To understand the basis for the market supply curve, it is useful to consider the supply decision from the point of view of an individual firm, which, for simplicity, we assume is an individual school. As shown in the right-hand panel of figure 4-2, the school is assumed to face a horizontal demand curve that is equal to the market-determined per pupil compensation. The horizontal nature of the demand curve represents the notion that the school is but one of many of similar quality and therefore has little influence over the pricing in the market as a whole. It can therefore "sell" as many educational slots as it wishes at the market determined price (tuition) but cannot increase its price above the market-determined one without losing all of its students, because those students can attend a number of alternatives at the market price.

Because the price of schooling is determined by the market as a whole, the school supply decision is going to be completely contingent on the cost to the school of supplying education. In particular, the school has an incentive to keep providing school slots as long as the additional revenue, called the

Figure 4-1. *Overall Market Demand and Supply and an Individual School's Supply Response*

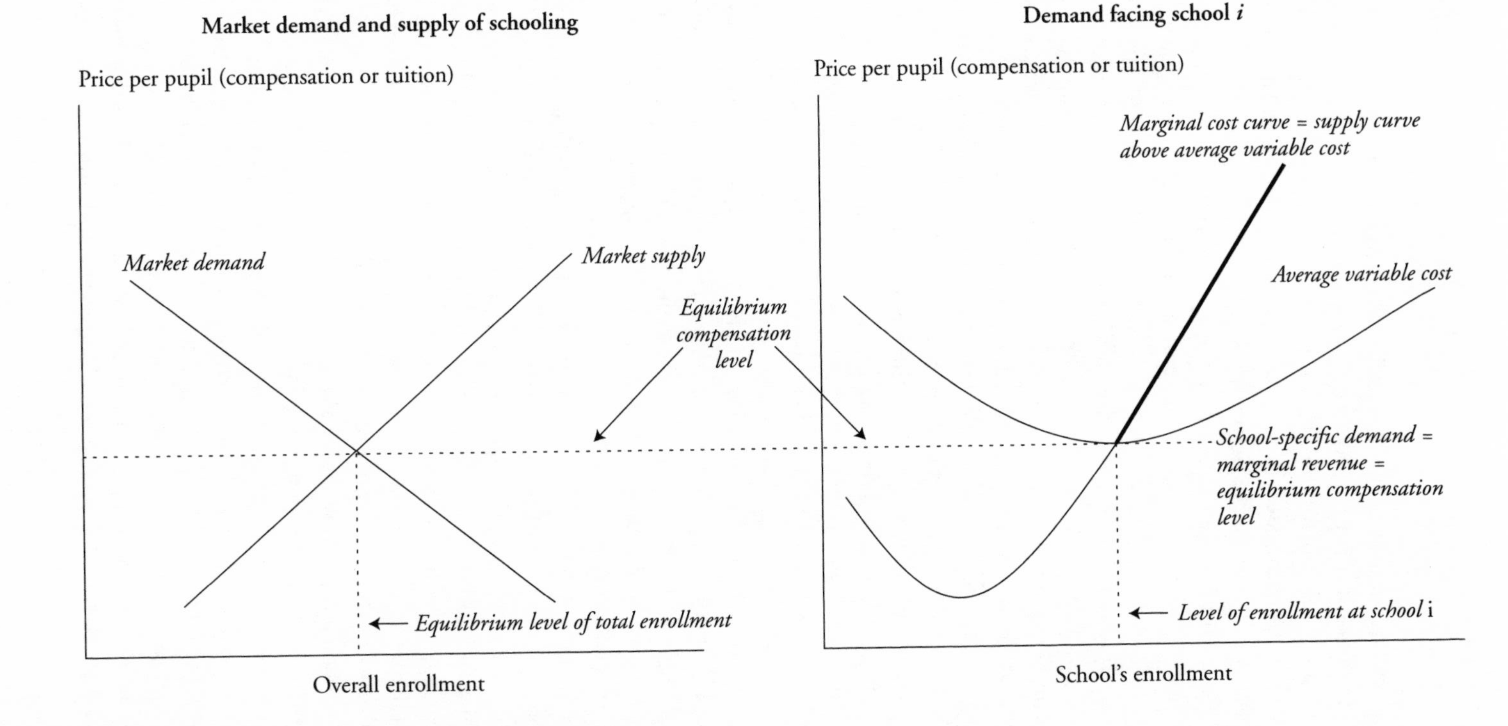

Figure 4-2. *Long-Run Decisions to Enter or Exit Market, by Average Total Cost and Revenue per Pupil*

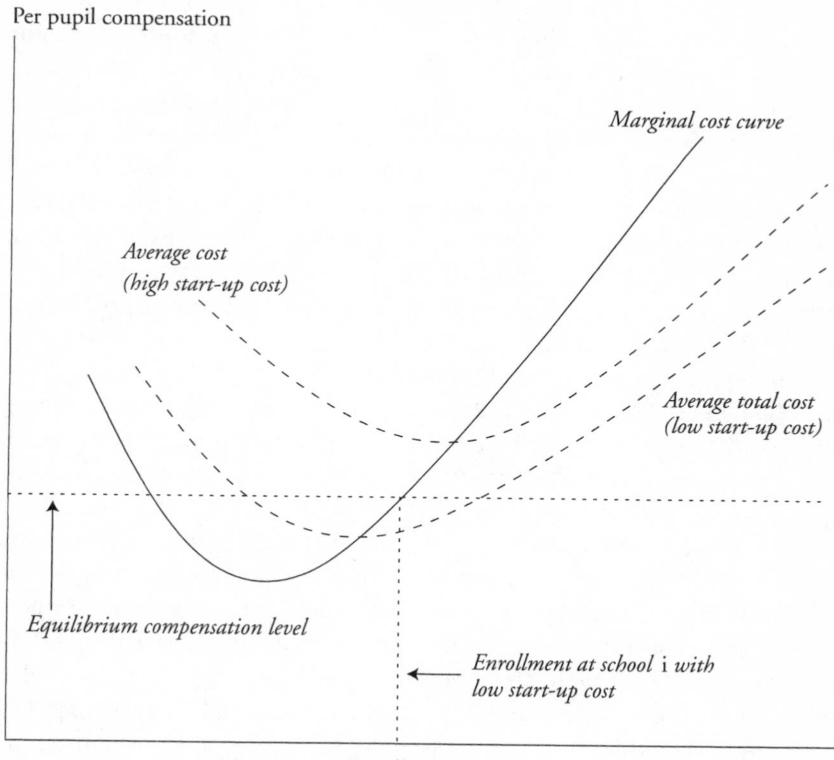

marginal revenue, it receives from the sale of an additional slot exceeds the cost of providing education to the student who fills that slot, referred to as the marginal cost. In other words, a school will continue to admit students as long as the tuition it receives exceeds the cost of educating the additional students. As shown in the figure, marginal cost is often a U-shaped curve, but in general increases at higher levels of enrollment, because of bottlenecks in production of services to students. For instance, with a fixed number of classrooms, it will become more costly to accommodate more students beyond a point. Thus the marginal cost curve represents the minimum tuition rate that would make it profitable for the school to admit another student. This marginal cost curve is the school's supply curve—but only that portion of the curve that lies above the average variable cost curve (the curve showing per student average cost, excluding fixed costs, of supplying education at different enrollment levels). A school will choose to shut down temporarily if the price drops below the average variable costs, because it will incur losses by opening its doors if it operates at an enrollment level where it is receiving less in compensation for each pupil served than the average cost of educating a pupil.

It is possible for school providers to earn significant profits in the short run; however, in the long run the supply response of individual school providers will be such that the aggregate supply and demand curves intersect at a point where the price (tuition, in the case of private schools) is set so that no school is earning more than "normal" profits. This means that no school provider will receive a rate of return on investment that exceeds the rate of return that would have been received had the investment been in the next best option. For example, if there are large profits to be made in the provision of schooling, more providers will opt to enter the schooling market, shifting the supply curve to the right, sending the equilibrium price of schooling downward, and hence diminishing those profits. This is an important economic concept because it implies that no providers are receiving "excess" profits and that only those providers that operate efficiently survive in the market. While this concept applies explicitly to for-profit school providers, it also implicitly dictates the level of efficiency that would be necessary for not-for-profit schools to remain open in the absence of any additional subsidies.

Figure 4-1 helps to illustrate how the specific provisions of any choice plan might greatly affect supply decisions. For example, any policy that enhances demand for new schools (such as public provision of transportation, increases in the size of a voucher, or expanded public funding per student for charter schools) would shift the market demand curve to the right, leading to an increase in the equilibrium price level in the market. This increases the per pupil amount that will be received by school *i,* leading to an intersection of marginal revenue and marginal cost that lies further to the right; therefore school *i* supplies more slots for students. It is also the case that changes in public school quality would be expected to affect the supply of nonpublic schools. One might anticipate, for instance, that the demand for nonpublic schools would vary inversely with the quality of public schools. Thus, all else equal, we should expect a higher demand and therefore a larger supply of nonpublic schools in areas with lower-quality public schools.

The long-run decision about whether to stay in the market or to enter the market depends on whether revenue per pupil is at least as large as average total cost. Average total cost is the sum of variable costs plus fixed costs (such as land leases or interest payments on permanent equipment), all divided by enrollment. Because average total cost includes fixed costs it is higher than average variable costs.

The decision over whether or not to enter the market is depicted more formally in figure 4-2. In this depiction, there are two average total-cost curves that a school could potentially face. One influence on the average total-cost curve is the costs associated with starting a school: high start-up costs are associated with a higher average total-cost curve, low start-up costs with a lower average total-cost curve. We can divide the total costs of operating the school into fixed costs, *F,* which do not vary with enrollment, and variable costs, *V,* which do vary with enrollment. Examples of fixed costs are the legal and regulatory costs of establishing a new school, the cost of new facilities, and basic maintenance. Examples of variable costs are teachers and supplies. It immediately becomes clear that average costs will plummet as a school increases its enrollment from zero, because, if E is enrollment, average cost will be $[F + V(E)] / E$, where $V(E)$ indicates that variable costs depend on E. For instance, a school that increases its enrollment from ten to twenty students may incur some minor additional variable costs, but this will probably be outweighed by the fact that the fixed costs are now being shared among twice the number of students. A rise in enrollment, which lowers the fixed costs per student, will lower the average cost per student—but only up to a point. At some point, as enrollment rises the school will begin to run out of space. At this point, adding more students could require the construction of new classrooms, overtime pay for teachers, and the like. Eventually, average cost per student should start to increase.

These competing patterns—declining fixed costs per student and rising marginal costs as enrollment rises—lead to the classic U-shaped average cost curve shown in figure 4-2, which has been observed repeatedly in many real-world studies of diverse industries. In essence, there is a single point that minimizes the operation's average cost per student. The figure shows two possible average cost curves, one reflecting high start-up costs and the other low start-up costs. The school with high start-up costs will have a higher average cost curve, and (as shown) the minimum point of the supply curve will be further to the right. In practice, this means that schools with higher fixed costs will, in general, be bigger, because they need a larger enrollment to absorb the fixed costs.

In the case of the high start-up costs shown in the figure (we discuss some real-world challenges to school start-ups in the following section), the school-specific demand curve intersects the marginal cost curve in the portion below the average total cost. At this point, the cost of providing this level of enrollment is greater than the revenue received, and the school will choose not to enter the market. By contrast, in the case of the low start-up costs, the same intersection point now lies above the average total cost curve. Schools will opt to enter the market in this case, since the cost of providing this level of enrollment is less than the revenue received, which indicates that the school would anticipate earning a profit from operation. High start-up costs imply that expanding existing schools will be far easier than building new schools.

It is also important to consider the implications of various regulations on both the decision to enter the market and the supply level. For example, regulation of the teacher labor market (such as credentialing) will potentially influence the costs of providing education. To the degree that these regulations increase the cost of provision, the average total-cost curve will be higher, therefore reducing the number of new school suppliers. In practice, there are several reasons that a competitive market structure may not always be the best one to consider in this context. For example, in rural areas there may be relatively few schooling options, which might imply that new school entrants will affect overall market conditions. Also, schools are distinct from one another in many ways, suggesting that they are not perfect substitutes for each other.

A market structure with large numbers of suppliers of a similar but somewhat differentiated product is referred to as monopolistic competition. The differentiation of product results in each school-specific demand curve having a downward tilt; the reason for this is that each school's product is a close—if not perfect—substitute for another. This downward slope signifies that a school is no longer a price taker and can choose the level of per pupil compensation that maximizes its profits.

This does not automatically mean that a school will be profitable, however. Although the school can determine the price, it cannot simultaneously determine the level of enrollment. Schools are still subject to the demand curve. In this case, the school will choose the level of enrollment such that the marginal cost of that level of enrollment is equal to the marginal revenue. As shown in figure 4-3, marginal revenue from admitting one more student is significantly below the demand curve. This pattern reflects the assumption in the monopolistic competition model that, to increase enrollment, the school must drop its price for *all* students. So if a school receives P dollars from one new student, its total increase in revenues is less than P.

The entry decision that monopolistic competitors face is similar to the decision that perfect competitors face: if the profit-maximizing price they set

Figure 4-3. *School Choice under Monopolistic Competition*

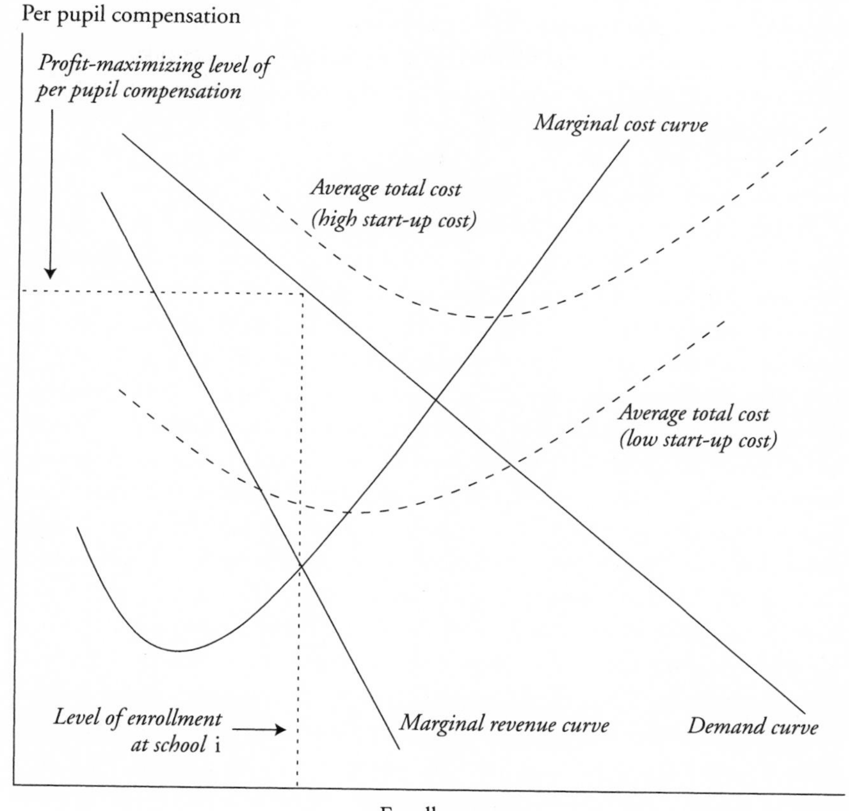

is above the average total cost, then it will be profitable to enter. If the price is below the average total cost, then they will incur losses upon entry and will likely choose not to do so. With monopolistic competition, the demand curve that the school faces depends on the number of competitors and the degree of differentiation among the competitors. Roughly speaking, a school facing a steeper demand curve (fewer substitutes) will have greater profits than one facing a flatter demand curve. In this case, a school has greater incentive to offer a different product than other schools, thus decreasing the amount of substitutability to their competitors.

From this analysis it is clear that schools tend to base entry decisions on their expected compensation as well as the marginal and average costs they face. We have simplified the analysis by looking at a static rather than a dynamic picture of the school decisions. In reality, the average costs that schools consider will be over the length of time that they expect to incur the costs and receive the revenues. Clearly, then, the time frame of these anticipated costs and benefits will affect the cost and revenue curves they face. For example, there are costs associated with uncertainty. Greater uncertainty over how long a choice system will exist increases the costs to potential market entrants, thus reducing the likelihood of entry.[3]

In the context of public school choice (that is, charter schools or private schools responding to voucher opportunities), the concept of price is a tricky one. From the school's point of view (which determines market entry), revenue per student is likely to be set by the state, either in the form of a voucher amount or per pupil funding for charters. Thus it would seem at first that all schools must be price takers and that price is determined not directly by market factors but by political power and institutional factors. However, in practice, successful charter schools are able to augment this revenue, or price, in a variety of ways. Many charter schools, though prohibited by law from charging tuition, do operate at a significantly higher cost per pupil than they are allocated by the state: successful schools are able to raise these funds from corporations, foundations, and individual giving by parents. Thus to the extent that charter schools can stimulate this kind of supplemental demand, they can influence the market price and thus increase average revenue. Though it is not the common practice under current voucher programs, voucher schools could, in theory, charge tuition and require parents to "top off" the voucher amount.

The unusual price structure described above is consistent with the monopolistic competition model: as more and more successful schools enter the market, it will become increasingly difficult to attract these extra funds, sending the equilibrium price of schooling downward. From the consumer's point of view, public education is free, so there is no price except in the rare case of private schools that require tuition in addition to a voucher. For the most part, consumers wishing to choose among publicly provided options (whether they be charters or private schools participating in a voucher program) are making their decision based on product differentiation, not on price. Choice schools, then, unlike other industries, have less of an incentive to lower their cost of production (since it will not necessarily result in selling more of their product) and more of an incentive to differentiate themselves and achieve measurable results that will attract parents and students.

Implications of the Theoretical Model

We must emphasize the importance of uncertainty in determining how many new schools will open should legislative changes result in greater school choice. In fact, we might not even be able to anticipate all the different types of institutional arrangement that might emerge under such a scenario. For example, one might imagine public-private partnerships engaged in the operation of schools. But, for convenience, the discussion below focuses primarily on schools of choice that have been started under existing choice plans: charter and private schools.

Typically, the enabling legislation for charter schools can be changed by state legislatures without notice. Many states have already done so in the last five years. Similarly, imagine that a voucher system is set up by state-level legislation that, again, can be changed without notice. The prediction that comes out of this immediately is that new entrants to the schooling industry are going to be unwilling to build new schools. After all, the state legislature could cut the funding by half next year, or it could outlaw private provision altogether a few years into the future. This represents a large business risk for potential operators of new charter schools or voucher-funded schools. Therefore, new entrants would likely prefer to take over existing school structures rather than to *increase* the number of schools. One for-profit school operator, Edison Schools, is now following exactly this model.

Similarly, uncertainty about whether a choice school will be allowed to operate over a long period without changes to the funding environment or the regulatory environment could lower the demand for slots in such schools. Dozens of studies confirm that most people are highly risk averse. If parents are considering moving their child out of a regular public school to a charter school, they may hesitate if they worry that its funding might be cut or that the chartering authority might fail to renew the school's charter. This in turn can have a negative effect on supply, as potential school operators take into account the impact of regulatory uncertainty on the demand for choice by parents and students.

What policy changes could be made to lower both the start-up (fixed) costs and the marginal costs of new schools? The regulatory requirements to charter a new school or to open a new voucher-funded school will have a significant effect on fixed costs. Of course, even in the most lax of regulatory environments, the fixed costs of building a new school are substantial. Thus there are opportunities both for government and philanthropists to engage in activities that would increase the likelihood of a supply response by pooling funding resources to finance the building of new schools of choice. Julian Betts (chapter 2, this volume), for instance, argues that—given the large fixed costs of building schools from scratch—creating small schools within an existing large school building could greatly increase competition and choice for parents without a need for new facilities.

As for the variable costs of operating a school, teacher and administrator salaries are typically the most important component. New charter and voucher schools generally do not have to adhere to collective bargaining agreements in their local districts. Also, teachers in independent schools will often accept slightly lower wage and benefits packages in return for greater autonomy. In addition, charter and voucher schools do not have tenure requirements, nor do they have the administrative overhead that districts carry, thus their marginal costs should be lower than regular public schools. However, they are still competing in a labor market that likely substantially overlaps the labor market that public schools draw upon, and thus they must offer reasonably competitive salaries to attract high-quality teachers.

Teacher licensure requirements also represent an important cost factor. If choice schools must follow the same guidelines in hiring teachers as regular schools, then this will, in general, increase the schools' costs. Of course, many argue that there are important reasons for requiring teachers to submit to lengthy credential processes. But this must be balanced against the claims of opponents of the current credentialing process, who argue that it creates a major barrier against entry of talented people into the teaching profession. Allowing recent college graduates, or midcareer professionals who have specialized in certain key subject areas such as math and science, to enter teaching through schools of choice without having first fulfilled the normal credentialing requirements has the potential to improve the quality of public education.[4]

In concluding this section on implications of the theoretical model, we point out that economic models of competition predict that education will be provided *efficiently* thanks to the rigors of competition, but the theory does not predict whether education will be provided *equitably*. Betts argues that competition can lead to unequal or equal allocations of outcomes across consumers, depending on how buying power is distributed across consumers. In the context of school choice, for instance, a voucher of $2,000 to every student in a state would arguably aggravate inequalities in the quality of education between affluent and less affluent families; the former would be able to top up these vouchers so that their children could attend the most elite (and expensive) private schools, leaving less affluent families with much more limited choice. In contrast, a voucher system that allocates substantially more per student but that gives vouchers only to less affluent families could arguably do much to lessen inequities in educational outcomes.

The scenario in which public funds are targeted toward less affluent families, via needs-based vouchers or charter schools, presupposes that there exist (potential) school operators who would be willing to provide slots to disadvantaged students. We address this issue, as well as the broader issue of the responsiveness of new schools to economic incentives, in the following section.

The Empirical Evidence on the Supply Side

There are two distinct ways in which supply restraints can slow the development of a school choice system. The first concerns the number of potential school operators who are willing to enter the market. The second concerns the extent to which talented people are willing to teach in schools of choice. We consider both of these issues briefly.

The charter school movement is too new for researchers to have yet grasped the extent to which laws enabling charters to operate induce the entry of new schools. This is even more true of the impact of voucher programs, which to date have been implemented in the United States in only a handful of cities. In spite of this, we have learned something about supply responses in these situations. More broadly, we can glean evidence from research that examines where and why private schools are established.

Supply of Choice Schools

Some of the best evidence to date on the supply of choice schools may come from a related but distinct literature that examines the location decisions of private schools. The most developed research in this regard, by Thomas Downes and Shane Greenstein, studied the location of private schools in California during 1978–80.[5] Downes and Greenstein find that private schools are more numerous in public school districts with more children living in poverty. The elasticity of private school slots with respect to the share of children living in poverty in the local area varies from 0.0 to 0.2. Thus the elasticity of 0.2, for instance, indicates that a 10 percent increase in child poverty is associated with a 2 percent increase in the provision of private school slots. (This and similar statements below all assume that nothing else changes.) This result suggests that, on average, private schools are more likely to locate in poorer areas. However, a countervailing finding is that private schools are more likely to locate in areas with a greater share of highly educated adults. For instance, they find the elasticity with respect to the share of high school graduates in the local population is about 1.0–4.0.

Another characteristic that the authors use is average income in the area. They do not find a strong link between income and provision of private schooling. There are many ways to interpret these results; one is that private schools (many of which are religious) are mission based and seek to serve needy students. Another is that in high-poverty districts with pockets of gentrification there is greater demand for private schools so the white middle class can escape sending their children to school with the poor children in the public school district. In suburban districts, where income is more uniform, there is not this demand, thus the finding of fewer private schools.

Downes and Greenstein also report that private schools are responsive to the level of crowding in public school classrooms. They find that the elasticity of private school slots with respect to the local public school pupil-teacher ratio is about 4.0. This is an extraordinarily high effect, suggesting, for instance, that a 10 percent increase in the local pupil-teacher ratio is related to a 40 percent increase in the provision of private school slots. To the extent that parents value smaller classes, this is exactly the sort of supply response that one would hope to engender in a broader system of school choice. It promises that private school provision could equalize school quality to some extent. The vast majority of private schools in the United States are religious, so it comes as little surprise that Downes and Greenstein find that the location of private schools is positively related to the percentage of the local population that is of the same religion and denomination.

More recently, Lisa Barrow has studied private school location in Chicago as a function of characteristics of the local zip code.[6] Her findings do not match those of Downes and Greenstein very closely. This could reflect the fact that the two sets of studies are of two different times and places. Furthermore, the Chicago study uses a relatively small sample as well as a very narrow definition of neighborhood that could well be much smaller than the attendance area for a typical private school, thereby missing some of the relations the California studies have found. One important area of agreement between the Downes and Greenstein and the Barrow studies is that private school location does not appear to respond much at all to the racial and ethnic mix of the local area. This finding is relevant, given concerns that increased school choice could spell increased racial segregation. Overall, these studies suggest that the supply of private school slots is quite responsive to the conditions of local public school districts, as one might expect.

Of course, this does not tell us much about how private schools would react to the provision of public funds through a wholesale voucher program, and these results do not say anything about charter school provision. Less formal evidence on voucher programs and charter schools suggests that the supply of these schools can be very responsive. For instance, charter school growth has been quite impressive nationally, suggesting that even with today's fairly strict rules, new schools enter the market. In Arizona, which has been among the most aggressive states in encouraging the development of charter schools, roughly 7–10 percent of public school students had enrolled in charters by 1998–99.[7] In Washington, D.C., more than 10 percent of students are enrolled in charter schools. Research by Jeffrey Henig and Jason MacDonald suggests that these charter schools are more likely to be established in high-minority, middle-income areas and that their establishment is sensitive to both economic and political considerations.[8] For example, they tend to locate in areas of the city with high need (in the sense that the achievement of public school students is poor) and with less competition from private schools.

Experiments with vouchers also provide important hints that a major voucher program could increase the supply of private school slots considerably. Brian Gill and co-authors report on Milwaukee's long-running voucher program.[9] Many of the new schools opened after the program was expanded to allow for the participation of religiously based schools, and many of these new schools tend to focus specifically on voucher students, signifying a strong supply-side response to vouchers.[10]

Supply of Teachers

We know surprisingly little about how the existence of private schools, charter schools, and voucher programs affects the supply of teachers. If teachers are unwilling to work in such environments, the development of a widespread choice system, even in the most generous of regulatory environments, could be constrained.

In one of the most relevant studies to date, Caroline M. Hoxby surveyed charter school teachers and merged this information with data from the Schools and Staffing Survey on private and public school teachers.[11] One of the central questions Hoxby asked was, Which types of school have a greater share of teachers with certain characteristics? Table 4-1, calculated from raw data in the unpublished version of Hoxby's study, provides some answers. Regular public schools ranked first in just two categories: the share of teachers who were fully credentialed and the share holding a master's degree (and

Table 4-1. *Ranking of U.S. Public, Charter, and Private Schools, by Characteristics of Their Teachers*

Characteristic	*Public school*	*Charter school*	*Private school*
College rank	3	1	2
Math or science major	2[a]	1	2[a]
Extra instructional hours	2[a]	1	2[a]
Teacher control over teaching methods	3	1[a]	1[a]
State certification	1	2	3
Master's degree	1[a]	1[a]	2

Source: Calculations based on Caroline M. Hoxby, "Would School Choice Change the Teaching Profession?" Working Paper 7866 (Cambridge, Mass.: National Bureau of Economic Research, 2000).
a. Tie.

charter schools were tied for first in the latter category). Charter schools ranked at the top of a number of other important categories, including the share of teachers with a math or science major in college and the selectivity of the college from which teachers graduated. Private schools also tended to outrank public schools. Hoxby used these rankings to conclude that the expansion of school choice could increase the average quality of teachers in the United States. Of course, an important limitation of this research is that the charter school movement is still so small that it is impossible to predict whether these patterns will persist if and when charters and other schools of choice become more prevalent.

Dale Ballou and Michael Podgursky suggest that a divergence in hiring practices between public and private schools could explain why private schools tend to employ teachers with greater skills in certain dimensions.[12] They found that private schools have a less compressed teacher pay schedule, allowing pay to be linked more closely to skills. For instance, teachers with subject mastery in areas that are perennially in short supply can be paid a premium. The authors also provide evidence that private schools are more likely than public schools to hire teachers with high ability (as measured by test scores).

While this literature is far too limited to allow for a prediction of the outcome should school choice expand in the future, it does suggest that private and charter schools may bring talented people into the teaching profession, especially if they are not governed by public school licensure requirements.

Practical Barriers to Market Entry

The previous sections outline a theoretical model and initial empirical data that help to predict which factors may stimulate or constrain a greater supply of schools. They also reveal how little is in fact known about the supply responses of private and charter schools. This section draws on the experience of school practitioners to illustrate the greatest barriers to entry faced by charter schools. It then focuses on case studies of three San Diego charter schools to show the complex circumstances and institutional alliances that give rise to and nurture successful charter schools.

Barriers

From a market standpoint, perhaps the number-one barrier to successfully operating a charter school is that initial approval and continuing oversight is by the local school district, whose schools are the charter's main competitors. If charter schools are successful and grow, they often are perceived as draining money from the district. In most states, charter school funding flows through school districts, which can apply fees and assessments based on the district's cost overruns, and charters have no recourse but to pay. As a result, charter schools cannot survive without the tolerance and, indeed, the support of their districts. One of the few districts with a different regulatory arrangement, Washington, D.C., also has the greatest market penetration of charter schools. The city has a separate charter board, which grants and oversees charters.

The market models outlined in the previous sections postulate fixed or start-up costs as another significant barrier to market entry, and this is indeed true in practice. Purchasing land and building a school adequate for 300 students typically costs between $3 million and $4 million. Anita Landecker of ExEd, a charter school developer in Los Angeles, points out that this barrier is especially high in California, where real estate values are exceedingly high, even in low-income areas. According to Landecker, to pay market rent or conventional debt service on a suitable property would cost approximately $1,500 per student, or 20–30 percent of total per pupil revenue. By contrast, in-district charters pay a fee of about 3 percent of their revenue to lease district space. This single factor keeps many choice schools out of the market.[13]

Zoning and building regulations create additional obstacles to opening a school. In some areas, these regulations are so prohibitive that schools without major funding will seek buildings previously occupied by other schools. Paul Hill worries that the supply of new choice schools may be limited in some cities to the "number of abandoned Catholic school buildings."[14] It should be noted that, although building regulations increase costs and thus constrain supply, many of them are necessary and serve the common good. Most of us want our children to go to school in a building with fire sprinklers, for example; yet if sprinklers were not required, a substantial number of schools would not have them.

The facilities barrier is perhaps the most recognized barrier in policy circles at both the state and federal levels, and there have been several attempts to ease it. A new federal program (New Markets Tax Credits) will provide tax credits to investors in charter school facilities in low-income neighborhoods; another program provides for a guarantee pool to entice more lenders into the unknown and risky market of charter school facilities financing. Both of these approaches are very promising though currently limited in scale. At the state level, efforts have focused on altering traditional public school bond programs to accommodate charter schools. In California these efforts have not borne fruit: districts that already have major space and financial woes are not willing to make room for charters. State-level bond allocation procedures are so complex, overregulated, and time consuming that most charter operators are unable to tackle them. Tying charters into district facilities may not be the most cost-efficient approach either. Eric Premack of the Charter Schools Development Center likens bond-financed school facilities to the huge public housing projects of the 1960s, when layers and layers of regulation and purported economies of scale gave rise to expensive behemoths like Cabrini Green and Robert Taylor Homes in Chicago. Private developers are now taking those projects apart, using flexible subsidies to create smaller-scale, more cost-effective housing that mixes income levels. Premack advocates "a flexible, 'Section 8–like' subsidy" that charters could use for rent or mortgage payment. The challenge would be to authorize such a subsidy for ten years. "California had it for one year, but it was wiped out by the budget crisis."[15]

A related barrier is simply the limited amount of per pupil funding that charters or voucher programs receive from the state. Charter schools are supposed to receive the same per pupil funding as public schools in their state or district do, but in practice they receive considerably less. Districts receive substantial transportation and special education funds, making their per pupil revenue significantly higher than the allocation that charters receive. These two are related, since facilities represent most schools' greatest expense, outside of wages and salaries. If facilities cost only 3 percent of a school's budget, instead of 20–30 percent, current per pupil funding would be adequate. Conversely, if per pupil funding were increased, charters could afford to pay market rates for facilities. Per pupil funding for charter schools does not provide for transportation, which can cost between $300 and $500 per pupil per year. Given the residential segregation of most major cities, implementing a widespread choice system without transportation assistance risks creating a system of segregated schools that mirrors residential patterns.

In addition to per pupil operating funding, schools need start-up working capital. Per pupil funding starts the day the school opens, but there are considerable earlier costs to planning and developing a school, on average about $400,000 per school. The federal government has a charter schools grant program, administered by the states, the purpose of which is to offset some of these costs, and it plays an extremely important role in enabling new schools to enter the market. However, the program is designed to fund a relatively small number of schools each year and would have to be considerably expanded were a full-scale choice program to be implemented nationwide.

A *Los Angeles Times* article tells the sad story of an approved charter school that closed its doors before admitting its first student, ostensibly due to "red tape and high costs."[16] Eric Premack calls this "re-regulatory creep" and confirms that it is taking place at both the federal and state levels.[17] Charters, which began as a way to deregulate education, are now facing new layers of regulation and reporting requirements related to funding streams, student assessment, and teacher credentialing.

A final barrier to market entry, and perhaps even more to sustaining a successful school, is the instability of funding for charters and the fragmentation of legislation and regulation. Every state has different authorizing legislation, and every district has complete power to regulate and extract fees. This makes it risky to enter the market and difficult to attract investors or lenders to the venture. It would likely take a nationwide program—and a number of years of stable funding—before operators would enter the market on a scale comparable to other public funding-stream markets, such as housing or health care.

Case Studies

The Preuss School, affiliated with the University of California at San Diego (UCSD), serves 750 limited-income students in grades 6–12.[18] The main impetus for the creation of the school was the perceived need to increase socioeconomic diversity on University of California campuses by providing a single-track, rigorous curriculum to students from less affluent families. To prepare high-achieving, low-income students for the university, UCSD faculty and administrators decided to create a charter school. Students are admitted to the school by lottery, and applicants are limited to those whose parents have no college degree; in addition, students must qualify for federal meal assistance. A major capital campaign was undertaken to raise funds for the $13 million facility, led by Peter Preuss, a University of California regent and local philanthropist.

The Preuss School was able to surmount the initial barriers to market entry through its affiliation with the university. It offsets limited per pupil funding through ongoing fundraising, helped out by its university link and by its widely perceived role in righting inequity and creating equality of educational opportunity. Favorable relations with the chartering school district, San Diego Unified School District, ensured transportation funding and made regulation and oversight relatively smooth during the 1999–2002 period. Students have performed well on the state test and are making unusually good progress on completing the "A–G" courses, which refer to the courses in seven subject areas required for students to become eligible to attend the University of California and California State University systems.

The Preuss School's charter was up for renewal in fall 2003. Facing a difficult budget situation, the chartering district did renew the charter in 2003, but rescinded all financial support for transportation. For the 2003–04 school year, the Preuss School instead leased buses from the district, paid for out of its general funds. This cutback by the district is clearly a costly blow to the school, as by design almost all students are bused to the UCSD campus from relatively disadvantaged neighborhoods, many of which are fifteen or more miles away. The cutback represents roughly a 7 percent cut in funding for the school, at a time when other (state) sources of funding that finance the school's longer school year and longer school day were also at some risk because of California's current fiscal crisis. This episode provides a vivid example of the budgetary uncertainties and risks that charter schools face.

Explorer Elementary Charter School, a K–6 school that focuses on individualized learning, interdisciplinary curriculum, and social intelligence was started in the context of a districtwide reform that standardized curriculum and teaching methods and was perceived by many as rigid. The initial planning group was then joined by a group of parents who were disaffected from their private school. Although it enrolls by lottery as well, due to its focus and its location in a relatively affluent area near a university, Explorer has attracted highly educated, high-income families. Thus while it has no affiliation with a powerful institution, it is able to draw on its parent body for ongoing fundraising to offset limited per pupil funding. An initially oppositional relationship with the district has now become more favorable due to several years of high and consistently improving test scores. Explorer has finally overcome its facilities barrier by locating in a building formerly owned by the Navy.

The initial idea for High Tech High came from corporate leaders who saw local labor shortages in the high-tech industry on the one hand and inadequately trained young people on the other. The 400-student high school focuses on project-based learning and integrating students of diverse backgrounds in nontracked classrooms. Initial success has led to the creation of a middle school for grades 6–8. Strong corporate relationships helped overcome start-up costs and continue to help with the ongoing challenges of limited per pupil funding. Even with these powerful connections, the facilities barrier is proving extremely challenging; banks shied away from long-range financing, given the school's five-year charter, and required either a personal guarantor, a shorter term loan, or a higher interest rate.

Because the students at High Tech High come from throughout the metropolitan area, transportation is a critical issue. Initially, the school rented buses from the district and expected the district to subsidize the cost, as the school paid an integration encroachment to the district and the school is integrated. The district balked, and the school sought and received a federal grant through the Workforce Investment Act. This grant covered transportation costs for the first three years of the school, but it ended early because of federal cutbacks. The school no longer provides transportation but subsidizes the bus passes of those students who qualify for federal meal assistance. This change will undoubtedly limit the student pool to those who are highly motivated and further illustrates the financial challenges that charter schools face, particularly if they are not neighborhood schools and seek to be integrated by race and class.

These three examples of highly successful charter schools, though quite different, share common features. Each responded to a very significant context and need, which then translated to a clear mission around which public support and funds could be rallied. Each had access to resources and power, either through the parent body or through affiliation with powerful institutions. Each has had consistently high test scores, helping them to weather criticism or attacks from regulators. What is most sobering though, is that each school, despite great success and significant advantages, is still struggling to operate comfortably.

Conclusions and Policy Recommendations

Market theory predicts that the supply of new schools depends crucially on market price and cost structure. Practical experience shows that these, in turn, are significantly influenced by the political and regulatory environment that schools face, both in terms of per pupil funding and ongoing regulations that can ultimately be prohibitive. In short, lower per pupil funding and greater regulatory costs will constrict the supply of new schools.

For a given infrastructure there is a unique ideal enrollment size such that lowering enrollment below that point will increase costs per pupil needlessly by spreading fixed costs across too small a number of students, and raising enrollment will increase costs per pupil due to overcrowding. However, economic theory cannot tell what the optimal size of schools might be. Real-world experience has convinced many practitioners that large schools are increasingly unable to deliver a high-quality education. The implication is that in a choice system there may be considerably more schools than currently exist in the United States.

The empirical literature is only beginning to study determinants of supply of choice schools and supply of teachers to those schools. Initial data suggest that private schools are responsive to local conditions such as overcrowding and that both private schools and charter schools are able to attract highly talented teachers. There are, however, significant barriers to opening new choice schools, which might limit a supply response under a choice program. Three broad areas of reform would do the most to increase the supply of choice schools while not sacrificing their quality: increases in funding, deregulation, and reducing uncertainty.

—Increases in funding: Although it would be politically difficult to achieve, a simple rise in the funding of charter schools and vouchers would do the most to increase the supply of choice schools. In market terms, it is equivalent to increasing the market price through stimulating the buying power of consumers, or effective demand. Unlike many other types of public service, where increased public funding can run the risk of simply reducing efficiency while not increasing quality, choice schools have a built-in accountability factor, since they are competing with each other and with public schools. Per pupil funding can only be collected for students who come to school, so funding increases cannot be translated into increased revenue unless the school is delivering an education which is good enough to keep attracting parents. Depending on policy aims, funding could be augmented through increasing the basic per pupil amount that schools receive, and it could be targeted to transportation, special education, or facilities assistance.

—Deregulation: Expanding the number of chartering authorities would eliminate district monopoly and encourage more school operators to enter the market. For example, state universities or community colleges could grant charters and oversee them. With multiple chartering authorities, individual schools would have more bargaining power and greater ability to resist extraordinary fees or arbitrary demands by their school districts. Relaxation of teacher licensing requirements would increase the supply of talented teachers to choice schools. Data on private schools, which face no credentialing requirements, show that these schools are able to attract high-achieving teachers. Because choice schools would still have to compete in the labor market with public schools, this deregulation might not translate immediately into lower costs. However, the ability to attract skilled teachers makes it easier to open new schools, sustain them, and deliver high-quality education.

—Reducing uncertainty: There is no guarantee in any industry against legislative changes that influence market conditions, nor perhaps would we want there to be, because the ballot box is the final arbiter of our priorities and thus of which market actors should thrive or fail. However, given that public school choice programs have been created by voters in many states, these programs should be implemented in such a way as to minimize uncertainty and thereby encourage more schools to enter the market. Charter schools could be given longer terms, and per pupil funding could be based on five-year contracts instead of fluctuating from year to year. For capital costs, districts or other (perhaps private) organizations could extend loan or bond guarantees to offer security to lenders.

Notes

This chapter is based on a paper prepared for the National Working Commission on Choice in K–12 Schools. We thank commission members Jean Kluver and Carol Wallace for many helpful comments.

1. For a discussion about the impetuses for entering the education market, see Frederick M. Hess, *Revolution at the Margins: The Impact of Competition on Urban School Systems* (Brookings, 2002), pp. 211–15.

2. The concept of market entrance encompasses both new schools and existing schools that expand their capacity.

3. Economic theory states that if firms are risk neutral, the degree of uncertainty should not influence entry decisions. However, it is likely that administrators are at least slightly risk averse. Risk aversion becomes important because, as we discuss below, charter schools have difficulty borrowing money specifically because they are viewed by the financial sector as having uncertain future cash flows.

4. The question of who should be allowed into the classroom is hotly debated. For a discussion of this issue and some empirical evidence on the relationship between teacher licensure credentials and student outcomes, see Linda Darling-Hammond, Barnett Berry, and Amy Thoreson, "Does Teacher Certification Matter? Evaluating the Evidence," *Educational Evaluation and Policy Analysis* 23, no. 1 (2001): 57–77; Dan Goldhaber and

Dominic J. Brewer, "Does Teacher Certification Matter? High School Teacher Certification Status and Student Achievement," *Educational Evaluation and Policy Analysis* 22, no. 2 (2000): 129–45; Dan Goldhaber and Dominic J. Brewer, "Evaluating the Evidence on Teacher Certification: A Rejoinder," *Educational Evaluation and Policy Analysis* 23, no. 1 (2001): 79–86; Margaret Raymond, Stephen Fletcher, and Javier Luque, *Teach for America: An Evaluation of Teacher Differences and Student Outcomes in Houston, Texas* (Center for Research on Education Outcomes, Stanford University, 2001); and Julian R. Betts, Andrew Zau, and Lorien Rice, *Determinants of Student Achievement: New Evidence from San Diego* (San Francisco: Public Policy Institute of California, 2003).

5. Thomas A. Downes and Shane M. Greenstein, "Understanding the Supply Decisions of Nonprofits: Modelling the Location of Private Schools," *RAND Journal of Economics* 27, no. 2 (1996): 365–90; Thomas A. Downes and Shane M. Greenstein, "Entry into the Schooling Market: How Is the Behaviour of Private Suppliers Influenced by Public Sector Decisions?" *Bulletin of Economic Research* 54, no. 4 (2002): 341–71.

6. Lisa Barrow, "Private School Location and Neighborhood Characteristics," *Economic Perspectives: A Review from the Federal Reserve Bank of Chicago* 25, no. 3 (2001): 13–30.

7. Caroline M. Hoxby, "School Choice and School Productivity; or, Could School Choice Be a Tide That Lifts All Boats?" Working Paper 8873 (Cambridge, Mass.: National Bureau of Economic Research, 2002).

8. Jeffrey R. Henig and Jason A. MacDonald, "Locational Decisions of Charter Schools: Probing the Market Metaphor," *Social Science Quarterly* 83, no. 4 (2002): 962–80.

9. Brian P. Gill and others, *Rhetoric versus Reality: What We Know and What We Need to Know about Vouchers and Charter Schools* (Santa Monica, Calif.: RAND, 2001).

10. Hess, *Revolution at the Margins;* Gill and others, *Rhetoric versus Reality.* Hess found schools with a missionary purpose to be a major source of new supply in a voucher program in Edgewood, Texas.

11. Caroline M. Hoxby, "Would School Choice Change the Teaching Profession?" *Journal of Human Resources* 37, no. 4 (2002): 846–91.

12. Dale Ballou, "Do Public Schools Hire the Best Applicants?" *Quarterly Journal of Economics* 111, no.1 (1996): 97–133; Dale Ballou and Michael Podgursky, "Teacher Recruitment and Retention in Public and Private Schools," *Journal of Policy Analysis and Management* 17, no. 3 (1998): 393–417.

13. Anita Landecker, personal conversation with Larry Rosenstock, June 30, 2003.

14. Paul T. Hill, "The Supply Side of School Choice," in *School Choice and Social Controversy: Politics, Policy, and Law,* edited by Stephen D. Sugarman and Frank R. Kemerer (Brookings, 1999).

15. Eric Premack, personal conversation with Larry Rosenstock, June 30, 2003.

16. Joe Mathews, "Charter Schools Choke on Rulebook: Red Tape and High Costs Are Stifling the Populist Trend, Discouraging Breakaway Educators, and Forcing Survivors to Mimic Public Districts," *Los Angeles Times,* June 1, 2003, p. A1.

17. Eric Premack, personal conversation with Larry Rosenstock, June 30, 2003.

18. The authors are familiar with the San Diego charter schools described here. Rosenstock is principal and chief executive officer of High Tech High, and Betts serves on the board of directors of the Preuss School at the University of California–San Diego.

5

How School Choice Affects Student Achievement

FREDERICK M. HESS AND TOM LOVELESS

In debates over charter schooling, school vouchers, and public school choice, policymakers look to the research documenting how choice arrangements affect participating students. Proponents point to studies that suggest school choice has produced positive effects; critics cite research showing choice to be harmful. Amidst these exchanges, the larger question tends to get lost: How have choice programs caused the benefits or harms that research has uncovered?

A curious vacuum exists at the heart of the research on school choice. Even as researchers seek to determine whether choice-based schools (primarily private schools and charter schools) educate children more effectively than conventional public schools, remarkably scant attention is given to the mechanisms producing these effects. Research on the effects of school choice proceeds as if school choice is an enormous black box that ought not be peered into.

This reticence has created several problems for policymakers, educators, and researchers. While scholars grope toward a consensus about how choice programs affect participants, our lack of knowledge as to how and why choice programs have the effects that they do makes it difficult to know whether positive results can be replicated and negative results remedied, or what kinds of choice-based reform are likely to do the most good for the largest number of children. For instance, what might studies of voucher programs or charter schools tell us about the benefits of children using public choice to attend another public school? Do existing findings accurately foretell the benefits of broader school choice? Do they overestimate the benefits? Might they actually underestimate the benefits? Under what circumstances do these contrasting scenarios occur?

The answers to these questions depend on a variety of considerations. Are the benefits of school choice due to the empowerment of being permitted to choose, to the comfort of being in a school where the child is happy, or to the qualities of the school itself? Depending on the forces at work, the public school choice contemplated by the No Child Left Behind Act may be expected to deliver major benefits or none at all. If one acknowledges this straightforward premise, understanding why school choice works (if and when it works) should be high on the education research agenda. It is not and has not been. That is a problem.

The issue is particularly salient because school choice encompasses an array of very different arrangements. On the one hand, it includes the choice of families to pay to enroll their children in essentially unregulated private schools, an arrangement that gives both family and school a great deal of leeway. At the other end of the spectrum, it involves the kind of highly regulated choice envisioned by No Child Left Behind—where families move their child from one conventional district school to another. In between are various arrangements, such as charter schools and school vouchers, that may themselves vary greatly in how much operational latitude schools are given, how much is demanded from participating families, and how independent schools are from public regulation. School choice is not one thing; it is an umbrella term that describes many things.

The effects of one kind of program may not necessarily reveal a lot about the consequences of another. Lessons learned from charter schools that can ignore curricular requirements, teacher licensure criteria, and staffing norms, for example, may not reveal a lot about charter schools functioning under different conditions—and even less about what happens at traditional public schools participating in public choice plans. This point is too often glossed over, as when studies evaluate charter schools en masse—without trying to understand why particular charter schools may be effective or ineffective.

This chapter examines these issues by focusing on two questions: What is it about school choice that matters for students exercising choice? And what do the elements that matter mean for using choice-based reform to improve educational opportunity for large numbers of children? The effect of choice programs upon participating students is not, of course, the only consideration in the choice debate. The competitive effects of choice arrangements, the impact on nonchoosers, the impact on class-based stratification or racial segregation, and the impact on the public weal are subjects that have received intense scrutiny in their own right. In this chapter, however, we focus on how choice benefits those students who actively choose their school.

What Is in the Black Box?

Are the benefits of school choice for participating students (stipulating, for the purposes of this discussion, that they do indeed exist) due to factors intrinsic to choice-based schooling, or are they a consequence of the kinds of schools that happen to serve students participating in choice programs? If it is the former, if the benefits are intrinsic to choice, then it will prove relatively simple to provide those same benefits in an expanded system. If, on the other hand, it is due to the characteristics of extant choice schools, then the critical question is whether or not those traits will continue to hold if choice is expanded and publicly supported. Finally, if the benefits are due to both factors, the relative significance of the two explanations—and how we might design programs to maximize the benefits for all children—raises important questions for policymakers.

There is an immediate objection from some proponents of choice-based reform to even raising the issues we address here. Some researchers suggest that to ask how or why choice programs benefit students is an unnecessary or politically motivated question, and one that may distract from the real issues of import. After all, proponents of choice-based reform suggest that choice may work for a variety of reasons, and many express disinterest in why or how it works in a specific context. Some of these advocates will regard the following as a pointless or futile exercise. "After all," they may say, "we're not always exactly sure how drugs or medical treatments work. Health scientists make discoveries, their handiwork is rigorously tested, and if the tests show convincing results we often approve the drug—whether or not we can explain exactly how and why it works."

Choice proponents, not unreasonably, suggest that enhanced autonomy or markets may work in a variety of ways and that there is no guarantee that those reasons will be systematic or readily visible. Students may benefit because they are now in schools that they wish to be in, because all schools now feel competitive pressure to improve, or because lack of centralized oversight permits educators to operate in more flexible and effective ways. Under such conditions, choice proponents suggest, it may not be possible or even necessary to determine precisely what is producing observed benefits.

We believe such an approach to school choice is unwise. The medical analogy is a dangerous guide because it assumes a constancy in treatment and patient conditions that does not hold for many social programs. Every aspirin tablet is pretty much identical to every other aspirin tablet, and the physiology of any one patient is similar to that of any other patient. Environmental factors do not strongly influence the effects of the treatment.

The situation is different with social remedies, like school choice or welfare reform. In these cases, the treatment often changes from one locale to the next, users have different characteristics and behave in different ways, and contextual factors can have a big influence. For instance, it may matter greatly whether a school voucher is worth $2,500 or $7,000, whether families are educated and whether they are engaged in their children's schooling, and whether a community has a lot of schools and good public transportation.

From the perspective of parents and policymakers, the questions of why and how choice-based reform serves participating children may be nearly as significant as efforts to discern whether they benefit. After all, schools are asked to do a number of things, and it is likely that choice programs will affect schools in a variety of ways. Whether choice programs work for a given student may be a difficult and complicated question. Only by understanding how and why these programs work will we be able to replicate their benefits. Consequently, parents and policymakers should care (and do care) about why choice-based schooling works, what the lessons might be for public schools, and whether new choice schools will provide the same benefits.

Considering the Evidence

There is a strong evidentiary record that, controlling for background characteristics like race and family economic well-being, students in private schools perform better than their peers.[1] The evidence particularly suggests that urban and minority children who attend private schools are much more likely than similar students in the public schools to graduate from high school and to attend college.[2] This research is complemented by a growing body of research on school voucher programs. This research, however, is less uniform in its findings. Although some research suggests that African American children who received school vouchers made significantly more academic gains than similar public school students who did not receive vouchers, one analysis of this scholarship suggests that the performance of voucher students was not significantly different from that of their peers.[3]

Research on charter schooling has yielded only limited insight into this question of outcomes. Charter research has been particularly hobbled by the fact that self-selection and the disparate missions of various schools have made it difficult to reach any general consensus about the effects on student performance.[4] However, even in the case of charter schooling, two studies that use value-added measures suggest that students in at least some charter programs are outperforming their public school peers.[5] Evaluations of magnet school programs suggest that magnets generally produce higher student achievement than do other public schools.[6]

While not all researchers are convinced that the observed gains are reliable or valid,[7] no systematic research contradicts these findings. Further, policymakers seem inclined to believe that choice-based schooling can help at least some children and legislate on the basis of that belief. That being the case, it is all the more important that we try to see inside the black box.

Can the Results Be Replicated?

Let's make this simple. Mary Smith shows up at a charter school or a traditional district school via public school choice. If one believes the research that finds benefits accruing to children who attend schools of choice, should we expect Mary to fare better than she would have otherwise?

This question highlights the critical difference between social policy and medical treatments. When asked the above question, most choice proponents will answer that it depends upon the quality of the school Mary is attending, whether the school is stifled by bureaucracy, and whether the school is able to impose discipline and require parental involvement. In other words, extrapolating from the findings on existing choice schools depends on our ability to replicate the characteristics of those schools. Determining whether a measles shot will affect Mary the way it has affected previous children is a far simpler process.

The most pressing question may be whether lessons from existing private schools or early charter schools can be emulated in public schools or can be replicated in new schools. For instance, in perhaps the most famous analysis of choice-based reform, John Chubb and Terry Moe suggest that the very autonomy that characterizes private schools leads to better educational practices and simply cannot be replicated within the public sector.[8] Proponents of choice also suggest that at least part of the benefits may be produced by the ability of private schools to demand behavior and foster heightened parental participation, focus on essential curricular content, use unlicensed teachers, or deliver a coherent curriculum. Meanwhile, critics argue that there are really no recognizable systematic differences between public and private schools and that any differences in observed student achievement are spurious and should not be taken to suggest that private schools or choice schools automatically improve student learning.[9]

There are three general ways to think about possible explanations for the observed findings—if we presume that the findings have substantive import.

First, specific pedagogical, curricular, or other educational characteristics of choice schools may themselves affect student outcomes. For instance, it may be that choice schools have smaller class sizes, more focused curricula, or more involved families. If this is the case, then it may be possible to design programs that deliver these benefits to more students.

Second, the organizational nature of choice schools may be responsible for the benefits observed. For instance, the ability to hire unlicensed teachers or operate outside the confines of state and federal red tape may allow schools to operate more effectively. If this is the case, then expanding school choice without providing choice schools with the requisite autonomy may fail to produce the anticipated benefits. Conversely, it may be possible to replicate the benefits of choice-based reform without necessarily adopting school choice—if policymakers are willing to take the necessary steps (a prospect about which many choice proponents are, for good reason, not optimistic).

Third, the effectiveness of individual elements may depend on the enabling power of choice. In other words, particular school elements may matter only if a student or a family has been empowered by having the opportunity to select that school, if the student is afraid of being sent to another school for irresponsibility, or if parents are more attentive to their student's performance because they feel invested in the school. If this is the case, efforts to replicate the benefits of choice programs in traditional district schools that do not offer choice would prove ineffective. This possibility is particularly important, as many critics of choice suggest that, if choice schools are effective, the key to systemic reform is simply to replicate those characteristics in traditional district schools. If individual school practices are effective only when conditioned on the presence of choice, such a strategy cannot work.

Peering into the black box will permit us to understand what is responsible for any apparent benefits and then determine whether the expansion of choice-based provision is likely to make those benefits more widely available.

Unpacking the Black Box

While some suggest that the benefits of choosing are so diffuse as to escape analysis, or that the structural advantages of school choice cannot be unpacked, the argument that we can never really understand how educational choice operates seems weak. In fact, when markets work as intended, economists have explanations for how and why that happens. There is no reason that the situation in education ought to be otherwise.

As noted in the previous section, there are a number of ways in which choice may benefit students who utilize it. In this section, it may be useful to group possible explanations into those that deal with the structure, the population, and the classroom instruction of choice schools.

The Structure

Several structural features of choice-based schools are hypothesized to matter. One is the sectoral autonomy enjoyed by private schools and, to a lesser extent, charter schools. John Chubb and Terry Moe offer the classic articulation of this point in their pathbreaking *Politics, Markets, and America's Schools*, where they argue that such schools enjoy the autonomy, flexibility, and operational latitude essential to effective school leadership and teaching.[10] If autonomy is important, choice plans must not impede the freedom of individual school communities.

Choice schools also tend to be significantly more flexible than traditional public schools in terms of hiring and compensating faculty, another consideration that may help explain the performance of these schools. While private and charter schools tend to pay teachers less than traditional district schools, because many are not required to hire certified teachers, they are able to draw on a pool of young, enthusiastic, and educated people only intending to teach for a few years and unwilling to pay the costs or endure the tedium of earning a license to teach in public schools. Moreover, private schools tend to be safer and more orderly than public schools—especially in urban areas—making them attractive to both nontraditional and traditional teachers. There is evidence that charter schools hire teachers who have graduated from good colleges and who are accomplished academically.[11] This freedom to tap a pool of effective teachers and spend less on salaries is only replicable if choice programs consciously ensure that participating schools also enjoy such freedom.

Private schools are able to demand a high degree of parental involvement.[12] Public schools are not. As choice is made more universal, it is likely to be more regulated (as in the case of charter schooling, public voucher programs, and public school choice), and participating schools will face limits on their ability to compel parental participation. Moreover, in programs like charter schooling or public school choice, families will no longer be required to pay tuition. In other words, the factors that traditionally elicit parental participation may disappear if choice is provided for all children through public funds.

Structural considerations are also involved in finances, facilities, and technology. The irony is that when the lay public thinks of private schools or charter schools, they often summon an image of expensive, elite Ivy League prep schools. Such schools, however, constitute less than 5 percent of the private school sector. Edison Schools and a few charter operators, for example, invest heavily up front on technology and facilities, but this approach is the exception. The vast majority of private and charter schools have significantly lower per pupil expenditures than traditional public schools, have less impressive facilities, and have less access to technology.[13] While none of these general statements ought to be taken as definitive, these considerations are certainly worth exploring and may well undercut any positive effects produced by choice-based programs.

The Population

It is possible that many of the benefits of enrollment in choice schools are largely a consequence of the students who are enrolled in those schools. The peer-effects literature makes clear that a child's fellow students have an impact upon that child's performance.[14] Private schools, especially those urban parochial schools at the heart of the choice conversation, tend to attract families that value education. The result is that choice school students are surrounded by classmates who are likely to do their homework, to graduate from high school, and to go on to college.[15]

In particular, choice school populations on the whole are wealthier and come from more educated families than do their local public school peers.[16] Such a pattern is only possible as long as choice schools enroll a select minority of the population. As choice programs expand, and especially if they continue to focus on serving low-income or disadvantaged students, these beneficial peer effects will dissipate.

The population of choice schools tends to be only a third or a quarter the population of comparable public schools. Some researchers believe that small schools facilitate school discipline, student-teacher interaction, and effective learning.[17] In a more expansive choice system, it is possible that increasing demand will encourage small schools to grow, erasing this advantage.

Choice schools, unlike traditional public schools, can expel or discipline students whom they consider troublemakers, thus keeping their population within the boundaries of their vision of an educational community. But could this freedom to determine the school population remain a characteristic of choice schools once they become the norm? Would there be another school to send these children to?

Because of their ability to limit their population to children of like-minded families, choice schools can match students, faculty, and academic program and do not face the conflicting demands that bedevil traditional public schools and lead to fragmented curricula and a proliferation of electives. An allocative efficiency rationale for the benefits of choice suggests that choice systems could be expanded in scope without sacrificing benefits.

Classroom Instruction

Several studies document the importance of teachers in producing student achievement.[18] It is reasonable to assume that the effectiveness or ineffectiveness of different teachers arises from differences in teaching. If the amount that students learn depends on how teachers teach, then a substantial portion of a choice program's effects, whether positive or negative, will be determined by the impact of parental choice on teachers' instruction. How might a choice regime affect instruction?

Our answer to that question is necessarily speculative. The element of choice with the strongest chance of affecting teaching is the casting of students and families in the role of customers. That does not mean that students and parents are completely powerless in the current system; educators certainly want to avoid alienating students and parents. Unhappy parents can complain to the school principal or district administration, triggering a round of meetings that consume enormous amounts of time and place all parties on the defensive. But since parents rarely resort to such tactics, in reality they possess limited leverage in getting teachers to change instructional approaches.

Choice alters that situation. Faced with customers who can readily leave if they are not satisfied, teachers will be motivated to teach in ways that students enjoy and that parents support. The altered teacher-student relationship could lead to more engaged students. The potential downside is that some teachers may adopt practices that are attractive but superficial, creating Potemkin village classrooms that keep everyone happy while educating no one. The moral authority of teachers, as the sociologist Willard Waller noted several decades ago, flows from the stature that society accords to the role of teacher and from the political legitimacy of serving as an agent of the state.[19] Both sources of authority could be undermined if teaching is seen primarily as an act of serving customers.

Viewing students as customers may also change the allocation of instructional time. Teachers divide their attention between groups and individual students. The typical elementary grade teacher instructs the whole class, teaches small groups of students (most often in reading), and works with individual students who need help. Balancing the three forms of teaching is a logistical challenge. The bulk of a teacher's instructional day is spent teaching the class as a whole. Small group instruction and individual help can only be given while the rest of the class is working independently. If educational customers value individual attention over being served in groups, the division of teaching time would be expected to swing toward more individualized instruction. Such a development would be significant in terms of what is currently known about individualized instruction. The individualized approaches evaluated to date have failed to boost student achievement.[20]

Viewed from another angle, whole-class instruction may flourish under a choice regime. Whole-class instruction is a mainstay of teaching because of its efficiency. Teachers with twenty-five students and six hours of instructional time can give each student a maximum of fifteen minutes of one-on-one time—and that is with no other instruction during the day. The idea of markets motivating teachers to adopt more efficient means of instruction is attractive: markets promote efficiency as businesses compete to provide the highest quality good or service at the lowest cost, and productivity is often increased by adopting new technologies, with fewer hours of labor required to produce a particular good. However, a body of reliable research that might guide teachers toward employing instructional approach *A* in situation *B* to attain outcome *C* simply does not exist. Research on the technology of teaching—technology here referring broadly to the tools and strategies teachers employ to produce learning—will have to be strengthened if teachers are to make the kind of well-informed instructional decisions that will lead to more efficient classrooms.[21]

Generalizing the Benefits

We began with the assumption that school choice is beneficial for students participating in existing schools of choice and then offered a few examples of why one should nonetheless be careful not to readily generalize from these findings by suggesting that choice would necessarily hold similar benefits for students in an expanded system. Stipulating that choice is beneficial does not mean that the question is settled—but it is a useful assumption if we are to think rigorously about the benefits of choice-based schooling.

To date, the vast majority of private school and voucher students have been enrolled in Catholic elementary schools. These schools are responsible for the surprisingly strong benefits of private schooling that researchers detailed in the 1980s and 1990s, for the results in Chubb and Moe's landmark 1990 study that made the case for school vouchers, and for most of the results of the voucher experiments in the 1990s. In other words, much of the research and many of the arguments that highlight the benefits of private schooling are based on Catholic schools.

As Tony Bryk and his colleagues point out, certain features of Catholic schooling appear to explain these positive effects, and it is not at all clear that these effects will be replicated by new private schools, even new Catholic schools.[22] Most of the new choice schools that open today are not Catholic schools but are nonsectarian charter schools or Evangelical Christian schools. The student outcomes of traditional Catholic schools, therefore, may not be predictors of the benefits of new choice schools.

The expansion of charter schooling during the 1990s was fueled by frustrated public school teachers and principals and by community leaders committed to an alternative vision of an educational community. These pioneers were able to draw upon an untapped body of philanthropic support and public monies. As charter schooling grows from 2,500 schools to 25,000, it is unlikely that the expansion will be able to continue drawing on the same sources of support. A fundamental shift in the composition of the charter school sector and the need to tap new resources means that the outcomes of the first wave may not say a lot about the outcomes of the next wave. In addition, as the system of school choice expands, it becomes increasingly likely that the community will impose limits on the freedom of individual schools to expel students. The whole community will tolerate such freedom only if there are schools that will admit the expelled students.

Many argue that the ability to foster homogeneous communities or to promote a faith-based mission are critical to making choice schools effective. These characteristics describe private schools today and they describe many charter schools, but these characteristics are not intrinsic to a choice-based school. They flourish in the absence of rules and regulation. However, as Terry Moe observes, the public indicates a desire to heavily regulate choice schools that are funded with public dollars.[23] In such a case, an expanded choice regime might require extensive regulation of participating schools and could eliminate the very qualities in choice schools that are responsible for producing the apparent benefits.

Understating the Benefits of Choice

Just as we should be cautious about projecting the benefits of choice-based reform from existing evidence, we should also recognize that private schools and charter schools currently operate under a number of limitations and disadvantages that would no longer hold in an expanded system of choice. In a world where choice-based schooling is more prevalent and where choice-based schools are more richly funded, the benefits of enrolling in a choice school could be significantly larger than they are today.

For instance, as mentioned, private schools and charter schools tend to spend significantly less per pupil than traditional public schools. While such calculations are somewhat complicated—for instance, Catholic schools are subsidized by local parishes, and some student populations are more expensive to educate than others—there appears to be a consensus that private and charter schools really do operate with less money than their traditional public counterparts. If this is the case, then the fact that choice schools are performing as well as public schools might suggest that these schools would do even better were they funded more adequately. Since these schools tend to operate on a shoestring and without the bonding authority enjoyed by traditional public school districts, they must make do with outdated facilities and a lack of educational technology and science equipment. Were these schools not operating in old or bare-bones environments, they might prove far more effective.

Because traditional public schools hire about 90 percent of the nation's teachers, those who contemplate a teaching career tend to fulfill the certification requirements that public schools demand. Once they have expended the time and energy to fulfill these, many are understandably hesitant to accept positions in charter or private schools that pay less, offer fewer benefits, and provide less security and stability. The result is a workforce that is less reliable and less proficient than it is likely to be in a world where traditional schools were a less dominant employer.

The relatively small size and fragmented nature of the choice sector also forces choice schools to shoulder logistical and cost burdens that would shrink with an expanded choice sector. For instance, few intermediaries have thus far emerged to provide bookkeeping assistance, accounting systems, transportation support, financing, and related services to charter schools—

largely due to the limited number of charters now in the market for such services. For traditional public schools, these services are provided by the central school district or by the state. Choice schools that obtain such services might prove more educationally effective.

Conclusion

This chapter has offered more questions than answers. When we try to see into the black box, it becomes clear just how much we do not know. Even the little we do know only dimly informs a future in which school choice may operate on a scale much greater than today.

To address the issues discussed here, we need more experiments and more efforts to draw upon lessons from other fields that have gone through the kind of radical makeover envisioned for schooling. It is only by peering into the black box and trying to learn what it conceals that we can begin to learn whether early findings point to the promise or the limitations of choice-based reform in education. Some traits responsible for the positive early effects of choice programs may not be replicable on a broader scale—or may only be replicable if programs are properly designed. Alternatively, benefits for participating students may be intrinsically produced by some element of the choice process or by the very nature of choice-driven schooling, suggesting that observed benefits can be readily extrapolated into larger choice programs.

Upon reflection, it is apparent that the aspirin analogy is more than a little problematic in the case of school choice. Choice-based reform is not a discrete treatment that can be expected to have consistent effects. Rather, choice-based reform encompasses a number of specific changes that may or may not be replicated in any other instance. While some of the changes produced by choice-based reform are a consequence of choice qua choice, many others are only incidentally related to choice and may or may not be replicated in any future choice-based arrangement. Rather than a treatment like a medication that is likely to have consistent results, choice-based reform is an arrangement—like altering hospital management—that will not necessarily produce consistent outcomes.

The black box—that is, the unknown and even the unknowable—illustrates why we should be cautious about extrapolating from findings, whether positive or negative, regarding the outcomes of existing school choice programs. Such warnings are not unique to the issue of school choice and are appropriately sounded whenever small-scale pilot efforts are considered as models for large-scale social interventions.

In the case of schooling, for instance, the same caution has been usefully applied to efforts to shrink class size. Although shrinking the size of classes in a particular school has obvious benefits, it has been found that reducing class size on a large scale can create a shortage of effective teachers, increase the use of unqualified or ineffective teachers, and result in higher costs without any corresponding benefits.[24] In other words, a promising strategy turned out to have very different results when implemented on a wide scale because the key condition that it required to be effective (enough competent teachers) turned out not to be met on a large scale (because of a shortage of competent teachers). Warning about the dangers of extrapolating from the results of pilot social programs is simply to acknowledge that the world is a complicated place and that social engineers ought to always exercise discretion.

All choice-based reforms are not created equal, and school choice is not simply school choice. If voucher schools aid students because the schools in question are cohesive and flexible, neither public school choice programs nor heavily regulated charter school programs are likely to deliver the desired benefits. If choice schools are successful because they are able to maintain discipline and expel troublemakers, expanding school choice while reducing the freedom of schools to discipline or expel students could prove a counterproductive policy. In other words, the desirability of choice-based reform and its broader lessons for reform depend in large part on how and why it works. These are issues that we do not know a lot about, but they will demand careful scrutiny in the years ahead.

Notes

1. James S. Coleman and Thomas Hoffer, *Public and Private High Schools: The Impact of Communities* (New York: Basic Books, 1987).

2. Derek Neal, "What Have We Learned about the Benefits of Private Schooling?" *Economic Policy Review* 4, no. 1 (1998): 3.

3. William G. Howell and Paul E. Peterson, with Patrick J. Wolf and David E. Campbell, *The Education Gap: Vouchers and Urban Schools* (Brookings, 2002); but see the reanalysis by Alan B. Krueger and Pei Zhu, "Another Look at the New York City School Voucher Experiment," Working Paper 470 (Industrial Relations Section, Princeton University, 2003). This research is particularly noteworthy because of its use of multiyear, randomized field trials, meeting a level of scientific rigor rare in educational research.

4. Tom Loveless, *Charter Schools,* Brown Center Report on American Education (Brookings, 2002).

5. Harold C. Doran and Darrel W. Drury, *Evaluating Success: KIPP Educational Program Evaluation* (Alexandria, Va.: New American Schools, 2002); Frederick M. Hess and

David L. Leal, "Evaluation of the National Heritage Academies Student Performance: 2000–02." Available online at www.heritageacademies.com/nha/assets/Hess_Report.pdf.

6. Adam Gamoran, "Student Achievement in Public Magnet, Public Comprehensive, and Private City High Schools," *Educational Evaluation and Policy Analysis* 18, no. 1 (1996): 1–18.

7. See, for instance, Brian Gill and others, *Rhetoric versus Reality: What We Know and What We Need to Know about Vouchers and Charter Schools* (Santa Monica, Calif.: Rand, 2001); Helen F. Ladd, *Market-Based Reforms in Education* (Washington: Economic Policy Institute, 2002).

8. John E. Chubb and Terry M. Moe, *Politics, Markets, and America's Schools* (Brookings, 1990).

9. Luis Benveniste, Martin Carnoy, and Richard Rothstein, *All Else Equal: Are Public and Private Schools Different?* (New York: Routledge Falmer, 2002).

10. Chubb and Moe, *Politics, Markets, and America's Schools.*

11. Caroline M. Hoxby, "Changing the Profession," *Education Next* 1, no. 1 (2001): 57–64.

12. Anthony S. Bryk, Valerie E. Lee, and Peter B. Holland, *Catholic Schools and the Common Good* (Harvard University Press, 1993).

13. Bryk, Lee, and Holland, *Catholic Schools and the Common Good.*

14. A strong case for peer effects is argued by Judith Rich Harris, *The Nurture Assumption: Why Children Turn Out the Way They Do* (New York: Touchstone, 1998).

15. Derek Neal, "The Effects of Catholic Secondary Schooling on Educational Achievement," *Journal of Labor Economics* 15, no. 1, pt. 1 (1997): 98–123.

16. James S. Coleman and Thomas Hoffer, *Public and Private High Schools: The Impact of Communities* (New York, Basic Books, 1987); also see U.S. Bureau of the Census, table 15, "Families with Children 5 to 24 Years Old by Enrollment Status in Kindergarten to College, by Control of School, Family Income, Type of Family, Race, and Hispanic Origin: October 2000." Internet release date June 1, 2001. Available online at www.census.gov/population/socdemo/school/ppl-148/tab15.txt.

17. Patricia Wasley and others, *Small Schools, Great Strides: A Study of New Small Schools in Chicago* (New York: Bank Street College of Education, 2000).

18. For example, June C. Rivers and William L. Sanders, "Teacher Quality and Equity in Educational Opportunity: Findings and Policy Implications," in *Teacher Quality,* edited by Lance T. Azumi and Williamson M. Evers (Stanford, Calif.: Hoover Institution Press, 2002); Steven G. Rivkin, Eric A. Hanushek, and John F. Kain, "Teachers, Schools, and Academic Achievement," Working Paper 6691 (Cambridge, Mass.: National Bureau of Economic Research, 2002).

19. Willard Waller, *Sociology of Teaching* (1932).

20. See Herbert J. Walberg and Jin-Shei Lai, "Meta-Analytic Effects for Policy," in *Handbook of Educational Policy,* edited by Gregory J. Cizek (San Diego: Academic Press, 1999), table 9.

21. Robert Dreeben, *The Nature of Teaching* (Glenview, Ill.: Scott, Foresman, 1970); Frederick M. Hess, *Tear Down This Wall* (Washington: Progressive Policy Institute, 2001); Tom Loveless, "The Regulation of Teaching and Learning," in *Stability and Change in American Education,* edited by Maureen T. Hallinan and others (Clinton Corners, N.Y.: Eliot Werner, 2003).

22. Bryk, Lee, and Holland, *Catholic Schools and the Common Good.*

23. Terry Moe, *Schools, Vouchers, and the American Public* (Brookings, 2001).

24. George W. Bohrnstedt and Brian M. Stecher, *What We Have Learned about Class Size Reduction in California* (Sacramento: California State Department of Education, 2002).

6

How School Choice Affects Students Who Do Not Choose

DAN GOLDHABER, KACEY GUIN, JEFFREY R. HENIG, FREDERICK M. HESS, AND JANET A. WEISS

Proponents of school choice often point to the benefits of competition in the private sector when positing that market-based education reform will yield academic benefits for all students. Critics of school choice, on the other hand, typically suggest that the education system is so different from the private sector that the market analogy is inappropriate. They voice concerns that students who do not avail themselves of options will be left isolated in schools stripped of the resources and personnel necessary for improvement. In this chapter, we address these two conflicting arguments. Though much of the debate about school choice has focused on the choosers—those students who actively choose their school—increasingly researchers and policymakers are concerned about the fate of the non-choosers, or those who are left behind. Our analysis attempts to explain when and how school choice policies may have positive and negative consequences for those students and families who do not actively exercise choice.[1]

The arguments for the benefits of choice among choosers are relatively clear. In theory, choice can expand to more students the options long available to those families with the wherewithal to exercise residential mobility or pay private school tuition. This may allow all families to select higher quality schools, or at least schools that best meet the needs of their children. At a system level, the cumulative effect of these choices would result in allocative efficiencies whereby students with varied needs, interests, and learning styles sort themselves into those learning communities most appropriate to their individual needs. Some propronents also suggest that benefits will result from stimulating student and family commitment and loyalty to schools, which will make them more supportive of the schools' efforts to promote educational achievement.

It is less clear whether school choice policies yield benefits for students who do not make active choices. So long as nonchoosers are not negatively affected by a choice system, benefits that accrue only to those students who exercise school choice may be sufficient to support a school choice platform; some students might benefit with no cost to others, resulting in a net improvement in American education. Yet there are some reasons to believe, at least in theory, that a choice system could be beneficial to both active choosers and nonchoosers. This "strong" claim about choice is based on the notion that choice can set into motion dynamics that influence school systems in ways that positively affect both groups.

The primary argument is that a market-based choice system will result in competition among schools, leading them to improve lest they lose students and the funding that accompanies them. Proponents suggest that the pressure upon educators to attract and retain students will force them to adopt previously neglected management, operational, or educational improvements. It is also possible that choice will provide educators with important diagnostic information that they would not otherwise have. For instance, they might learn something about what makes often-chosen schools "successful" and apply these lessons to schools that are not chosen. Choice could also lead to allocative efficiency benefits for nonchoosers. In one possible scenario, students who do not actively choose options may end up in schools with other students who are similar to them academically. These students may then benefit from pedagogical strategies tailored to their needs. Finally, one might argue that a choice system would bolster confidence in education among the public at large; increased public confidence might in turn lead to stronger public support for public school funding, benefiting all students.

To the extent that many or most students do not actively use school choice, the broader impact of choice depends in large part on whether schools do indeed react in ways that benefit nonchoosers. However, little of the scholarly research examining school choice as an educational reform strategy has explicitly explored these claims about how choice may affect the experience of nonchoosers. While advocates argue that choice and competition may be the keys to improving traditional public schools for everyone, and detractors suggest that they might help those who actually choose a school but will surely hurt those who are left behind in traditional public schools, rigorous analysis of the various assumptions has languished.[2]

We believe that this debate will be far more useful when it focuses on the policy design of the choice system itself. The simple truth is that the concept of choice is neither good nor bad. In practice, choice policies may have positive or negative consequences, depending on the specific circumstances under which these policies are implemented. In this chapter we attempt to explain the conditions under which we might expect choice policies to have positive or negative consequences for those students who are not active choosers. Only by coming to understand these conditions can we map the causal pathways that connect choice and competition to school performance and student achievement.

Why Choice Initiatives Might Help Nonchoosers

Why might school choice help nonchoosers? The answer to this question is of significant policy importance in understanding the systemic effects of large-scale choice programs. It may be of particular importance to those disadvantaged students who are performing poorly under the prevailing arrangement of neighborhood school assignment, since these are probably the students least likely to be active choosers.

Most discussions about the competitive consequences of school choice are framed in terms of economic theories about how competition, supply, and demand play out through markets. Our analysis draws on these discussions but expands upon them in two ways. First, we identify some potential market consequences that have not received due attention. Second, we move beyond the conventional economic perspective to consider how competitive effects may have consequences because of the ways they are channeled through political processes and institutions. In other words, public systems may not respond directly to market pressures but may instead be motivated by political pressures articulated through electoral, interest group, and bureaucratic channels.

Competitive Responses

One reason to anticipate positive effects for nonchoosers involves competitive responses from traditional public schools eager to hold onto their students. Part of the original rationale for market-oriented proposals for school restructuring was that traditional public schools had no direct incentive to strive to satisfy their students.[3] As public monopolies with revenues guaranteed through taxes, public schools could afford to be indifferent to the possibility that families would take their business elsewhere. A choice system could break down the buffers that shield traditional public education systems from competition, exposing them to incentives to improve. As this is a market-based argument, it is useful to consider the conditions under which markets function efficiently and the degree to which the education system might be made to work like a market.

As Julian Betts (chapter 2, this volume) discusses, classical economic theory holds that perfectly competitive markets lead to socially optimal outcomes. Perfectly competitive markets, however, are defined by very specific conditions that seldom hold even in the private sector and vary substantially from the reality of the public education sector. Of course even imperfect market systems may result in socially beneficial outcomes, and this becomes more likely as the market more closely approximates perfect competition. Choice advocates, in drawing the market analogy, assume that public schools today are not as efficient as they could be; that parents, given greater options, would vote with their feet to support "good" schools; and that the appropriate connection between resources and students would pressure public schools to change policies, practices, and resource allocations in ways that would enhance the achievement of all students.

All this presumes that at least some public schools are inefficient, so there is room for improvement. Public schools may be technically inefficient, meaning they could achieve more with existing resources. For instance, they may be overly bureaucratic and rule bound, prohibiting teachers from teaching in the most effective ways. Or school personnel may not work as hard as they might if they knew their jobs would be in jeopardy if large numbers of parents select other schools.[4] Public schools may also make inefficient decisions, by purchasing a suboptimal mix of educational resources.[5] The market model of education suggests that competition would compel schools to wring out these sources of inefficiency.

In theory, school choice makes the public education system function more like a market: consumers of education (parents and students) select schools based on their preferences, and producers of education face negative consequences if their product fails to sell. Nonchoosers may benefit from the market pressures induced by even a small number of choosers.[6]

Two aspects of this market model of education are worth stressing. First, it is not necessarily the case that students actually need to exercise choice for the benefits of competition to accrue. The mere threat of losing students (and this threat is more potent if the accompanying consequences are direct and big) may induce institutional responses from schools or behavioral responses from school officials. Second, to the degree that educators do not selectively educate students within schools, nonchoosers benefit from the choices made by choosers: schools become better for all students as a result of the invisible hand principle. This is the central argument to the notion that a rising tide (due to choice) would lift all boats.

Allocative Efficiency Gains

A second argument that choice would benefit nonchoosers is that sorting students across schools according to their needs and interests would allow schools and teachers to tailor educational programs and practices to the students they are serving. This argument is typically made for those who are active choosers; however, there is room to argue that nonchoosers would benefit as well. A narrowing of academic proficiency levels or learning styles within a school or classroom may be beneficial. For instance, it is possible to imagine nonchoosers benefiting from choice programs that draw other (possibly more vocal and demanding) students away from the nonchoosers' classrooms. Proponents of teaching techniques like phonics and directed instruction sometimes argue that the benefits of these pedagogical approaches are most apparent for students who are struggling academically[7] and that teachers may be better able or more willing to utilize these instructional methods or to set and maintain a consistent tone and level of instruction when students have roughly similar academic preparation. Such arguments rest on the assumption—as yet untested—that nonchoosers as a group are more similar to one another than they are to the students who actively seek choice opportunities.

Investment in Public Education

Finally, one might imagine important links between confidence in public schools in the public at large and the electorate's willingness to support public schools through taxation. To the degree that school choice instills greater public confidence that public schools will use resources effectively, the public may be more willing to invest in public education. School choice systems might therefore serve as a safety valve for dissatisfied families, allowing them to leave an inadequate public school without necessarily leaving the public schools altogether. Keeping families attached to publicly funded schooling may benefit those left in schools primarily serving nonchoosers by adding political muscle to the constituency supporting funding for public school budgets. Parents who currently send their children to private schools do not have a direct private incentive to support public school expenditures. With a choice system, private school parents may have greater private incentive to support greater public school spending—if, for instance, the size of private school vouchers were tied to public school expenditure levels.

How School Choice Initiatives Could Hurt Nonchoosers

Just as there are theoretical reasons to believe that choice initiatives might help nonchoosers, there are theoretical reasons to believe that nonchoosers would be harmed by school choice. Many worry that choice would harm both choosers and nonchoosers by leading to a diminishment of social cohesion. Increased choice may foster values-based segregation leading to social fragmentation.[8] This concern goes to the heart of basic concepts regarding the roles of individuals and society. In its extreme, this perspective regards society as somewhat fragile and as dependent on collective and shared institutions for socialization and cohesion.

Even if choice does not lead to values-based segregation, there are routes by which expanded choice and competition could set the stage for educational decline. One possibility is that increased student and teacher mobility, combined with increased fluidity on the supply side, might induce greater educational inefficiencies. A second is associated with the regulatory costs involved in administering a choice system. A third is related to spillover or peer effects and the possibility that choice could lead to a redistribution of students that might be less advantageous to society as a whole and to nonchoosers in particular. A fourth possibility is a more indirect chain of events through which competition erodes the constituency that supports funding public schools. A final possibility is that the competition arising from a choice system would be based on attributes other than academic outcomes.

Educational Inefficiencies

Expanded school choice programs might reduce aggregate student learning due to inefficiencies associated with either facilities costs or student and teacher mobility. The market model assumes that schools that are unable to compete effectively for students will close. However, communities do not have good mechanisms for knowing when a school has become such a competitive failure that it should be closed. During a period of decline, when a school loses enrollment, the costs of the building and grounds (and their maintenance) remain relatively fixed. A building that is half full costs nearly as much to heat and cool and secure from vandalism and crime, for example, as one that is fully enrolled. School choice initiatives deliberately invite students to move from unattractive schools to more attractive ones. This necessarily leads to underutilization of some school buildings, which is likely to result in increased per pupil costs. While markets may correct for this over time, political and regulatory restraints may make it difficult to close those schools with low enrollment, implying greater inefficiencies.

Student mobility associated with school choice may also cause inefficiencies. As school choice invites students to move from one school to another, any given school experiences considerable turnover in the student body. A high rate of student mobility complicates the educational mission of schools, forcing teachers to educate students arriving from schools with wide variation in curricula and levels of preparation.[9] Furthermore, teachers may be more effective when they know more about their students as individuals. To the degree that choice leads to greater turnover, teachers have less time to become familiar with their students.[10]

Inefficiencies may also result from the way in which competitive effects are channeled through political institutions. Elected officials may respond to political pressures with symbolic, rather than substantive, changes[11] because such changes are often easier, given technological complexities, fiscal constraints, or political controversy. Recourse to symbolic and superficial policies may be particularly common in the education arena. School choice initiatives may appeal to political leaders precisely because they present the image that they are taking dramatic actions.[12] But choice schemes may be especially damaging to nonchoosers if, in practice, they divert efforts from educating nonchoosers toward merely symbolic gestures.

Regulatory Costs

The costs of regulating a choice system may also produce harmful effects to nonchoosers by diverting resources from educational improvement to regulatory oversight. Even an unregulated voucher scheme of the type Milton Friedman proposed requires a level of government capacity sufficient to raise the revenues needed to realize the collective goods aspects of education and to monitor and regulate so as to avoid fraud and abuse, civil rights violations, and threats to public health. Any choice program that is remotely feasible in the current political environment places even greater responsibilities on government to ensure that choice is exercised within the proper bounds. For example, most choice proposals assume that the government will be responsible for monitoring schools receiving public monies to limit fraud, mismanagement, and inappropriate teachings (for example, government will intervene if schools teach hatred or intolerance). There may be significant costs associated with this government role.

While some proponents of choice believe that elimination of waste can create substantial savings, most imagine that government at the very least will maintain a public funding commitment sufficient to preserve existing levels of educational attainment, and some believe that any savings due to elimination of waste should be reinvested in order to achieve even better outcomes. However, it is plausible that the cost associated with regulatory oversight would exceed the value of having a choice system[13] and might be better spent on other educational investments. This could be particularly true for nonchoosers, who are likely to be heavily dependent upon public investment for their education.

Peer Effects

Considerable and compelling evidence shows that peer effects play an important role in the education of students. When some students and families make active choices, the pattern of choices might result in compatible student groupings across schools, leading to positive educational effects. However, it might result in a distribution of students across schools that would be educationally harmful to nonchoosers. For example, if nonchoosers tend to be lower achieving students, if there are benefits for lower achieving students from close contact with higher achieving students, and if the choice policy leads to less mixing of high- and low-achieving students, then nonchoosers are likely to be harmed by the peer environment that follows from school choice.

Nonchoosers might also be harmed if school officials adopt grouping practices within schools in response to competitive pressure. If school officials seek to be competitive by offering selective benefits to active choosers, then nonchoosers may find themselves isolated from their peers within the school. Resources within the school may be drained away from those students who do not choose, in order to satisfy the needs of the more assertive families.

Provision of Public Education

Economic theory predicts underprovision and underconsumption of goods that generate positive externalities. Education is the classic case of this type of good. Education clearly provides private benefit to those who receive it, but also offers significant benefits to society as a whole. For example, all members of society benefit from the increased skill and knowledge of individuals who receive high-quality schooling, as citizens with more education are more productive in the workplace, more likely to vote, less likely to commit crimes or require public assistance, and so on. When education is framed as a public good, the political argument for public provision is compelling. As we move toward a market model, with education framed as a private good, with educational choices to be made by individuals and families rather than by public officials, then we may lose sight of its broader benefits.

While some argue that choice would enhance public confidence in schools leading to more enthusiastic public support for school funding, it is also possible to argue that choice policies could undermine such support. While school choice does not necessarily imply the privatization of the provision of education, public willingness to support public schools may be influenced by a focus on the private benefits offered by an education system organized around competition for student enrollment. If the choice system also provides options for families to choose private schools, then, depending on its structure, more families might have a reduced stake in the public system. This may weaken the political voice articulating and promoting a vision of collective investment in education.[14] The expansion of choice may create cleavages within the constituencies that traditionally support expenditures on public education, leading to lower levels of aggregate public school spending than otherwise would be the case.[15] For all of these reasons, nonchoosers may find themselves in a public school system with fewer resources to provide them with high-quality education.

The Wrong Type of Competition

In the discussion above on how the market may help nonchoosers, we assume that parents choose schools primarily for academic reasons and generate pressures for schools to respond with academic improvement; however, this may not be the case. There are two reasons why competition may not lead to systematic improvements in academic quality at all or to improvements for some at the expense of others. First, parents may not have the information necessary to make good decisions about academic quality. To the degree that they are ill informed, they may respond to visible proxies more than to substantive differences in school quality. This could impel public systems to compete through visible and symbolic actions that seem to indicate an attractive program but that have little effect on the quality of education offered by the school. For example, schools might seek to attract enrollment by investing in new facilities or extracurricular activities, without ensuring that these investments actually improve student achievement. Second, parental preferences may be such that the competition to attract students is not primarily based on school quality. For example, if proximity to a school is more important to parents than the academic environment, we might observe that a choice program results in, on average, lower quality schools that are more conveniently located.

The Importance of Context

If choice policies may have such a wide range of effects on students and families who do not choose, how can we design policies that make positive effects more likely and negative effects less likely? As we examined the policy design choices that might buffer nonchoosers from the risks of school choice, we quickly realized that these choices are constrained in important ways by characteristics of the school district and community involved. Schools, districts, and states vary in ways that bear directly upon how choice programs work and the likelihood that the risks for nonchoosers can be mitigated. Thus we expect the same policy design, launched in different settings, to lead to quite different results.

In this section, we discuss some variables in the policy environment that play an important role in mediating the impact of choice policies on students. The discussion is suggestive, rather than exhaustive. Exploring these mediating variables, which we call contextual effects, may point the way to some areas in which disagreements about school choice can be narrowed through a more thorough investigation of the right empirical questions. Attention to context could lead policymakers to design choice policies to serve local circumstances. Considerations of context could even lead policymakers to conclude that choice programs should not be implemented in their community given the risks.

Whether choice-induced competition will benefit nonchoosers depends both on whether schools seek to compete by improving their programs for everyone and also on whether schools have the resources, institutional flexibility, and the know-how to do so. Contextual factors that blunt incentives or sap capacity are likely to block the anticipated competitive effect. While some contextual variables are embedded in the demographic, cultural, and historical attributes of communities, others are more subject to deliberate intervention by government. The following discussion takes up contextual factors that we find especially relevant to the effects of school choice on nonchoosers.

—*Education policies and practices:* information, school transportation, school and district financial practices, school start-up costs and facilities, and the capacity of school and district leadership.

—*General public sector conditions:* public transportation, strength of public employee unions, city-suburb relations, size and number of districts, wealth and business climate, public opinion, and political and legal history of school reform.

—*Demographic and social capital conditions:* population density, school-age population trends, racial and ethnic composition and segregation, religious composition and private schools, generalized trust, and public sector capacity.

Education Policies and Practices

Policymakers who wish to proceed with choice initiatives need to consider factors that will enable the community, district, region, or state to implement education policy in ways that will benefit even those who do not actively choose among schools.

Information is essential if parents and students are to know how to shop intelligently for a school. Ignorance or misinformation may cause parents to choose schools for the wrong reasons. The measures used to describe different schools or different options are important and depend on the capacity of the school and the district to generate accurate, reliable, and valid information. The kinds of information provided to families will influence the choices that they are likely to make.[16] Absent useful and objective measures provided by the district, parents are likely to rely on their social networks (which vary widely in the criteria they use and the accuracy of their information) or on heuristic shortcuts (such as the racial composition of the student body or the presence of graffiti on school walls) to make judgments about school quality. Such informal sources of information can be valuable, but they also have the potential to mislead parents or reinforce social biases.[17]

Schools and districts not only need to provide good information to families, they also need to be able to track and analyze the choices that families make. The theory underlying choice is that schools that are losing students will adapt in educationally beneficial ways. In doing so, they help nonchoosers. If, however, school personnel do not make the effort or do not have the capacity to monitor what choices families are making or why they are making them, they lose the ability to translate mobility patterns into useful signals about what needs to be done to improve all schools. Thus they may fail to make educationally beneficial changes.

Choice systems also assume that schools and districts may learn from one another. Schools and districts that are losing students are presumably doing the "wrong" things and could learn from those schools and districts that are gaining students because they are presumably doing the "right" things. However, information that is available at one point in an organization may not be distributed to other people who may need or want to learn from it. This unreliable information flow is one reason that competition may not influence school administrators. At the school level, information technology, information management, and money management systems are often relatively rudimentary. This limits a district's ability to make tough decisions regarding resource allocation, to know what is working and what is not, and to effectively drive organizational change.

Transportation costs are a second important factor. If costs of transporting students to school are high and must be borne by families, families may be discouraged from switching schools. Schools may have little incentive to improve their performance if school administrators conclude that they have a captive clientele. This factor is especially important in rural areas, where schools are geographically dispersed. Only changes in funding policies for transportation (for example, busing students at district expense to whichever school they choose) are likely to allow competitive pressures to emerge.

School and district financial practices are a third important factor. Exit and entry of students will not have the planned impact on school performance unless financial systems are in place that closely link revenues to enrollment. School and district budgets need to be responsive to changes in enrollment and the revenue that is driven by enrollment. In traditional educational budgeting, costs do not automatically adjust to enrollment changes. Schools losing students cannot instantaneously cut staff, reduce facilities costs, or cut programs—and if they *could,* the risks would be great that this would simply lead to additional student migration out of the school. Out-migration may undermine school or system capacity to undertake remedial action, spurring a dysfunctional spiral of decline.[18] Strong financial systems and the political will and capacity to manage costs aggressively are important to ensuring that money follows students, but there needs to be sufficient lag time so that schools losing students are not forced to deliver even weaker service to their remaining students.

A fourth important factor is the difficulty of starting up new schools. Choice is likely to generate competitive pressures only if new schools emerge or if existing schools expand to meet families' demands. High start-up costs (due perhaps to a lack of suitable facilities or strict regulatory standards) may limit the number of new providers who enter the educational market. Given that the threat to any single school posed by competition will be a function of how many students can be educated outside of that school, high start-up costs that result in few schooling options will limit competition. If there is no place for students to move, there is little threat that they will leave.

To some extent, a community's potential for new providers may depend on the presence of a pool of private schools with vacant seats or the availability of start-up capital for alternatives. But other start-up costs may be under the control of policymakers—for example, schools and districts may have policies or practices that make underutilized public buildings available for new school options. Or they may subsidize, insure, or otherwise encourage private investment in school facilities; or they may allow nontraditional providers to rent space in existing public school buildings. The feasibility and cost of these options, in turn, can be affected by the age and condition of the existing stock of public school buildings.

The fifth contextual factor is the capacity for leadership at the district and school levels. Market competition affects the behavior of organizations by influencing the behavior of officials in positions of leadership. Where school district leadership is weak, politically divided, and subject to rapid turnover, a school or district will have limited capacity to generate effective responses to competitive pressures. Similarly, unskilled or indifferent principals and teachers will be unable to rise to the occasion, even if the market incentive is powerful.[19]

When private sector executives grapple with competition, they have many tools at their disposal: promotions, salaries, bonuses, perks, job titles, working conditions, geographic assignment, scope of responsibilities, and other job elements. Most school system officials do not have the same arsenal of tools to support their efforts to improve performance. The relatively flat organization of schools, and the resulting lack of opportunity for upward movement within teaching, means that administrators cannot easily threaten to withhold promotions or other opportunities for advancement. The performance of teachers is difficult for administrators to assess. This makes it difficult to decide how to reward or sanction school employees. Teachers are sometimes invisible in their separate classrooms, and direct observation of teachers in action may be perfunctory and infrequent. Moreover, teacher reliance on student preparation and cooperation complicates efforts to determine when a teacher is working hard and effectively. This challenge is heightened in the urban school context, where teachers and principals must overcome significant environmental challenges. As organizations, school systems have not been constructed with much attention to efficiency or top-down control.[20] The structural constraints on leadership make it all the more essential that school and district administrators take the initiative to protect or, better yet, improve the experience of students who are nonchoosers.

While the organizational constraints on leadership may be daunting, the extent to which they constrain competitive response may vary from community to community and over time. For example, the ability of administrators to wield termination as a threat will depend on such factors as the size of the teacher labor force, the relative availability of teaching slots, and the desirability of local positions. The need for qualified teachers in the past decade has made threats of termination less imposing than they might otherwise be.[21]

In any case, the capacity of the district and school leadership to make the organizational changes required to improve is a key factor in determining whether competition will lead to more effective schooling. The broader success of a choice program depends on the willingness of the leadership to look beyond the immediate incentives to satisfy the choosers and to take up the additional work of attending to the concerns about the educational experiences for nonchoosers.

General Public Sector Conditions

The contextual factors that we discuss in this section influence the ways that choice programs are likely to play out in particular places. They have an important role in determining whether choice benefits or harms those who do not actively exercise the option to choose schools. General governance, political and policy legacies, and market conditions are much stickier to change than the education-specific policies discussed above, although they can reasonably be expected to change in response to concerted efforts. From the perspective of those considering school choice initiatives, that distinction can be important. Where the context is not conducive, reformers who are concerned about nonchoosers need not abandon their interest in choice options, but they may need to be prepared to undertake major efforts to create the conditions under which a choice system would work better.

The existence of a comprehensive and well-functioning public transportation system substantially reduces the costs of student mobility for school choice. All else equal, this will tend to increase the proportion of families who do actively choose a school for their children. This, in turn, will increase the pressure on schools to meet the needs even of families who are slow to choose, because the prospect that they *might* exit is realistic. To the extent that such a communitywide transportation system reduces the need for school districts to direct more money into busing, it may also mean that there is a greater prospect that these schools will be able to obtain the financial resources to make internal reforms.

The strength of public employee unions (and the laws that protect them) vary considerably across the states and communities. The flexibility for school administrators to respond to the loss of students is attenuated (or eliminated) when teachers and principals have strong contract protection against termination and mandatory reassignment. Similarly, schools' capacity to innovate and improve may be constrained when union contracts include restrictions on personnel policies and working conditions, such as the length of the workday or year, class sizes, and compensation policies.[22] Even when district leaders have the incentive and desire to act, they may lack the tools necessary to compel the cooperation of subordinates. Moreover, administrators generally have little power to reward or sanction teachers monetarily because teachers are compensated by contract according to a single salary schedule, in which teachers are paid solely on the basis of the degrees they hold and the length of time they have taught. This system provides little incentive for teachers to improve their performance. In these ways, restrictive collective bargaining agreements and statutory regulation present significant barriers to the capacity of districts to respond to competitive pressure.[23]

Political and economic relationships between city and suburbs become significant factors when choice proposals are designed to encourage or accommodate moves of students across district boundaries. Although the market logic of choice does not stop at the border of the local school district, suburban communities have tended to resist plans that would open their school doors to inner-city children. Suburban reluctance has not stopped some state legislatures from passing laws permitting interdistrict public school choice. But in most instances legislatures have allowed local jurisdictions considerable discretion in determining whether to take part in interdistrict transfers. For instance, Ohio's law establishing a voucher program in Cleveland explicitly included suburban public schools as potential providers for voucher students, but not a single one opted to participate.

The size and number of school districts in a metropolitan area can affect school choice dynamics as well. A metropolitan area that is divided into many small districts provides families with more opportunities to vote with their feet.[24] Research suggests that these opportunities matter to education;

multiple districts in close proximity effectively create a public school choice option (albeit one that requires residential mobility to put into effect).[25] Thus policymakers who seek to create competitive pressure to stimulate school improvement have less work to do when their community already has many districts within easy traveling distance—and more work to do when there are few districts spread over large geographical swaths.

The overall wealth of a community and the climate for investment may have important effects on the likelihood that new providers will emerge to serve dissatisfied families. In communities generally considered to have an inviting climate for private investment (lower taxes, less burdensome regulation, greater willingness to invest public funds in economic development), the private sector may be more likely to generate new educational options and, therefore, more likely to apply competitive pressure to public schools serving families that do not actively choose. Wealthier communities may also be more likely to raise funds for new educational options, whether these are new programs within public schools, charters, or private schools.

Public opinion toward public education might also influence the manner in which choice policies play out. For example, strong community support for traditional public education (students attending publicly operated schools) is likely to limit the use of the exit option. This in turn dilutes the incentives for schools to reform.[26] Similarly, tight social networks may make families relatively unlikely to change schools based simply on conventional assessments of school quality. To the degree that this is true, we might expect a limited reaction to school choice options and, thus, relatively little competition as a result of choice.

Local history may also influence choice programs. Past litigation focused on school segregation or school finance, or major efforts to adopt systemic school reform, may create a legacy that will change the response of many constituency groups to school choice. Litigation may directly constrain choice when the courts impose mandates and oversight structures that limit student mobility or the linkage of funding to enrollments. Past litigation may indirectly constrain choice by creating wariness among officials and the public about the prospect of resource-intensive and controversial battles that risk future legal action. A history of failed civic efforts to reform public schools may induce a cynicism about the prospects for an effective public school response to competitive pressures, escalating the spiral of out-migration and depleting the capacity of schools to rise to the challenge posed by school choice policies.

Demography and Social Capital Conditions

Demographic and social factors, although seldom susceptible to policy intervention, need to be taken into account in designing school choice policies so that the resulting policies are suited to the communities involved.

Jurisdictions vary substantially in their population density, rates of growth or decline, mobility rates, and the heterogeneity of their populations. These demographic characteristics may influence the extent to which choice will generate substantial competitive effects as well as whether those effects benefit or harm students who are not active choosers. The costs of exercising choice are likely to be lower when the population is denser; in cities, parents can more readily examine alternative schools, and transportation costs are likely to be lower. Moreover, denser communities, because they present a richer target of potential customers, are more likely to attract new schools, further increasing competitive pressure and the likelihood that existing schools take seriously the risks of losing students. The total number of students and schools in a community might also be important, independent of density. For instance, all other things equal, we might expect larger districts to be more bureaucratic and to confront greater logistical challenges in implementing and monitoring change. Furthermore, larger districts are more likely than smaller districts to devote less attention to schools serving large numbers of nonchoosers, attenuating incentives to improve. By contrast, larger-size districts might increase the incentive and capacity to change in at least one important way. Districts with many schools may be better able to introduce variation in what schools offer, making it possible for entrepreneurial school leaders to develop specialized niches—thus creating additional pressure on schools to keep their curriculum up-to-date and attractive to students.

Just as relevant as the current population density and scale are the rate and direction of population change. In rapidly growing communities, school choice programs may spur the opening of new schools that attract many students, but they do so without generating any threat to the existing schools. One might argue that public schools in rapidly growing districts will welcome the loss of students, to alleviate the pressure of student enrollment. Under such circumstances, school choice would not be expected to generate improvement in response to competitive pressure, because existing schools may not actually feel any pressure. Choice may introduce a very different dynamic in areas undergoing population loss. Educators and communities already concerned about declining enrollment, layoffs of teachers, and possible school closings are likely to feel considerable pressure to do what it takes to retain their current students and attract new ones.

School systems with steady enrollment might vary substantially in the extent to which individual schools experience high student mobility rates. Residential instability (for example, associated with renters, lower incomes, and many households with changes in marital and employment status, as well as with dynamic economies) might disrupt efforts to sustain a coherent and successful school program. High mobility, with the attendant rapid comings and goings, creates "noise" that makes it difficult for school staff to notice and learn from market signals about consumer preferences and satisfaction. On the other hand, school choice may have the positive consequence of reducing transfers from one school to another when families move; school choice would permit students to remain in the school they prefer. This increased stability may help to improve conditions for learning in all schools, with clear benefits for nonchoosers.[27]

The extent of racial and ethnic heterogeneity is also an important contextual factor. Historically, racial and ethnic identities and antipathies have considerable power to influence family decisions about schools. Furthermore, race and ethnicity tend to be associated with other phenomena that parents care about (for example, peers' socioeconomic status, family background, special needs, friendship and conflict patterns, teacher expectations, academic achievement, and college attendance). Because racial composition is often easier to discern than these other phenomena, parents may rely on the racial composition of the student population as a proxy in making decisions about where to send their children to school. This can undermine both the incentive and capacity of schools to respond to competitive pressure associated with school choice. If parents are making school choices based on racial and ethnic composition of schools rather than school policies, practices, and performance, schools serving large numbers of students from racial minorities will have trouble attracting new students, with reduced incentives to improve their quality. To the extent that nonchoosers are disproportionately attending schools with large minority enrollment, they may be least likely to benefit from school choice.

Religious diversity can play a contextual role similar to race and ethnicity. Communities with many parents who seek to send their children to school with other children of the same religion (and avoid children with different religious beliefs) may be less attentive to school quality and therefore will undermine the incentives of schools to improve. The religious composition of the community raises a host of other issues, including the likelihood that the community supports a thriving sector of religious private schools. The commitment to religious schooling may affect voter support for school choice, especially when choice plans are designed to incorporate nonsecular private schools.[28]

The literature on social capital emphasizes the importance that generalized trust may play in determining whether collective endeavors flourish or fail.[29] High levels of generalized trust may give school decisionmakers a more forgiving zone of discretion within which to innovate and take risks. Absent such trust, families capable of exercising choice may be more prone to flee a school either out of personal dissatisfaction or—more socially pernicious—out of fear that *others* will exit (and possibly fill up available alternatives) before they do.[30]

Public sector capacity—an amalgam of the knowledge and judgment of public officials and the authoritativeness, coordination, and adaptability of the formal institutions in which they are housed—constitutes a final contextual parameter having to do with demographic or social capital features that are relatively impervious to policy intervention except over the (very) long run. Well-designed constitutions and laws; deep-seated practices for recruiting, electing, and appointing able and judicious public leaders; broad popular support for investing in government and providing its agencies with the resources needed to do their job well—these are all factors that can increase the likelihood that schools will respond effectively to competition and find the help they need to respond to exit signals.

Contextual Factors, Summary

To citizens and policymakers weighing the potential benefits and risks of expanding school choice options, the contextual factors discussed above for the most part present themselves as fixed elements of the local landscape or as considerations outside the boundaries of school choice. We argue, however, that these contextual factors may have substantial influence on the dynamics of choice—influences that assert themselves regardless of the specifics of school choice policies. Policymakers should carefully consider these contextual factors in jurisdictions where they appear likely to undermine the incentive or capacity to improve for schools serving nonchoosers. In those jurisdictions even well-intentioned and well-designed initiatives may exacerbate inequities between active choosers and those who are left behind. In such districts, policymakers may want to take extra care to build in precautions to protect nonchoosers. In districts where these factors are less evident, policymakers can anticipate that the rewards of choice will flow more easily and that potential risks associated with choice can be more readily managed.

Designing Choice Policies That Protect Nonchoosers

Since the effects of school choice on nonchoosers are likely to be closely tied to the context in which choice is implemented, it is important to consider the policy design choices that would lead to better student outcomes in different contexts. We note again that some contextual variables may be influenced by policies while others are less malleable. This clearly implies that choice will have different impacts in different community settings. The set of specific policy interventions most likely to yield benefits, or mitigate the harm, of choice will therefore vary with the setting. In this section we focus on policies that we believe are central to the success of choice across a variety of contexts. Furthermore, we exclusively focus on those design elements that we believe are most consequential for nonchoosers.

Information and Oversight

As we discuss earlier, choice presumes that properly aligned incentives will, through a complex causal chain, drive improvement across the universe of schools—by forcing schools to improve or to give way to more effective competitors. Of course, the critical link in this process is the decisions that parents make about schools. The underlying assumption of choice proponents is that parents will make decisions that reflect the best educational interests of children and that this means choosing high-quality schooling. The competition between schools is then based on educational quality. High-quality schools will attract students and funding, and low-quality schools will improve, either through greater effort by school employees or by the adoption of educational practices and policies that lead to improvement. All this will occur only if choosers (and their parents) take the first step of choosing good schools. Thus though our focus here is on nonchoosers, it is critical that choosers make good decisions in order that nonchoosers may benefit.

While we can reasonably assume that all parents will seek to make decisions that are educationally beneficial for their children, not all parents know how to make informed choices or judge educational quality on the merits. Some studies show a strong correlation between school selection and the demographic characteristics of students.[31] One explanation for this is that parents do not always have good information on school quality so they use other cues when making decisions. These cues may be correlated with educational achievement even when they are not correlated with the contribution that *schools* make toward student achievement. Both common sense and empirical evidence suggest that the more "good" information parents have about school quality, the more likely they are to select schools on the basis of quality.[32]

Prohibiting schools from practicing discriminatory admissions that make them appear to be high performing by virtue of their selection of students is one key to increasing the likelihood that schools are judged by their performance. Another key is the development of data and accountability systems (at the federal, state, and local levels) that are sophisticated enough to detect the contribution that *schools* make toward students' learning growth. Finally, information is only valuable in decisionmaking to the extent that it can easily be accessed by those who need it to make decisions. Thus information about schools must be communicated in a form that is clear and easily accessible to parents and the wider community.[33]

Just as parents are likely to make better decisions about schools with better information, so too are school personnel likely to make better decisions if they are provided with good information. In order to understand why student enrollment is declining, school administrators need to be aware where students are choosing to go, what kinds of program and instruction they are seeking, and how their school's performance on various criteria stacks up to the competition. If school administrators do not have access to information about the flow of students to schools, then they will be less likely to make serious efforts to respond by adopting promising educational practices.

Ensuring the Emergence of Schooling Options

The second link in the causal chain is the assumption that choice will result in pressure to improve on schools that are losing enrollment. This will only occur if parents have viable schooling options. As we describe above, there are many factors—some of which are largely outside the control of policymakers—that will help determine whether a community can generate a rich set of alternatives to the existing public schools. Though the number of school choices will clearly vary depending on the community in question, all communities could make options more accessible to students in several ways. First, policymakers might provide funding that allows for the formation of new schools or the expansion of existing schools; they might also establish policies and procedures conducive to the establishment of small schools, sometimes sharing a single building. These steps would help to create the competition envisioned by school choice supporters. Second, transportation to schools is central to providing parents with real schooling options. Strong public transportation systems or guaranteed publicly provided transportation to schools would both encourage new start-up schools (since they might be able to attract students from a wide geographic area) and allow parents a wider variety of schooling options.

Incentives: The Link between Student Flows and School Resources

The third link in the causal chain is a mechanism that creates incentives for school improvement. This mechanism is a linkage between student enrollment and financial support provided to schools.[34] By linking student choices to consequences for school administrators, leaders of ineffective schools are given concrete incentives to take the hard steps necessary to improve in order to attract students.

It is one thing to say that resources ought to be tied to student flows. It is far more difficult to design that connection so that it works effectively. Significant questions arise about the amount of money that ought to flow with individual students and about when schools ought to receive the resources that flow with students. The structuring of appropriate incentives is a very complex issue, particularly when one is concerned about the effects of the incentives on nonchoosers.

If increased competition is to result in increased efficiency of schools, incentives must be structured so that a choice policy penalizes schools that are judged by parents, by virtue of their school selections, to be unsuccessful. In particular, the loss of revenue associated with the loss of a student has to be greater than the marginal cost associated with educating that particular student. Otherwise the choice system creates the perverse incentive whereby schools benefit financially from losing students. This, however, raises a seeming dilemma. Providing schools with appropriate financial incentives to improve in effect undermines the capacity for school improvement. For example, there is the very real possibility that schools that are losing enrollment may find it difficult to recruit or retain the high-quality teachers they need to become more successful. The incentive-capacity dilemma is less of a concern if significant capacity for improvement already exists within failing schools. The dilemma is also less stark when schools are viewed within the organizational framework of districts. If one of the benefits associated with choice is diagnostic, then changes in student enrollment provide a ready means for school districts to identify when particular schools are succeeding or failing. This benefit assumes that the district will respond by identifying policies and practices that make schools successful and ensuring their implementation in less successful schools. In addition, if financial sanctions are applied at the district level and not in the budgets of individual schools, there is a greater incentive for the district to make appropriate changes.

The incentive-capacity dilemma may also be addressed by structuring the amount of funding schools lose with each student departure, so that it gradually increases with time. For instance, schools that lose students might initially lose less than the marginal cost of educating the departed students, so that the school will actually have slightly more to spend on each remaining student as school administrators face the initial challenge of responding to market signals. If, over time, the school does not make improvements sufficient to stanch the outflow of students, the loss of revenue would then begin to exceed the marginal cost of educating the departed students. In this way, schools have an opportunity to make improvements, knowing that if such improvements are not made there will be increasingly severe financial consequences. In contrast, schools that receive students will always have to receive at least the marginal cost to educate those students, in order to provide an incentive for those schools to recruit and accept students who wish to enroll. These policy recommendations clearly imply that a choice program will increase educational costs in the short run. The hope is that, in the long run, increased educational efficiencies brought about by choice will offset the transition costs. We are not necessarily recommending this approach—a tack that initially rewards schools for losing students raises its own concerns—but are positing this example as one reasonable way that policymakers might negotiate the complexities they must address.

Provision of Educational Funding

Related to the linkage between student flows and school resources is the issue of public monies flowing to private schools. One worry about any public subsidy of private school tuition is that increased enrollment in private schools would erode the overall willingness of the public to support educational expenditures. There is an extensive literature about the potential for underprovision of goods when individuals fail to account for the social benefits associated with the consumption of those goods, as can happen in a purely private sector market. While a choice system does not necessarily move the provision of education to the private sector, it does move the education system in the direction of a market system. Consequently, over time it could alter public opinion about education as a social good, which in turn may reduce the public's willingness to support it. Thus we argue that any educational voucher (the term we use to signify the connection between students and public funding for education) be tied directly to per pupil spending in public schools. This would help to make explicit the stake that the entire society has in public schooling.

Flexibility and Capacity for Change

The above discussion of school change assumes that all schools have the capacity and flexibility to make beneficial changes; however, this may not be the case. A variety of legal and institutional constraints may inhibit the extent to which schools can change their policies and practices. We have discussed some of the ways in which public schools are constrained in their institutional responses to competitive threats. While research offers only limited and conflicting theoretical and empirical findings to support the relaxation of specific federal, state, and local policies that constrain schools, a choice policy ought to be constructed in conjunction with a review of other education-related policies that create rigidity in the practices of schools and districts.

Conclusion

This chapter addresses the concern of many critics of school choice that increased competition among schools will leave substantial groups of students behind. These students, predict the critics, will neither benefit from newly created options nor will their schools improve under pressure of competition. Our theoretical analysis suggests that such concerns have a plausible basis. Given what we know about schools, especially urban schools, the worries about nonchoosers need to be taken seriously. However the analysis also suggests that critics who predict a necessarily grim fate for nonchoosers may be overstating the challenges and overlooking the ability of policymakers to minimize adverse consequences through sensible policy decisions. There are plausible reasons to anticipate that choice-based reform might very well help nonchoosers, though proponents of choice tend to underestimate the significance of program design in producing happy outcomes. Our discussion of contextual factors emphasizes a number of the contextual variables that can help determine the consequences of choice regimes for nonchoosers, and it is precisely this kind of analysis that demands increased attention from both proponents and critics of choice.

Given that school choice might work either to the benefit or to the detriment of students who do not avail themselves of choice options, our discussion explores large and small ways to protect nonchoosers from the risks of school choice. These methods focus on modifying some of the key design elements of the choice policy: incentives, capacity, new competitors, and supports for families.

—The competitive pressure created by school choice pushes school officials to respond to students and families that make active choices. We suggest that sensible school choice policies attend to the second-order effects of these incentives. For example, schools might be prohibited from marketing themselves in ways that distract attention from school quality. For another example, even schools that lose enrollment must have a way to garner the resources and political support to improve.

—The capacity of schools and districts to respond to the choices made by active choosers depends in part on substantial political and organizational resources within the community. Responding to the needs of the nonchoosers requires systematic investment of attention, commitment, and resources, even beyond the rigorous demands of competition. For example, care in assigning quality teachers to schools serving large numbers of nonchoosers or the deliberate inclusion of nonchoosers in innovative programming within schools are two active steps that permit schools to respond to competition and simultaneously improve the educational experience of nonchoosers.

—The introduction of competitors to provide schooling is one important element in creating competitive pressure. The regulation of new entrants should be done in ways that minimize disruption for nonchoosers and that are less likely to exacerbate segregation of nonchoosers (for example by rules governing the timing of permissible transfers to charter schools or schools in other districts).

—Supports for families are critical to effective choice. Although all families will not actively choose, all families may benefit from better information about the schools their children attend. More effective and inclusive information relayed to parents may therefore benefit schools serving nonchoosers.

This analysis highlights a fundamental tension. On the one hand, only strong and direct incentives that mightily reward schools that attract enrollment (and force schools with declining enrollment to close their doors) are likely to produce the across-the-board transformation in the public schools that will lift the performance of all schools—and thus benefit the nonchoosers. On the other hand, a competitive free-for-all puts the nonchoosers at considerable risk of falling between the cracks, as schools are forced to focus their energies on attracting new students. We try to define a middle ground, in which important elements of competition are deployed, while their risks are counterbalanced with supports for families and students. School choice policies that craft an amalgam of competition and support in ways that are tailored to the particular context of the local community are most likely to strike a reasonable balance between the needs of nonchoosers and of those striving for institutional reform.

Notes

1. Claims about the potential benefits of school choice come in both a weak and a strong form. The weak form holds that choice will provide benefits to the students and families who seek out the best available school option. The strong form suggests that choice will lead to competition among schools and programs that will improve education for everyone, choosers and nonchoosers alike.

2. It is not clear under some choice policies what is meant by traditional public schools. This issue is discussed below.

3. Milton Friedman, *Capitalism and Freedom* (University of Chicago Press, 1962).

4. The theory is that school choice would move public schools from operation within the production possibilities frontier onto the frontier itself.

5. Allocative efficiency implies that the mix of inputs chosen is such that all inputs have the same marginal product per dollar. Thus allocative inefficiency in schools or school districts would suggest that educational resources are not utilized in the correct proportions. For more detail on these sources of inefficiency, see Dan Goldhaber and Eric Eide, "Methodological Thoughts on Measuring the Impact of Private Sector Competition on the Educational Workplace," *Educational Evaluation and Policy Analysis* 25, no. 2 (2003): 217–32; and Dan Goldhaber and Eric Eide, "What Do We Know (and Need to Know) about the Impact of School Choice Reforms on Disadvantaged Students?" *Harvard Educational Review* 72, no. 2 (2002): 157–76.

6. As elucidated in Mark Schneider, Paul Teske, and Melissa Marschall, *Choosing Schools: Consumer Choice and the Quality of American Schools* (Princeton University Press, 2000), p. 173, "The marginal consumer, by making the best choices for herself, provides a positive externality to other consumers by her behavior, even without directly communicating information to less-informed citizens." A cadre of alert choosers can monitor school performance and wield a credible threat of exit if school administrators fail to respond. That most of the parents do not themselves devote the time and energy to learn about test scores, or behavior problems, or poor guidance, or inept teachers does not matter much, according to this perspective, as long as these proxy consumers are speaking up. That said, having all parents fully informed would be even more efficient and preferable on other grounds as well.

7. Jeanne S. Chall, *The Academic Achievement Challenge: What Really Works in the Classroom?* (London: Guilford Press, 2000); James Traub, "New York's New Approach," *New York Times,* August 3, 2003, p. 4A20.

8. Research based on what parents say they consider when selecting schools suggests that fears of value-based segregation may be overstated. For example, Schneider, Teske, and Marschall, *Choosing Schools,* find that white and minority and suburban and central-city parents all tend to say that academic quality is what is important and tend to dismiss as peripheral any consideration of the racial composition of schools. Studies looking at choice as exercised are less sanguine, with support for the notion that families rely on the race and

socioeconomic status of student populations as cognitive shortcuts to finding more homogeneous settings even at the expense of leaving "better" schools, at least as measured by test score performance. See also Jeffrey R. Henig, "The Local Dynamics of Choice: Ethnic Preferences and Institutional Responses," in *Who Chooses? Who Loses? Culture, Institutions, and the Unequal Effects of School Choice,* edited by Bruce Fuller and Richard F. Elmore (New York: Teachers College Press, 1996); Mark Schneider and Jack Buckley, "What Do Parents Want from Schools? Evidence from the Internet," *Educational Evaluation and Policy Analysis* 24, no. 2 (2002): 113–44; Gregory R. Weiher and Kent L. Tedin, "Does Choice Lead to Racially Distinctive Schools? Charter Schools and Household Preferences," *Journal of Policy Analysis and Management* 21, no. 1 (2002): 79–92.

9. If turnover introduces inefficiencies, an important empirical question is whether choice reduces or increases student turnover. There are reasons to believe that choice might reduce turnover. To the extent that turnover is induced by residential relocation across fixed attendance zones within a given school system, choice policies could enable students to remain in a school even if their family moves.

10. Teacher and administrator mobility also poses a potential inefficiency problem. Although the point receives little consideration, efficiencies may be lost as educators adapt to new surroundings (start-up costs). In addition, some efficiencies may depend upon fit between skills and a stable and familiar context (thus some principals who succeed in one educational environment can fail dramatically in another).

11. Murray J. Edelman, *The Symbolic Uses of Politics* (University of Illinois Press, 1985).

12. Frederick M. Hess, *Revolution at the Margins: The Impact of Competition on Urban School Systems* (Brookings, 2002).

13. Henry M. Levin and Cyrus E. Driver, "Costs of an Educational Voucher System," *Education Economics* 5, no. 3 (1997): 265–84.

14. Albert O. Hirschman, *Exit, Voice, and Loyalty: Responses to Decline in Firms, Organizations, and States* (Harvard University Press, 1970), p. 43, writes that "the presence of the exit alternative can . . . tend to atrophy the development of the art of voice." School choice systems that remain encapsulated within public institutions, by this reasoning, may atrophy voice at the school level but retain it at the system level.

15. See Jeffrey R. Henig, chapter 9, this volume

16. Hess, *Revolution at the Margins.*

17. Schneider and others, *Choosing Schools;* Schneider and Buckley, "What Do Parents Want from Schools?"; Weiher and Tedin, "Does Choice Lead to Racially Distinctive Schools?"

18. Hirschman, *Exit, Voice, and Loyalty.*

19. Hess, *Revolution at the Margins.*

20. Janet A. Weiss, "Control in School Organizations: Theoretical Perspectives," in *Choice and Control in American Education,* edited by John Witte and William Clune (Philadelphia: Falmer, 1990); Eliot Freidson, *Professionalism: The Third Logic* (University of Chicago Press, 2001).

21. Nationally, annual teacher turnover exceeded 8 percent in the mid-1990s, as the nation's schools sought to hire over 150,000 new teachers a year. In urban areas the situation was even more daunting, with teacher turnover routinely amounting to 10–15 percent each year. Moreover, the nation's schools anticipated needing 2 million or more new

teachers during the first decade of the twenty-first century. Thus veteran teachers had little reason to fear layoffs or to be forced out of their existing school due to enrollment changes. Moreover, teaching conditions in most urban districts are harsh, and many, or even most, urban teachers could find more pleasant jobs elsewhere if they had to. Significantly, the context is very different in suburban communities, where high demand for pleasant and relatively high-paying teaching jobs may create a much lower rate of turnover, may create much more competition for positions, and may make teachers much more sensitive to the possibility of downsizing or to the potential loss of their job. Ironically, this suggests that school leaders might be better equipped to answer competition in those very districts where families are more satisfied with the current condition of schooling.

22. Frederick M. Hess and Patrick J. McGuinn, "Muffled by the Din: The Competitive Noneffects of the Cleveland Voucher Program," *Teachers College Record* 104, no. 4 (2002): 727-64.

23. Hess, *Revolution at the Margins.*

24. Charles M. Tiebout, "A Pure Theory of Local Expenditures," *Journal of Political Economy* 64, no. 5 (1956): 416–24.

25. Caroline M. Hoxby, ed., *The Economics of School Choice* (University of Chicago Press, 2003).

26. This could be the case if that support manifested itself as "loyalty" (Hirschman, *Exit, Voice, and Loyalty*) by families to their neighborhood school (therefore making school administrators less worried about potential out-movement) or by the community at large (making the community less willing to allow out-movement to result in disinvestment in particular public schools or the system at large).

27. Nonchoosers, in this sense, include some who rotate among schools due to family and residential changes largely outside the capacity of the family to control.

28. For example, Jesse H. Choper, "Federal Constitutional Issues," in *School Choice and Social Controversy,* edited by Steven D. Sugarman and Frank R. Kemerer (Brookings, 1999); and R. Kenneth Godwin and Frank R. Kemerer, *School Choice Tradeoffs: Liberty, Equity, and Diversity* (University of Texas Press, 2002), chapter 5.

29. Valerie Braithwaite and Margaret Levi, *Trust and Governance* (New York: Russell Sage, 1998); Anthony S. Bryk and Barbara Schneider, *Trust in Schools: A Core Resource for Improvement* (New York: Russell Sage, 2002); Karen S. Cook, ed., *Trust in Society* (New York: Russell Sage, 2000); Robert D. Putnam, *Making Democracy Work: Civic Traditions in Modern Italy* (Princeton University Press, 1993); Robert D. Putnam, *Bowling Alone: The Collapse and Revival of American Community* (New York: Simon and Schuster, 2000).

30. On the dysfunctional consequences of exit when it is exercised too rapidly, see Hirschman, *Exit, Voice, and Loyalty.*

31. Henig, "The Local Dynamics of Choice"; and Weiher and Tedin, "Does Choice Lead to Racially Distinctive Schools?"

32. For the empirical method, see for example Kent L. Tedin and Gregory R. Weiher, "Racial/Ethnic Diversity and Academic Quality as Components of School Choice," *Journal of Politics* 60, no. 4 (2004): 1109–33.

33. In Florida, the simple change (brought about by the passage of the A+ program) from "level" school ratings to an easily understood grading system, whereby schools are

assigned a letter grade of A through F, appears to have had a profound impact on perceptions of schools, despite the fact that the underlying way in which schools were judged and held accountable did not immediately change.

34. Policymakers may also consider structuring a choice program in such a way that it clearly creates incentives that are explicitly student-achievement oriented. As an example, the Florida A+ program—which is not a universal choice program—only allows for choice if schools have failed to achieve specified performance objectives. A school that is "voucher eligible" may move out of voucher eligible status by increasing the achievement levels of its students. Such a system serves to explicitly narrow the basis of the competition between schools to criteria established by the choice policy itself.

7

School Choice and Integration

BRIAN GILL

One of the key empirical questions about school choice programs is how they will affect the way students are sorted into schools and classrooms. This chapter does not present new empirical evidence about the relationship between choice and integration, but it seeks to establish a conceptual framework for future empirical work. It begins by briefly examining the purpose and meaning of integration and argues that the empirical study of integration must be informed by a deep understanding of the concept and its place in the history of American public education. It hypothesizes a number of causal models that can explain integration—in a hypothetical system lacking choice entirely, in a system of constitutionally protected choice like that in place in most American communities today, and under various policies promoting choice. And it describes how the effects of choice on integration are likely to depend both on local context and on the details of the design of a choice policy, offering guidance for policymakers interested in promoting integration in choice programs, and proposing guidelines for researchers in measuring the effects of choice on integration.

What Is Integration For?

The integration of students from a variety of backgrounds is one of the traditional purposes of American public schools. Indeed, the century-and-a-half-old idea of the common school evokes an ideal in which all students in a community are educated together. Although American public schools have frequently failed to live up to the integrationist ideal—most notably when they systematically segregated black students into separate schools—the ideal remains widely held.

Integration is sometimes viewed as a goal to be sought in its own right, but its widespread support is based on implicit or explicit assumptions about the favorable effects that it may produce. Integration of the schools is hoped, first, to promote equitable access to educational opportunities. This was the major focus of the desegregation efforts of the 1950s and 1960s, which recognized that, despite the claims of "separate but equal," the intentionally segregated black schools of many communities did not provide African American students with opportunities equivalent to those of white students.[1] Integration is intended to promote educational opportunity for disadvantaged children not only by ensuring equitable access to educational resources (including highly qualified teachers) but also by promoting healthy peer effects (that is, giving disadvantaged children the opportunity to learn alongside more advantaged classmates).

Second, integration is hoped to promote healthy social interaction among students of different backgrounds, ultimately leading to a more tolerant and open-minded citizenry.[2] In this sense, integration is intended to benefit not only disadvantaged minority children but also middle-class, white children. All children, suggests the theory, are more likely to learn to appreciate diversity if they personally interact in school with children who are different from themselves. Moreover, the positive attitudes that integration aims to promote will ultimately (it is hoped) benefit all of society by increasing social cohesion and reducing racial tension. The fact that Americans care more about integration in school than in other contexts (such as housing) suggests the importance of this second purpose: integration of schools is directly related to the schools' function in educating children to become good citizens.

The fact that integration is a means to other ends complicates its empirical study. A thorough empirical assessment of integration requires not only an accurate count of the distribution of students among schools but also other kinds of information relevant to the purposes of integration. The basic question is this: What kind of integration is needed to promote equity and citizenship? A number of more detailed questions follow:

—What features are relevant and important for integration? Race and ethnicity are most frequently the dimensions of interest in discussion of integration, but other dimensions may be important as well—including social class, religion, and sex. Each of these dimensions should be considered with respect to the purposes of integration. For example, is equity promoted by schools that admit only girls? Can good citizenship be inculcated in a school that offers an Afrocentric curriculum to an African American student population or a school that offers a Catholic curriculum to a Catholic student population?

—Within schools, what characteristics of student interaction are important to promote the ends associated with integration? Is it sufficient to ensure schoolwide representation of each group, or are additional steps needed to promote positive interaction between and among groups? How important is the integration of individual classrooms (or academic tracks), extracurricular activities, or the cafeteria? Do different methods of integration (that is, integration resulting from family choice versus integration by assignment of the school district) produce different social interaction among students?

—What counts as integrated? What is the numerical standard to be measured against (for example, city, metropolitan area, state, nation)? In the case of the Cleveland voucher program, for example, disputes over integration have arisen because competing studies disagree about using the demographics of the city or the metropolitan area as the standard for measuring integration.[3] The appropriate standard should presumably depend on the ultimate effects of integration.[4]

To the extent that there are cracks in the integrationist consensus, they often result from doubts about the extent to which integration is achieving its aims. Perceptions that integration has failed to achieve its aims also raise the worrisome possibility that integration may be in tension with other educational goals. The dismantling of systems of de jure segregation has not eliminated racial achievement gaps, and charter schools offering Afrocentric curricula aim to demonstrate that African American children can be effectively educated in the absence of nominal integration. Meanwhile, some advocates argue that girls' schools can effectively promote gender equity, and the Bush administration is moving to remove restrictions on same-sex education. In many cities, schools that are nominally integrated are highly segregated internally, with racial minorities underrepresented in college preparatory courses. In this context, a deep understanding of how choice affects integration requires much more than merely counting students in schools.

Integration in the Absence of School Choice Policies

The integration of students in schools is affected by a variety of factors independent of choice, and it is useful to consider some of the factors that produce integration or segregation in the absence of a school choice policy. First, consider a system in which families have no choices whatsoever that can affect their children's school placement. Such a system, it should be noted, is purely hypothetical. In reality, even in communities without policies promoting choice of schools, families can exercise choice by sending their children to private schools or by choosing to live in a different attendance zone or school district. Nevertheless, consideration of a hypothetical nonchoice system is a useful place to start.

In a nonchoice system with school assignment based on residence, the most important factor contributing to the integration of schools is the integration of housing. Indeed, this factor is not merely hypothetical: public schools with neighborhood-based assignment enroll three-fourths of American students.[5] As a consequence, the stratification of housing by race leads directly to racially stratified schools.

A second factor that contributes to school integration in a nonchoice system, of course, is the school assignment policy itself. Neighborhood-based assignment policies will replicate patterns of housing integration in the schools. Neighborhood-based policies, however, are not the only possibilities, even in a nonchoice system. Alternatives can be devised that have the specific intention of promoting integration (or segregation). If families have no choice but to accept the school assigned to their child, then creating a system of nominally integrated schools is merely a logistical problem. But schools that are integrated entirely by coercive policies may not produce the social benefits assumed to result from mixing students of different backgrounds. Schools that are integrated involuntarily may lose their defining character and thus be less attractive to the middle class, which may then either leave or demand an internally differentiated program.

In a nonchoice system, the extent to which school district assignment policies can promote integration is constrained by school district boundaries. If student populations vary systematically across district lines (as they do in many metropolitan areas, where central cities have overrepresentation of minorities and suburbs have overrepresentation of whites), then there is little that districts can do to promote full integration. In a nonchoice system that is residentially segregated by district, promotion of integration across a metropolitan area would require an assignment policy that crosses district lines, presumably imposed by the state.[6]

Integration in a nonchoice system will be affected not only by the size of school districts but also by the size of schools. If students are assigned residentially and housing is not integrated, then small schools are less likely to enroll a diverse mix of students than are large schools. Nevertheless, while this proposition is mathematically inevitable, it does not tell us anything about the quality of integration within schools. (It is possible, for example, that it is easier to promote healthy integration of classrooms and lunchrooms in small schools than in large schools.)

Indeed, all of the preceding factors relate almost entirely to surface-level, numerical integration at the level of school buildings. Other factors related to substantive educational decisions, however, may have important effects on internal integration within schools and on the quality of that integration. Most obviously, the creation of multiple academic tracks can easily undermine integration at the classroom level. In contrast, active efforts to promote constructive interaction across student groups may help to make nominal integration into the kind of integration that produces equal opportunity and socially desirable values and attitudes.

As noted above, there are no systems in the United States that truly preclude all family choice in education. First of all, the U.S. Supreme Court made clear long ago (in 1923 in *Pierce* v. *Society of Sisters*) that states could not preclude the private school option. Second, some choice among public schools is implicit in the fact that families can choose where they live—another constitutionally protected right. Both of these varieties of school choice—via residential mobility and private school tuition—depend on having the financial means to pursue them. These kinds of choice are therefore likely, in many instances, to reduce school integration by social class and by race (which are strongly correlated with each other). The extent to which the availability of these two forms of constitutionally protected choice may undermine integration depends on several other factors.

Integration may be affected by the ease of mobility across attendance zones and school districts. If districts are small and regional transportation infrastructure is good, families will have more residential options among districts. Similarly, the supply and cost of private schools determines the number of tuition-paying options available to families. Across all schools, levels of integration may be lower in metropolitan areas with large numbers of school districts or large numbers of students enrolled in private schools.[7]

The effect of constitutionally protected choices on integration will depend not only on the number of options available but also on the perceived characteristics of schools and the preferences of families. If school quality—among districts or between public and private schools—is not perceived to vary much, then the availability of residential choice and private schools may not have much of an effect on integration. If some districts are perceived as much better than others, or if private schools are perceived as much better than public schools, then the availability of constitutionally protected choices is likely to reduce integration as choices are made by families with the means to choose.

Moreover, parents may care about a variety of factors other than school quality. Parents may care about the kind of peers their children have, with preferences that could increase or reduce integration. Indeed, in some circumstances, parental preferences about peers may systematically undermine policies promoting integration, as when white flight follows the institution of a desegregation plan. Parental preferences about other school factors, such as religious instruction, may also have the effect of reducing integration.

In sum, a wide variety of factors influence the level of integration in schools in the absence of explicit school-choice policies, factors both external and policy related:

The external factors include
—residential patterns,
—ease of mobility,
—supply, characteristics, and cost of private schools, and
—parental preferences.

The policy-related factors include
—student assignment policy,
—district size,
—school size, and
—student tracking within schools.

Thus even in the absence of choice policies, choices will be made by families choosing their places of residence or private schools. Those choices, however, are more easily made by higher income families, choices that in many communities will undermine integration by race as well as social class. Indeed, the high levels of racial and class stratification now evident in many areas are the result of the accumulation of such choices. Any analysis of the effect of school choice policies on integration must keep in mind that current levels of stratification are driven to a great extent by choices made by those with the means to choose.

The Possible Effects of School Choice Policies

In the context of an existing system in which residential patterns are often highly stratified and private school choice and residential mobility are constitutionally protected, the introduction of an explicit policy of school choice might either increase integration or reduce it. Again, there are a number of possible causal relationships, suggesting hypotheses to explore in empirical work. A school choice policy might increase integration in several ways.

First, it breaks the connection between residence and school assignment, so that patterns of housing stratification need not be reinforced in the schools. Indeed, it is even possible that a school choice policy could ultimately increase the integration of housing, because it permits families to select schools independently of neighborhoods.[8]

Second, a school choice policy opens to lower income families those schools currently available only to families with the means to purchase a house in the suburbs or to pay private school tuition. If suburban and private schools were open to all students rather than to only those from higher income families, they might end up more integrated.[9]

Third, a school-choice policy might promote smaller schools that are less likely to separate students into different academic tracks. Academic tracking often segregates children by race in their classrooms, even if the schools are nominally integrated.[10] A school integrated by choice might have a very different social environment than one that is integrated by imposed assignment.[11] Such schools may avoid group resentments that can result from coercive placements and may be able to maintain the features that keep them attractive to middle-class parents.

Alternately, there are a variety of ways that a school choice policy could worsen integration. For example, some school choice policies would largely have the effect of expanding options for middle- and upper-income families rather than extending options to low-income families.[12] More generally, school choice policies may permit highly motivated parents and high-achieving students to separate themselves from other students (particularly if the policy permits schools to select students).[13]

School choice policies may also reduce integration—at least in crude numerical terms—if they encourage the growth of schools with well-defined missions that cater to a niche market. Religious schools may be especially likely to serve only a subset of a community's population. Some school choice policies would permit single-sex schools to participate, systematically separating boys from girls. Other schools of choice may decide to offer an Afrocentric curriculum or instruction in Spanish, for example; such schools are likely to serve student populations that are not racially or ethnically diverse.

These examples raise questions about the purposes that integration serves. How should we think about voluntary self-segregation by a minority group? A school that serves an African American population that has chosen to attend in order to enjoy an Afrocentric curriculum is quite different from a pre-*Brown* school that serves an African American population as a result of segregationist policies imposed by white school boards. The actual environments and effects of such schools—as well as religious schools and same-sex schools—on the values, attitudes, and behavior of their students and graduates merit serious empirical examination.

The mechanisms by which the introduction of choice might either increase or reduce segregation are summarized here:

Choice may increase integration by
—opening private schools to low-income families,
—promoting schools with less tracking,
—promoting schools that operate as voluntary communities, and
—breaking the connection between residence and schooling.

Choice may decrease integration by
—creating options available largely to upper-income families,
—permitting schools to skim off the most desirable students,
—promoting schools that serve narrow interest groups, and
—undermining desegregation plans.

As the competing possibilities suggest, choice may affect integration in complicated ways. Whether the introduction of school choice has favorable or unfavorable effects on integration is affected by the local context—in particular, the level of school integration before the introduction of a choice policy. That is, school choice might improve integration in a community where schools are highly segregated but might reduce integration in a community where schools are highly integrated. In many central cities, racial stratification is so pronounced that a school choice policy could hardly make it worse.

Another local contextual factor that is relevant to the effect choice will have on integration is the existing and potential supply of schools available for families to choose. A choice policy will have little effect on integration—positively or negatively—if few schools are actually open for new families to choose. A larger supply of choice schools will permit a choice policy to have larger effects on integration. As I discuss below, the supply of schools available can be influenced by the design of the choice policy.

Finally, the preferences of parents are even more important in the context of a choice policy than when choice is limited to residential mobility and private school tuition.[14] In the context of a choice policy, the critical question relates to the preferences of parents newly enabled to choose by the policy—which may or may not be similar to those of parents who choose via residential mobility or private school tuition.

Implications for Policy Design

The myriad causal mechanisms described above make clear that it is difficult to predict, in the abstract, whether the introduction of a school choice policy will have favorable or unfavorable effects on integration. Indeed, the various causal possibilities suggest that different choice policies may produce different effects (a lesson that holds true not only with respect to integration but also with respect to many other outcomes associated with school choice).[15] The specifics of choice policies vary widely, and policymakers designing choice policies have an array of tools by which to influence outcomes. With respect to integration, a number of specific differences may lead to positive or negative outcomes.

Admissions

Policies that permit schools to select students may reduce integration, depending on the preferences of the schools and the correlation between the measure of selection and race or ethnicity. Given the pervasive racial gap in achievement, it is likely that integration will be reduced if schools select students based on academic achievement—but with one caveat: it may be possible to promote integration if the schools succeed in attracting students who would otherwise opt out by moving to the suburbs or enrolling in private schools. In contrast, a requirement that schools admit students by lottery (as in many charter laws as well as the voucher programs in Milwaukee and Cleveland), with a simple and transparent application process, may reduce the likelihood of stratification.

Integration can be actively encouraged either by direct regulation of admissions (for example, with a requirement to match local demographics) or by incentives. Controlled choice systems that have been put in place in some school districts (such as Cambridge, Mass.) control school preferences at the district level and constrain family choices so that they do not reduce integration. Systems designed to promote integration by providing diversity incentives to schools have not been tried in the Unites States (as far as I know), but it is possible to imagine policies that provide bonuses to schools with enrollments that reach specified diversity targets. Both direct regulation and incentive systems would have to be carefully designed to avoid legal challenges.

Policies promoting schools that focus on serving at-risk students (like, for example, the Texas charter law) may reduce integration—even if they are effective at serving the at-risk population. In this instance there may be a trade-off between integration per se and the desire to provide services specifically to at-risk populations.

Funding

Policies that are universally available to all students but funded at low levels may reduce integration. Low-subsidy vouchers are likely to benefit higher income families more than lower income families, because the subsidy amounts are often well short of the full cost of tuition.

Policies that operate as income tax benefits (for example, tuition tax credits) may reduce integration, because they are more likely to be used by higher income families. They generally require families to have the means to pay tuition up front, with the tax reduction coming only later. Income tax subsidies for tuition payments are often worthless to families with little or no tax liability. Indeed, income tax subsidies that operate as deductions or exclusions (such as the federal government's education savings accounts) are actually worth more money to higher income families, because their value depends on the family's tax bracket.[16]

Policies that provide transportation funding are more likely to be usable by low-income families and therefore more likely to promote integration than policies requiring students to find their own transportation.

Supply

If they are targeted to low-income students, policies that permit existing private schools to participate may increase integration. There is good evidence that targeted voucher policies can in fact serve low-income families.[17] By doing so, they may be able to improve integration levels in both public and private schools, by moving low-income children from public schools to private schools with tuition-paying classmates. The inclusion of private schools in the choice program can bring tuition-paying, middle-class students into the mix.[18] Because income is highly correlated with race, such programs may improve racial integration as well as integration by social class.[19]

Policies that promote formation of new schools (or the participation of existing private schools) may increase integration by creating a buyer's market. If most existing public schools are stratified, new schools can allow parents who prefer some integration to move. This will not increase the segregation of segregated existing schools, and it will increase the numbers of students in integrated schools.

If low-income and minority students are concentrated in the worst schools, policies that close and replace low-performing schools may promote integration by giving them new options in more integrated schools (unless such integration leads to white flight).

Information

Policies that maximize the availability of information to low-income parents may increase integration. Choice policies inevitably favor those with more information, and low-income families often have less access to good information.[20] Active efforts to disseminate information (such as Massachusetts' parent information centers) may reduce the likelihood of stratification.[21]

Policies that protect children even if their parents do not express a choice could improve integration. Generally, if parents do not express a choice their children are assigned to schools with low enrollment, which are often heavily minority and low performing. An alternative policy might establish an ombudsperson to choose schools for children whose parents have not expressed preferences, or an active lottery that assigns nonchoosing children to schools of choice (although I am not aware of any existing examples of such policies).

In sum, despite the large uncertainties about how school choice policies will affect integration, it is nevertheless possible to provide substantial guidance to policymakers on the specific design details that are likely to promote integration.

Implications for Empirical Study

Discussions of school choice and integration are often plagued by a failure to appreciate the challenges of adequately assessing the effects of choice on integration empirically. In fact, only a small number of empirical studies have rigorously examined the issue, and few of these involve programs operating in the United States.[22] Fortunately, the discussion in the preceding pages provides at least some guidance for avoiding some of the conceptual mistakes that researchers or commentators can make in empirical discussions of integration. Ideally, empirical studies of the effects of choice on integration would observe the following guidelines:

—Compare apples to apples (that is, ensure that units of analysis are consistent). Examinations of charter schools sometimes compare group representations in a charter school to average group representations in the surrounding district. Although such a comparison can tell us whether groups are over- or underrepresented, it tells us nothing about relative levels of integration, because the average representation for a district may obscure wide variations in representation in individual district schools. Consider, for example, a charter school that enrolls 70 percent minority students in a district that is 50 percent white and 50 percent minority. It would be a mistake to conclude that the charter school is less integrated than district schools, because we do not know the composition of individual district schools. It is unlikely that every district school is racially balanced, and it is even possible that every district school is less racially balanced than the charter school (for example, if the district includes ten schools, five of which are all white and five of which are all minority). School-to-school comparisons or, better yet, classroom-to-classroom comparisons (not school-to-district or school-to-state comparisons) are needed to assess relative integration levels.

—Examine what goes on inside schools. If integration is important for the ends it serves (in terms of equity and the inculcation of values), then merely counting the number of students of different groups present in a school cannot tell us whether integration is effective. A school that is nominally integrated may be quite stratified at the classroom level, particularly if it places students in differentiated academic tracks. More generally, nominal counts of the representation of different groups may obscure important differences in how those groups actually interact in the school. Examining what goes on inside schools is essential to determine whether integration is succeeding in promoting equity and civic cohesion.

—Avoid generalizing from current integration levels in public and private schools. Discussions about vouchers often make reference to empirical evidence comparing existing public and private schools in the absence of vouchers.[23] In the case of integration, however, such comparisons may be deceptive. Existing patterns result from the choices made by those with the means to pay tuition, while many voucher programs are designed to give choices to lower income families; vouchers might therefore cause patterns of integration to be different from existing patterns.

—Fully consider all counterfactual possibilities in the context of constitutionally protected choice. Even if existing schools of choice (such as charters or magnets) serve populations that are less diverse than conventional public schools, it does not necessarily follow that the choice program has worsened integration or that abolishing it would improve integration. Given the existence of constitutionally protected choice, many parents may respond to the absence of policy choice by opting out of the system (by moving to the suburbs, sending their children to private schools, or homeschooling their children). If so, a choice policy may paradoxically improve levels of integration even if the chosen schools are less integrated than conventional public schools. Consider this example: a community's student population is 50 percent minority, the public schools are 55 percent minority, and the private schools are 10 percent minority. If a magnet school opens with a population that is 40 percent minority, drawing a substantial number of white students from private schools, then it will have improved levels of integration across the system, even though it is nominally less integrated than the conventional public schools. Magnet schools, as the name suggests, are generally intended to induce middle-class (often white) parents to enroll in urban public schools rather than opting for private schools or a move to the suburbs. By the same token, the establishment of a charter law may permit racially homogeneous private schools to become more diverse by converting to charter status and eliminating tuition payments.[24]

—Use an appropriate measure of integration. Conceptually, integration is surprisingly difficult to measure. (Measuring access by a minority group, by contrast, is much more straightforward, because it requires merely representational counts rather than an assessment of how different groups are mixed.) Measurement becomes even more challenging when the number of relevant groups involved is greater than two (such as black, white, Latino, and Asian). In consequence, discussions of integration are frequently muddled. Fortunately, however, sociologists have given substantial thought to measuring integration, most notably in a methodological paper by Sean F. Reardon and Glenn Firebaugh.[25]

In sum, assessing the effect of choice on integration empirically requires a dynamic model that examines over time all of the changes in the distribution of students across educational settings—public and private, chosen and assigned—that might be induced by choice. Static comparisons of the demographic composition of choice and nonchoice schools are insufficient to assess the *effect* of introducing a choice policy. And the dynamic analysis can and should account for the fact that many families make residential and private school choices even in the absence of a choice policy. What is needed is a longitudinal examination of how choice affects the distribution of—and interactions among—students in all of the schools and classrooms of a community.

Notes

1. The Supreme Court's opinion in *Plessy* v. *Ferguson* from a half century earlier had endorsed the view that separate public facilities for blacks and whites were constitutionally permissible as long as they were given equal resources.

2. A report advocating the use of controlled, public school choice to promote integration cites both of these purposes. See Task Force on the Common School, *Divided We*

Fail: Coming Together through Public School Choice (New York: Century Foundation, 2002); see also Michal Kurlaender and John T. Yun, "The Impact of Racial and Ethnic Diversity on Educational Outcomes: Cambridge, Mass., School District" (Civil Rights Project, Harvard University 2002).

3. See Jay P. Greene, "Choice and Community: The Racial, Economic, and Religious Context of Parental Choice in Cleveland" (Columbus, Ohio: Buckeye Institute), for a discussion of how the standard affects the interpretation.

4. See Douglas A. Archbald, "School Choice and School Stratification: Shortcomings of the Stratification Critique and Recommendations for Theory and Research," *Educational Policy* 14, no. 2 (2000): 214–40.

5. Task Force on the Common School, *Divided We Fail.*

6. Of course, a state-imposed, multidistrict coercive integration policy might carry unintended negative consequences and, in any case, is likely to be politically unviable in most states.

7. Erika Frankenberg and Chungmei Lee, "Race in American Public Schools: Rapidly Resegregating School Districts" (Civil Rights Project, Harvard University, 2002).

8. Thomas J. Nechyba, "Public School Finance in a General Equilibrium Tiebout World: Equalization Programs, Peer Effects, and Private School Vouchers" (Cambridge, Mass.: National Bureau of Economic Research, 1996), points out this possibility via modeling methods.

9. This argument is made, for example, by Greene, "Choice and Community."

10. Valerie E. Lee and Anthony S. Bryk, "Curriculum Tracking as Mediating the Social Distribution of High School Achievement," *Sociology of Education* 61 (April 1988): 78–94; Tom Loveless, "The Tracking and Ability Grouping Debate" (Washington: Thomas B. Fordham Foundation, 1998); Samuel R. Lucas and Adam Gamoran, "Tracking and the Achievement Gap," in *Bridging the Achievement Gap,* edited by John E. Chubb and Tom Loveless (Brookings, 2002); Jeannie Oakes, "Multiplying Inequalities: The Effects of Race, Social Class, and Tracking on Opportunities to Learn" (Santa Monica, Calif.: RAND, 1990).

11. Jay P. Greene and Nicole Mellow, *Integration Where It Counts: A Study of Racial Integration in Public and Private School Lunchrooms* (Public Policy Clinic of the Government Department, University of Texas at Austin, 1998). Available at www.la.utexas.edu/research/ppc/lunch.html (accessed 9/26/2000).

12. For this perspective, see Bruce Fuller and Richard F. Elmore, eds. *Who Chooses? Who Loses? Culture, Institutions, and the Unequal Effects of School Choice* (Brookings, 1996); and Bruce Fuller, Luis Huerta, and David Ruenzel, "A Costly Gamble or Serious Reform? California's School Voucher Initiative—Proposition 38" (Berkeley: Policy Analysis for California Education, 2000).

13. For empirical and theoretical discussion of this concern, see David Arsen, "Does Choice Enhance the Educational Opportunities Available to Poor Children?" in *The School Choice Debate: Framing the Issues,* edited by David N. Plank and Gary Sykes (Education Policy Center, Michigan State University, 2000); Valerie E. Lee, Robert G. Croninger, and Julia B. Smith, "Parental Choice of Schools and Social Stratification in Education: The Paradox of Detroit," *Educational Evaluation and Policy Analysis* 16, no. 4 (1994): 434–57; Henry M. Levin, "Educational Vouchers: Effectiveness, Choice, and Costs," *Journal of Policy Analysis and Management* 17, no. 3 (1998): 373–92; Donald R.

Moore and Suzanne Davenport, "School Choice: The New Improved Sorting Machine," in *Choice in Education: Potential and Problems,* edited by William Lowe Boyd and Herbert J. Walberg (Berkeley, Calif.: McCutchan, 1990); and Amy Stuart Wells, "The Sociology of School Choice: Why Some Win and Others Lose in the Educational Marketplace," in *School Choice: Examining the Evidence,* edited by Edith Rassell and Richard Rothstein (Washington: Economic Policy Institute, 1993).

14. For a variety of views on parental preferences with respect to school choice, see David L. Armor and Brett M. Peiser, "Interdistrict Choice in Massachusetts," in *Learning from School Choice,* edited by Paul E. Peterson and Bryan C. Hassel (Brookings, 1998); Caroline M. Hoxby, "The Effects of School Choice on Curriculum and Atmosphere," in *Earning and Learning: How Schools Matter,* edited by Susan E. Mayer and Paul E. Peterson (Brookings, 1999); Mark Schneider, Paul Teske, and Melissa Marschall, *Choosing Schools: Parents, School Choice, and the Quality of American Schools* (Princeton University Press, 2000); Paul Teske and Mark Schneider, "What Research Can Tell Policymakers about School Choice," *Journal of Policy Analysis and Management* 20 (2001): 609–31; and John F. Witte, *The Market Approach to Education* (Princeton University Press, 2000).

15. See Brian P. Gill and others, *Rhetoric versus Reality: What We Know and What We Need to Know about Vouchers and Charter Schools* (Santa Monica, Calif.: RAND, 2001).

16. Establishing an income tax subsidy in the form of a refundable credit could reduce its regressivity but might still provide access for some low-income families.

17. For a summary of the evidence, see Gill and others, *Rhetoric versus Reality.*

18. If however the private schools that are actually made available via vouchers are those that already serve a segregated minority population, then vouchers will not improve integration; see Sean F. Reardon and John T. Yun, "Private School Racial Enrollments and Segregation" (Civil Rights Project, Harvard University, 2002).

19. Howard L. Fuller and George A. Mitchell, *The Impact of School Choice on Integration in Milwaukee Private Schools* (Institute for the Transformation of Learning, Marquette University, 2000), argue that private schools in Milwaukee are more integrated than Milwaukee public schools as a result of vouchers targeted to low-income families. Available at www.schoolchoiceinfo.org/servlets/SendArticle/4/integ1299.pdf (accessed 10/20/2000).

20. Schneider, Teske, and Marschall, *Choosing Schools,* provide good empirical evidence on this point.

21. The Massachusetts centers are described in Charles Glenn, K. McLaughlin, and Laura Salganik, "Parent Information for School Choice" (Boston: Center on Families, Communities, Schools, and Children's Learning, 1993).

22. For a review, see ibid.

23. One article, for example, examines existing levels of integration in public and private schools while using the provocative but misleading title, "How Might School Choice Affect Racial Integration in Schools?" See Gary W. Ritter, Alison Rush, and Joel Rush, "How Might School Choice Affect Racial Integration in Schools? New Evidence from the ECLS-K," *Georgetown Public Policy Review* 7 (2002): 125–36. Another report likewise draws fairly strong implications about the likely effect of vouchers from data on existing integration in the absence of vouchers, but it at least uses more finely grained data to make plausible implications about the specific schools likely to enroll minority voucher students. See Reardon and Yun, "Private School Racial Enrollments and Segregation."

24. For example, if a private school with 10 percent minority enrollment converts to charter status, increasing its minority enrollment by bringing in a substantial number of minority students from conventional public schools, then it will have improved levels of integration throughout the system, even if it remains less integrated than conventional public schools nearby.

25. Sean F. Reardon and Glenn Firebaugh, "Measures of Multigroup Segregation," *Sociological Methodology* 32 (2002): 33–67.

8

Charter Schools and Integration: The Experience in Michigan

Karen E. Ross

When President Bush signed No Child Left Behind into law on January 8, 2002, an already highly charged debate over school choice got an extra boost. The most contentious debates previously surrounded the issue of vouchers for private (and often religious) schooling. The new education law has, however, brought charter schools and other forms of public school choice to the center of the debate. Although much of the controversy over school choice revolves around the ability of school choice to improve student achievement, the impact of increased choice on the integration of schools may be dramatic. Opponents argue that choice will lead to increased segregation via "cream-skimming," but in the abstract it is possible that increased choice may lead to greater integration by easing the historically tight link between residence and school attendance.

Although there has been a tremendous amount of both academic and political debate over the consequences of increased school choice, there is much we do not know about the actual consequences of the school choice policies that are operating today. Both voucher programs and charter school laws vary considerably across cities and states, making it impossible to definitively answer the many questions we have with one national study.[1] However, this variation also serves as an important source of information about the potential impact of policy design, particularly when it comes to investigating the effects of the charter school movement on public school segregation. Three states (Connecticut, North Carolina, and California) include racial balance provisions in their charter school legislation, but most states do not. Combine this lack of legislative oversight with declining support for school desegregation plans and high levels of residential and school segregation, and one can see why there is cause for concern over the impact of unrestrained public school choice.

The state of Michigan is a prime example: it is unique in allowing public state universities and community colleges to authorize charter schools, which has led to a boom in the supply of new schools that are unconstrained by traditional bureaucratic structures. In addition, its metropolitan areas are among the most segregated in the nation. The combination of these demographic and legislative characteristics makes Michigan a promising context in which to uncover the potential effects of the charter school movement on segregation.

This chapter aims to take advantage of Michigan's unique policy context to address the following three research questions:

—How does the racial composition of charter schools compare to nearby traditional public and private schools? Is there any evidence that charter schools may be serving distinct populations with respect to race, ethnicity, and poverty status?

—Which characteristics of school districts predict charter school location? How do the locational decisions of charter schools relate to the demographic characteristics of the district's residents and the attributes of their traditional public schools? Do charter schools choose to locate in districts that are more or less racially segregated in the years preceding their opening?

—Are charter schools leading to greater racial segregation among traditional public schools within districts?[2]

Background

Michigan's charter school law was signed on January 1, 1994. Relative to other states with active charter school legislation, Michigan's charter school law is unique in several respects, leading it to rather closely resemble a voucher-like system of education. First off, when a student leaves a traditional public school for a charter school, 100 percent of the per pupil funding for that student is transferred from the traditional public school to the charter school. Taken in tandem with Michigan's efforts to equalize per pupil revenues across districts, the financial incentives of the charter school movement work to create a truly competitive environment, which many argue is required to induce systemic educational improvement.[3]

Second, Michigan allows a variety of groups to authorize charter schools, including public state universities and community colleges, and allows private schools to convert to charter school status. By expanding the list of potential authorizers beyond school districts and state education boards, Michigan has encouraged a strong supply response from groups that are not entrenched in the bureaucracy of public education. This supply response is critical to the ability of charter schools to affect the system as a whole, given that the parents most likely to benefit from public school choice are those that cannot afford private schools or cannot afford to move to a district with higher quality public schools. Therefore, the schools must come to them. At least from a legislative standpoint, it appears as if Michigan has succeeded in making this more likely to occur.

As of the 2002–03 school year, there were 196 charter schools in Michigan, enrolling 60,236 students.[4] Several researchers have done extensive work on the nature of Michigan charter schools, covering critical areas such as student demographics, school resources and governance, and student and parent satisfaction, among others.[5] With respect to the racial composition of charter schools relative to traditional public schools, all groups of researchers find that, as of 1996–97, charter schools were enrolling higher proportions of minority students. Similarly, David Arsen and colleagues' examination of the geography of school choice illustrates that charter schools are much more likely to locate in central-city districts.[6] However, as Jerry Horn and Gary Miron show, it is important to consider the context in which the schools are located; in comparison to their host districts, charter schools were actually enrolling slightly higher proportions of white students.[7]

Descriptive analyses, while important in understanding the context of choice in Michigan, are not evidence of segregation per se. One of the most potentially misleading paths of the school choice debate is the tendency to accept discrepancies in the racial composition of schools and districts as evidence of segregation. For example, a charter school may serve primarily black students even though it is located in a district with a percentage of black students substantially lower than average. However, this comparison ignores the fact that there is tremendous variation in the racial composition of schools within districts, which is masked by using the district average as a benchmark. A district may serve 50 percent white students, but this average may be a result of a cluster of predominantly white schools balanced out by a cluster of predominantly black schools.

It is also critical to take into account the location of charter schools. To date there is little work that analyzes the locational decisions of charter schools.[8] Given that charters are more likely to locate in central cities, one might infer that they are more likely to serve higher proportions of minority students without creating higher levels of segregation. Yet mere descriptive differences, even based on appropriate comparisons, do not capture the spatial dynamics that are critical to segregation. Further, in assessing the impacts of choice on segregation, one must acknowledge that the supply response of choice schools may be affected by the demographic composition of neighborhoods and districts, which in turn structures the potential impacts of parental choice of schools.

Data and Methods

The analyses presented here rely on observations of Michigan schools and districts in the 1989–90 through 1999–2000 school years. For the sake of consistency and policy relevancy, the analyses exclude public schools of a specialized nature, such as special education schools, vocational schools, and alternative schools. In addition, schools reporting enrollments of fewer than ten students and districts with a single school are excluded. The final sample includes approximately 489 districts in each year.[9]

I rely on the U.S. Department of Education's *Common Core of Data* for school-level measures of racial composition, student eligibility for free or reduced-price lunch, student-teacher ratios, and school size.[10] These data have been aggregated to provide district-level averages of these measures.[11] Measures of school segregation are also derived from the *Common Core of Data,* relying on information on the racial composition of individual traditional public schools to provide an indicator of segregation at the district level.[12] Therefore, even though a great deal of school-level data have been used in these analyses, the district is the unit of analysis for most of the results presented here.

An often ignored yet critical component of the racial dynamics of public education is the racial and socioeconomic composition of the population residing in the school district. I use decennial census data for 1990 and 2000, based on school district boundaries, to capture relevant characteristics of the residential population.[13] I base measures of racial composition, poverty status, and percentage of district residents enrolled in private schools on the population of school-aged children enrolled in public or private schools and residing in the district. Measures of urbanicity, median income, and homeownership are based on the entire population of the district, while educational attainment is calculated for the population over age twenty-five.

Further information regarding public school districts is derived from the Michigan Department of Education's online databases, including average teacher salary, district per pupil revenues, and student achievement in mathematics and reading. Student achievement is measured by the percentage of students in a district scoring satisfactorily on the state's educational assessment, the Michigan Educational Assessment Program. To capture the effect on districts of the 1994 school funding reform, I use data on the amount of per pupil revenue each district received from state and local sources in 1993–94, before the change, and compared it to the 1994–95 amounts.[14] Given that the reform was intended to equalize spending across districts by replacing local funding based on property taxes with a state block grant, the net effect on districts' per pupil revenues will be crudely captured by the change in state plus local revenues over these two periods. Finally, I use data from the Private School Survey to gauge the racial composition of Michigan's private schools relative to charter and traditional public schools.[15]

The first stage of the analysis aims to assess the extent to which charter schools may be racially distinct from comparable traditional public schools. The 1999–2000 data were analyzed using geographic information science (GIS) techniques, which enabled me to compare charter schools to private and traditional public schools located within a particular distance. This relatively simple descriptive analysis is powerful in enabling one to make the appropriate comparisons among schools that could potentially serve the same student populations.

The next step of the analysis seeks to understand the locational decisions of charter schools, using precharter characteristics of districts to predict their likelihood of having a charter school by the 1999–2000 school year. Given the uneven distribution of the count of charter schools at the district level, the most reasonable measurement of charter presence was zero, one, or multiple charter schools. Preliminary investigations indicated that quite different processes led to single versus multiple charter schools. Therefore I chose to use a multinomial logit specification to allow a district's precharter characteristics to have different impacts on the likelihood of having a single charter school or multiple charter schools, each versus zero charter schools. These models allow for clustering of schools within districts, and standard errors are adjusted accordingly.

The goal of the final stage of the analysis is to estimate the effect of charter school presence on the segregation of traditional public schools within districts. One of the most stubborn problems in this type of analysis is the issue of endogeneity of charter location. Given that charter schools are not randomly distributed across Michigan's school districts, estimates of their impact on segregation may be biased. This analysis, unlike research that uses an instrumental variable approach, relies on a difference-in-differences approach.[16] By taking the difference of pre- and post-charter measures, the potential influence of time-invariant omitted factors that may have affected both a district's level of segregation and their likelihood of having a charter school are differenced out, leaving unbiased estimates of the effect of charter presence on changes in segregation.

Results

Table 8-1 shows the characteristics of Michigan's charter schools as of 1999, compared to both private and traditional public schools. These results clearly show that charter schools are serving a distinct population: with respect to race and ethnicity, 47 percent of charter school students are black, compared to 17 percent of traditional public school students. This gap mirrors the discrepancy in the percentage of white students served by charter and traditional public schools (47 and 77 percent white, respectively). Michigan's student population is becoming more diverse over time, even though the percentages of other racial and ethnic groups remain small. Latino students make up nearly 4 percent of the traditional public school population, and Asian and American Indian each make up less than 2 percent. Charter schools serve slightly higher percentages of Latino and American Indian students, and a lower percentage of Asian students, relative to traditional public schools. Private schools appear to be the least diverse: 84 percent of their students are white, 11 percent black, and the remaining 5 percent are either Latino, Asian, or American Indian.

With respect to socioeconomic status, measured by the percentage of students eligible for free or reduced-price lunch, it appears that fewer charter students are eligible, about one-quarter versus one-third for traditional public schools.[17] However, an examination of the schools that report having at least one student participating in the Free and Reduced Price Lunch Program

Table 8-1. *Characteristics of Michigan Schools, by School Type, 1999*
Percent except as noted

Characteristic	*Charter schools*	*Traditional public schools*	*Private schools*
Racial composition			
American Indian	1.63	1.25	0.44
Asian	0.72	1.58	1.46
Black	46.62	16.89	11.38
Latino	4.14	3.56	2.74
White	46.89	76.72	83.97
Student-teacher ratio	17.77	18.10	15.63
Free or reduced price lunch			
All schools	25.09	33.59	n.a.
Schools reporting at least one student eligible	53.32[a]	35.80[b]	n.a.
Size (number of students)	270.50	479.26	181.09
Level			
Elementary	64.12	59.23	82.66
Middle/junior high	3.53	19.03	0.00
High school	13.53	18.79	0.00
K–12	7.06	1.79	17.34
Other grade spans	11.76	1.16	0.00
Summary statistic			
N schools	170	3,358	692
N districts	75	484	272

Source: National Center for Education Statistics, *Common Core of Data, 1999–2000* (U.S. Department of Education); National Center for Education Statistics, *Private School Survey, 1999–2000* (U.S. Department of Education).

a. Based on 47 percent of schools.

b. Based on 94 percent of schools.

indicates that more than half of charter school students are eligible, compared to slightly more than one-third of traditional public school students.[18] Relative to traditional public schools, charter schools are also substantially smaller by approximately 200 students, have similar student-teacher ratios, and are slightly more likely to serve elementary grades or alternative combinations of grades.

Overall, these results alleviate the fear that charter schools serve largely white and affluent student populations. However, the size of the discrepancy in the proportion of black students drawn into charter schools does raise some questions. Are charter schools explicitly targeting black populations through their curricula and recruitment strategies? Or are black parents less satisfied with their current educational options and most likely to seek new opportunities? These questions are difficult to answer with existing data, but one may start by analyzing the locational decisions of charter schools. Other researchers note that, since charter schools must accept all applicants, one way that they may shape their populations is through their choice of location. There may also be more practical considerations involved in these decisions, such as cost and building availability to name just two. However, one can learn quite a bit from a simple comparison of schools within a geographic area. Table 8-2 shows the racial composition of charter schools relative to other types of schools within their immediate vicinity.

Local Contexts

The data in table 8-2 show that the higher percentage of black students in charter schools is based in large part on their physical location: in 1999–2000, 49 percent of charter elementary students were black; the corresponding figure was 52 percent for traditional public schools within two miles. Interestingly, when one examines a five-mile radius, one sees a large drop in the percentage of black students in traditional public schools, down to 37 percent, reflecting the tremendous variation in the racial composition of schools within limited geographic areas. In contrast, charter schools seem to be serving smaller percentages of Latino students, 3 percent versus 5 percent for traditional public schools within two miles and within five miles. The same patterns are seen in the racial composition of private schools, with those within two and five miles of charter schools serving 37 and 23 percent black students, respectively, double and triple the percentage of black students in private schools statewide. With respect to socioeconomic status, it appears at first as if charter schools are only serving half the percentage of poor students as traditional schools nearby (27 versus 55 percent); however, once we consider only schools reporting participation in the lunch program, we see that charter schools are serving only slightly fewer poor students (53 versus 62 percent).

The table also compares schools located within two miles of a private school serving elementary grades. Charter schools located within two miles of private schools (approximately two-thirds of charter schools serving the elementary grades) have black populations that are 10 percentage points higher than all charter schools, yet again they look quite similar—with respect to racial composition—to traditional public schools that are also

Table 8-2. *Racial Composition of Schools, by Physical Proximity*[a]

Percent except as noted

School and proximity measure (N; *size*)	*American Indian*	*Asian*	*Black*	*Latino*	*White*	*Student-teacher ratio*	*Socioeconomic status*[b]	
							All schools	*One eligible*
All schools								
Charter (121; 295)	2.01	0.84	48.96	3.31	44.88	17.91	25.09	53.37[c]
Traditional public (2,170; 375)	1.25	1.63	20.48	3.82	72.82	18.23	33.59	40.58[d]
Private (692; 181)	0.44	1.46	11.38	2.74	83.97	15.63	...	...
Traditional public, private relative to charter								
Charter (121; 295)	2.01	0.84	48.96	3.31	44.88	17.91	25.09	53.37[c]
Traditional public within two miles of charter (583; 391)	1.00	1.54	52.12	5.28	40.06	17.63	55.35	61.94[e]
Traditional public within five miles of charter (1,061; 386)	0.97	1.99	37.43	4.93	54.68	17.99	47.44	50.94[f]
Private within two miles of charter (140; 202)	0.65	1.63	36.66	3.79	57.28	16.85	...	...
Private within five miles of charter (316; 225)	0.49	1.82	22.88	3.59	71.22	16.66	...	...
Charter, traditional public relative to private								
Charter (121; 295)	2.01	0.84	48.96	3.31	44.88	17.91	25.09	53.37[c]
Charter within two miles of private (87; 306)	0.90	1.44	59.20	3.85	34.62	18.28	31.44	56.99[g]
Charter within five miles of private (104; 310)	0.91	1.31	55.79	3.60	38.38	18.27	29.56	54.88[h]
Traditional public within two miles of private & charter (500; 401)	1.61	0.96	57.41	5.73	34.29	17.71	59.21	64.92[e]
Traditional public within five miles of private & charter (1,031; 388)	2.02	0.97	38.29	5.01	53.71	18.01	47.91	51.08

Source: See table 8-1.

a. To capture the appropriate comparison groups, only schools serving elementary grades, including K–12, are included.

b. Socioeconomic status is measured by eligibility of students for free or reduced-price lunch. "One eligible" indicates schools reporting at least one eligible student.

c. Based on 51 percent of schools.

d. Based on 94 percent of schools.

e. Based on 89 percent of schools.

f. Based on 93 percent of schools.

g. Based on 55 percent of schools.

h. Based on 54 percent of schools.

within two miles of a private school. This similarity of charter and traditional public schools located within a two-mile radius of a private school suggests that charter schools are targeting students in public rather than private schools, although this issue requires far more rigorous investigation.

In conclusion, these descriptive data based on the physical location of schools imply two trends. First, charter schools are enrolling disproportionately high proportions of black students, a result of their choice to locate in areas with large black populations. Second, the similarities in the makeup of charter schools and local traditional public schools suggest that charter schools are not creating racially distinct schools relative to their local contexts and are likely drawing students of similar socioeconomic backgrounds as well.

Predicting Charter Presence

The goal of this analysis is to determine whether charter schools are significantly more likely to locate in districts where public school segregation is high. This is an important policy question in its own right, in that the locational decisions of charter schools provide a measure of the supply response to the charter school movement, but the answer is also critical in understanding the nature of the relationship between charter schools and trends in public school segregation. The previous section illustrates that charter schools are choosing to locate in areas with larger black populations; whether these areas are significantly more segregated than districts without charter schools is another question.

Tables 8-3 through 8-9 present a series of multinomial logit models that examine the influence of district characteristics on charter school presence.[19] (The means and standard deviations of the measures used in the model are presented in table 8-10.) The first column of each model shows the marginal effect of each predictor on the probability of a positive outcome (a single charter school or multiple charter schools), followed by the coefficient and its standard error. These models use characteristics of schools and districts that predate the charter movement to predict a district's likelihood of having a single charter school or multiple charter schools versus no charter schools by the 1999–2000 school year. Characteristics of the residential population, which come from the decennial census, are only available for 1990, while the other predictors represent averages over the period of 1989–90 through 1993–94, except for teacher salary and achievement, which each span 1991–92 through 1994–95.

The first model (the baseline model, table 8-3) includes no controls for segregation, while the following models (tables 8-4 through 8-9) examine

Table 8-3. *Predicting Charter Presence, Baseline Model*

	Zero vs. 1 charter			*Zero vs. 2+ charters*		
	$\partial y/\partial x$	*Coef.*	*SE*	$\partial y/\partial x$	*Coef.*	*SE*
Constant		–3.343			–1.362	
Demographics of school district residents, 1990						
Poor (relevant children in poverty)	–0.004	–0.026	0.035	0.001	0.022	0.054
Housing in urban areas	0.001	0.004	0.007	–0.000[a]	–0.008	0.014
Some college or higher	–0.001	–0.003	0.025	0.003	0.057	0.032*
Homeowners	–0.002	–0.018	0.018	–0.002	–0.058	0.033*
Enrolled in private school	–0.002	–0.016	0.018	0.006	0.126	0.067*
Characteristics of school districts, 1989–94 [b]						
Number of traditional public schools	0.014	0.110	0.037*	0.008	0.202	0.040***
Average student-teacher ratio	0.000	–0.007	0.090	–0.006	–0.125	0.161
Satisfactory in math, 4th-grade students	–0.001	–0.008	0.042	0.000	0.004	0.070
Satisfactory in reading, 4th-grade students	0.003	0.015	0.044	–0.005	–0.098	0.083
Average teacher salary (1999 dollars)	0.004	0.032	0.077	0.002	0.048	0.115
Net effect of finance reform (1999 dollars)	0.279	2.039	0.617***	0.051	1.500	1.057

Addendum

Model X^2 (df): 120.05 (22).
R^2/pseudo R^2: 0.3893.
N schools (districts): 2,638 (484).

Source: U.S. Bureau of the Census, 1990 Decennial Census School District Special Tabulation (National Center for Education Statistics); U.S. Bureau of the Census, 2000 Decennial Census School District Special Tabulation (National Center for Education Statistics); Michigan K–12 Student Database, 1989–94 (Michigan Department of Education); National Center for Education Statistics, Common Core of Data, 1989–94 (U.S. Department of Education).

$^*p < .10$, $^{**}p < .05$, $^{***}p < .01$.

a. Actual figure is –0.00038.

b. Predictors are averages for the period 1989–90 through 1993–94.

isolation and exposure in traditional public schools within districts. Tables 8-4 through 8-6 examine exposure rates; black-white exposure (table 8-5), for example, indicates the percentage of white students in the school attended by an average black student. Isolation measures (tables 8-7 through 8-9) capture the extent to which students attend schools primarily with students of their own racial or ethnic group; for example, Latino isolation represents the average percentage of Latino students in schools attended by an average Latino student.

One of the most interesting things to note about these results is that the array of factors leading to a district housing multiple charter schools is quite

Table 8-4. *Predicting Charter Presence, White-Black Exposure*

	Zero vs. 1 charter			*Zero vs. 2+ charters*		
	∂y/∂x	*Coef.*	*SE*	*∂y/∂x*	*Coef.*	*SE*
Constant		–2.089			–1.111	
Dimensions of segregation						
Exposure of white to black	0.600	4.330	1.817**	0.041	1.655	2.483
Demographics of school district residents, 1990						
Poor (relevant children in poverty)	–0.011	–0.074	0.038**	0.001	0.006	0.057
Housing in urban areas	0.000	0.002	0.007	0.000	–0.009	0.014
Some college or higher	–0.003	–0.020	0.027	0.002	0.050	0.033
Homeowners	–0.002	–0.020	0.017	–0.003	–0.061	0.033*
Enrolled in private school	–0.005	–0.029	0.034	0.006	0.126	0.066*
Characteristics of school districts, 1989–94[a]						
Number of traditional public schools	0.016	0.123	0.038***	0.009	0.206	0.041***
Average student-teacher ratio	0.001	–0.003	0.089	–0.005	–0.114	0.162
Satisfactory in math, 4th-grade students	0.001	0.006	0.043	0.000	0.004	0.070
Satisfactory in reading, 4th-grade students	0.003	0.017	0.043	–0.004	–0.090	0.083
Average teacher salary (1999 dollars)	0.001	0.010	0.074	0.002	0.045	0.110
Net effect of finance reform (1999 dollars)	0.262	1.935	0.610**	0.052	1.462	1.090
Addendum						
Model X^2 (df): 146.27 (24).						
R^2/pseudo R^2: 0.3975.						
N schools (districts): 2,638 (484).						

Source: See table 8-3.
*$p < .10$, **$p < .05$, ***$p < .01$.
a. Predictors are averages for the period 1989–90 through 1993–94.

different from that leading to a single charter school. The only factor that is consistently related to a district's likelihood of having both a single charter school and multiple charter schools is district size, indicated by the count of traditional public schools located in the district: larger districts are significantly more likely to have both single and multiple charter schools by 1999. Districts that were more favorably affected by Michigan's school finance reform were more likely to get a single charter school but not multiple charters, while higher poverty districts had significantly lower probabilities of having a single charter. Relative to districts without charter schools, districts with multiple charters had marginally significantly lower homeownership rates and higher private school attendance rates, possibly representing less affluent populations that place a high priority on education; alternatively,

Table 8-5. *Predicting Charter Presence, Black-White Exposure*

	Zero vs. 1 charter			*Zero vs. 2+ charters*		
	$\partial y/\partial x$	*Coef.*	*SE*	$\partial y/\partial x$	*Coef.*	*SE*
Constant		1.9646			–11.713	
Dimensions of segregation						
Exposure of black to white	–0.579	–4.2953	1.860**	–0.312	–7.132	2.597***
Demographics of school district residents, 1990						
Poor (relevant children in poverty)	–0.012	–0.0863	0.044**	–0.003	–0.083	0.077
Housing in urban areas	0.000	–0.0002	0.007	–0.001	–0.016	0.014
Some college or higher	–0.004	–0.0225	0.028	0.002	0.032	0.037
Homeowners	–0.003	–0.0262	0.018	–0.002	–0.053	0.029*
Enrolled in private school	–0.005	–0.0245	0.035	0.006	0.109	0.069
Characteristics of school districts, 1989–94[a]						
Number of traditional public schools	0.015	0.1161	0.038**	0.010	0.220	0.045***
Average student-teacher ratio	0.004	0.0157	0.094	–0.006	–0.121	0.168
Satisfactory in math, 4th-grade students	–0.001	–0.0046	0.041	0.001	0.017	0.075
Satisfactory in reading, 4th-grade students	0.005	0.0296	0.044	–0.004	–0.084	0.091
Average teacher salary (1999 dollars)	0.004	0.0242	0.075	0.000	0.002	0.107
Net effect of finance reform (1999 dollars)	0.285	1.9617	0.617***	0.038	1.141	1.049
Addendum						
Model X^2 (df): 126.15 (24).						
R^2/pseudo R^2: 0.4055.						
N schools (districts): 2,600 (417).						

Source: See table 8-3.
$^*p < .10$, $^{**}p < .05$, $^{***}p < .01$.
a. Predictors are averages for the period 1989–90 through 1993–94.

there may be a high concentration of families desiring religious education for their children. Interestingly, few of the factors we tend to think of as associated with school quality are predictive of charter school presence, such as student achievement, student-teacher ratios, and average teacher salaries.

With respect to race, these models show an interesting pattern. In districts where black students are more exposed to white students, there is a significantly lower likelihood of both single and multiple charter schools. The sizes of these effects are not trivial; for example, a district that is one standard deviation higher than the mean for black-white exposure faces a .17 drop in the probability of having a single charter school and a .09 drop in the probability of having multiple charter schools.[20] Further, greater black isolation increases the likelihood of both a single charter and multiple charters; districts with

Table 8-6. *Predicting Charter Presence, Latino-White Exposure*

	Zero vs. 1 charter			*Zero vs. 2+ charters*		
	∂y/∂x	*Coef.*	*SE*	*∂y/∂x*	*Coef.*	*SE*
Constant		2.022			4.607	
Dimensions of segregation						
Exposure of Latino to white	–0.596	–4.335	1.877**	–0.203	–4.983	2.448**
Demographics of school district residents, 1990						
Poor (relevant children in poverty)	–0.011	–0.079	0.042*	–0.001	–0.035	0.067
Housing in urban areas	0.000	0.001	0.007	–0.001	–0.013	0.014
Some college or higher	–0.004	–0.022	0.028	0.002	0.036	0.035
Homeowners	–0.003	–0.022	0.018	–0.002	–0.054	0.031*
Enrolled in private school	–0.005	–0.027	0.035	0.006	0.114	0.067*
Characteristics of school districts, 1989–94[a]						
Number of traditional public schools	0.016	0.120	0.038	0.010	0.222	0.044***
Average student-teacher ratio	0.002	0.004	0.086	–0.006	–0.126	0.164
Satisfactory in math, 4th-grade students	0.000	–0.001	0.041	0.001	0.024	0.073
Satisfactory in reading, 4th-grade students	0.005	0.024	0.044	–0.005	–0.098	0.089
Average teacher salary (1999 dollars)	0.003	0.020	0.075	0.001	0.024	0.108
Net effect of finance reform (1999 dollars)	0.276	1.943	0.623**	0.042	1.237	1.107
Addendum						
Model X^2 (df): 133.52 (24).						
R^2/pseudo R^2: 0.3997.						
N schools (districts): 2,607 (445).						

Source: See table 8-3.

*$p < .10$, **$p < .05$, ***$p < .01$.

a. Predictors are averages for the period 1989–90 through 1993–94.

higher levels of black isolation (one standard deviation above the mean) have .15 and .06 higher probabilities of having a single charter and multiple charters, respectively. The same pattern is found with respect to Latino-white exposure, with both single and multiple charter schools being less likely in districts where Latino-white exposure is high. Further, districts with high levels of Latino isolation are significantly more likely to house multiple charter schools. With respect to exposure, districts that are one standard deviation above the mean face a decline of .13 in the probability of a single charter school. The marginal effects of isolation on charter school presence are not substantial.

In contrast, in districts where white students are more exposed to black students, there is a significantly higher probability of having a single charter

Table 8-7. *Predicting Charter Presence, Black Isolation*

	Zero vs. 1 charter			*Zero vs. 2+ charters*		
	$\partial y/\partial x$	*Coef.*	*SE*	$\partial y/\partial x$	*Coef.*	*SE*
Constant		−1.837			0.761	
Dimensions of segregation						
Black isolation	0.525	3.854	1.693**	0.219	5.078	2.444**
Demographics of school district residents, 1990						
Poor (relevant children in poverty)	−0.011	−0.080	0.040**	−0.002	−0.052	0.069
Housing in urban areas	0.000	0.001	0.007	−0.001	−0.013	0.015
Some college or higher	−0.003	−0.020	0.027	0.002	0.042	0.035
Homeowners	−0.003	−0.026	0.018	−0.003	−0.058	0.030*
Enrolled in private school	−0.005	−0.025	0.035	0.006	0.115	0.067*
Characteristics of school districts, 1989–94[a]						
Number of traditional public schools	0.015	0.113	0.038**	0.010	0.211	0.043**
Average student-teacher ratio	0.001	0.002	0.096	−0.006	−0.120	0.169
Satisfactory in math, 4th-grade students	0.000	−0.002	0.042	0.001	0.016	0.073
Satisfactory in reading, 4th-grade students	0.005	0.025	0.044	−0.005	−0.090	0.087
Average teacher salary (1999 dollars)	0.003	0.019	0.075	0.000	0.007	0.110
Net effect of finance reform (1999 dollars)	0.275	1.926	0.604***	0.042	1.212	1.123
Addendum						
Model X^2 (df): 135 (24).						
R^2/pseudo R^2: 0.3991.						
N schools (districts): 2,600 (417).						

Source: See table 8-3.

*$p < .10$, **$p < .05$, ***$p < .01$.

a. Predictors are averages for the period 1989–90 through 1993–94.

but no higher likelihood of multiple charter schools. Similarly, districts with higher levels of white isolation have lower probabilities of a single charter but are no more or less likely to house multiple charter schools. In terms of magnitude, a district has a .11 higher probability of a single charter school if its white-black exposure rate is one standard deviation above the mean and a .13 lower probability for a comparable level of white isolation.

These results cannot tell us the true reasons, but clearly there is a desire for alternative educational options in districts where both Latino and black students are more segregated from white students. Further, there appears to be less motivation toward charter schools in districts where white isolation is high and exposure to black students is low, although these results are not as robust. Given these findings—that charter school location is far more

Table 8-8. *Predicting Charter Presence, White Isolation*

	Zero vs. 1 charter			*Zero vs. 2+ charters*		
	$\partial y/\partial x$	*Coef.*	*SE*	$\partial y/\partial x$	*Coef.*	*SE*
Constant		1.778			2.242	
Dimensions of segregation						
White isolation	–0.613	–4.464	1.858**	–0.114	–3.237	2.477
Demographics of school district residents, 1990						
Poor (relevant children in poverty)	–0.011	–0.077	0.040*	0.000	–0.011	0.061
Housing in urban areas	0.000	0.001	0.007	0.000	–0.010	0.014
Some college or higher	–0.003	–0.021	0.028	0.002	0.043	0.034
Homeowners	–0.002	–0.019	0.018	–0.003	–0.058	0.032*
Enrolled in private school	–0.005	–0.027	0.034	0.006	0.121	0.066*
Characteristics of school districts, 1989–94[a]						
Number of traditional public schools	0.016	0.125	0.039***	0.009	0.216	0.043***
Average student-teacher ratio	0.002	0.010	0.086	–0.005	–0.113	0.160
Satisfactory in math, 4th-grade students	0.000	0.003	0.042	0.001	0.015	0.071
Satisfactory in reading, 4th-grade students	0.004	0.021	0.044	–0.005	–0.094	0.086
Average teacher salary (1999 dollars)	0.002	0.015	0.075	0.002	0.035	0.110
Net effect of finance reform (1999 dollars)	0.270	1.961	0.620**	0.046	1.335	1.091
Addendum						
Model X^2 (df): 137.76 (24).						
R^2/pseudo R^2: 0.3991.						
N schools (districts): 2,638 (484).						

Source: See table 8-3.
*$p < .10$, **$p < .05$, ***$p < .01$.
a. Predictors are averages for the period 1989–90 through 1993–94.

responsive to racial composition than to other characteristics of school districts—the next step of the analysis assesses the extent to which the presence of charter schools works to worsen or ameliorate levels of segregation within their chosen districts.

Changes in Segregation over Time

Tables 8-11 through 8-16 present difference-in-difference estimates of the effects of charter presence on the segregation of traditional public schools within districts. The outcomes are changes in within-district segregation between 1990 and 2000.[21] In these models, charter school presence is first measured as it was in the previous analysis, comparing districts with a single or multiple charter schools to those without. Although these models control

Table 8-9. *Predicting Charter Presence, Latino Isolation*

	Zero vs. 1 charter			*Zero vs. 2+ charters*		
	$\partial y/\partial x$	*Coef.*	*SE*	$\partial y/\partial x$	*Coef.*	*SE*
Constant		−3.118			−1.607	
Dimensions of segregation						
Latino isolation	0.020	0.810	5.758	0.517	11.015	4.279**
Demographics of school district residents, 1990						
Poor (relevant children in poverty)	−0.004	−0.026	0.037	0.001	0.013	0.055
Housing in urban areas	0.001	0.004	0.007	0.000	−0.007	0.014
Some college or higher	−0.001	−0.003	0.025	0.002	0.051	0.033
Homeowners	−0.002	−0.020	0.018	−0.003	−0.060	0.033*
Enrolled in private school	−0.003	−0.016	0.035	0.006	0.117	0.069*
Characteristics of school districts, 1989–94[a]						
Number of traditional public schools	0.014	0.110	0.037**	0.008	0.195	0.042***
Average student-teacher ratio	0.000	−0.011	0.091	−0.007	−0.142	0.161
Satisfactory in math, 4th-grade students	−0.001	−0.009	0.042	−0.001	−0.017	0.070
Satisfactory in reading, 4th-grade students	0.003	0.017	0.044	−0.003	−0.067	0.086
Average teacher salary (1999 dollars)	0.004	0.030	0.078	0.003	0.069	0.109
Net effect of finance reform (1999 dollars)	0.282	2.025	0.611***	0.055	1.536	1.070
Addendum						
Model X^2 (df): 123.27 (24).						
R^2/pseudo R^2: 0.3956.						
N schools (districts): 2,607 (445).						

Source: See table 8-3.
**p* < .10, ***p* < .05, ****p* < .01.
a. Predictors are averages for the period 1989–90 through 1993–94.

for the size of district, the share of public school population enrolled in charter schools may be a better indicator of charter school presence. Therefore districts are also categorized based on their percentage of public school students that are enrolled in charter schools in 1999: zero, below the median of 7 percent, or at or above the median.[22] Many demographic characteristics are likely to influence changing segregation patterns, such as the racial composition of the resident population, levels of poverty, and educational attainment. Changes in these characteristics of the resident population are controlled for in these models, as are changes in the size of the private school population, the percentage of white residents attending private schools, and characteristics of traditional public schools in the district.

Table 8-10. *Summary Statistics*

Factor	1990		Precharter average[a]		2000	
	Mean	SD	Mean	SD	Mean	SD
Charter school presence						
Number of schools	...	...	...	...	3.72	10.70
Percentage of district enrollment	...	...	...	...	0.02	0.04
Percentage of district enrollment, conditional on having a charter	...	...	...	...	6.46	5.33
Dimensions of segregation						
Exposure of black to white	0.78	0.30	0.78	0.30	0.75	0.31
Exposure of white to black	0.11	0.19	0.11	0.19	0.12	0.20
Exposure of Latino to white	0.83	0.22	0.82	0.22	0.78	0.26
Black isolation	0.17	0.30	0.17	0.29	0.19	0.31
White isolation	0.84	0.21	0.84	0.22	0.80	0.24
Latino isolation	0.05	0.08	0.05	0.08	0.08	0.14
Demographics of school district residents, 1990						
American Indian	0.86	0.02	...	...	0.79	0.02
Asian	1.30	0.02	...	...	1.57	0.02
Black	12.88	0.25	...	...	14.31	0.26
Latino	2.91	0.03	...	...	4.27	0.04
White	81.93	0.26	...	...	76.31	0.28
Other races	0.13	0.00	...	...	2.76	0.02
Poor (relevant children in poverty)	16.98	0.13	...	...	12.93	0.10
Housing in urban area	53.00	0.47	...	...	58.12	0.46
Some college or higher	43.63	0.13	...	...	50.08	0.13
Homeowners	65.35	0.13	...	...	75.04	0.12
Enrolled in private school	11.45	0.06	...	...	11.01	0.05
White residents enrolled in private schools	14.05	0.10	...	...	13.82	0.09
Population size	22,358	54,499	...	...	24,818	60,504
Characteristics of school districts						
Number of traditional public schools	28.56	61.23	28.00	59.26	30.88	66.12
Average student-teacher ratio	15.54	2.49	18.97	2.45	18.24	2.18
Satisfactory in math, all students	43.60	13.09	51.75	12.23	72.37	13.33
Satisfactory in reading, all students	37.35	11.49	41.40	10.99	59.83	12.78
Average teacher salary (1999 dollars)	49,619	7,146	32,679	4,682	48,448	6,979
Net effect of finance reform, 1993–94 (1999 dollars)	...	...	578.17	326.32	...	...
Summary statistic						
N (schools)	2,778–852		2,814–52		2,787–852	

Source: See table 8-3.

a. Precharter averages are based on data from 1989–93, except for teacher salary and achievement, which are based on 1991–94 data.

Table 8-11. *Change in Black-White Exposure, Difference-in-Difference Estimates of Segregation*[a]

	Count		Median	
Variable	*Coef.*	*SE*	*Coef.*	*SE*
Intercept	–2.138		–2.149	
Charter school presence				
Zero charters	...	...	...	...
One charter	0.072	0.701	...	...
Multiple charters	–0.565	1.304	...	...
Charter share of public enrollment				
Zero charters	...	...	...	...
Less than median (6.6 percent)	...	...	0.659	0.756
Median or greater	...	...	–1.937	0.984**
1990–2000 changes in residential population of school districts				
Δ Residential population enrolled in school	–0.812	0.336**	–0.844	0.338**
Δ Percent residents enrolled in private schools	0.323	0.221	0.238	0.218
Δ Percent white residents enrolled in private schools	–0.205	0.223	–0.139	0.214
Δ Percent black	–0.980	0.149***	–0.949	0.150***
Δ Percent Latino	–0.765	0.120***	–0.743	0.114***
Δ Percent housing units in urban areas	0.012	0.016	0.015	0.016
Δ Percent poor	–0.043	0.072	–0.046	0.070
Δ Percent homeowners	0.025	0.022	0.024	0.022
Δ Percent residents with some college or higher	0.033	0.073	0.035	0.069
1990–2000 changes in characteristics of schools and districts				
Δ Number of traditional public schools in district	0.158	0.091*	0.111	0.086
Δ Average student-teacher ratio	–0.142	0.101	–0.165	0.097*
Δ Percent students scoring satisfactory				
Satisfactory in math, 4th-grade students	–0.025	0.032	–0.021	0.033
Satisfactory in reading, 4th-grade students	0.073	0.036**	0.066	0.038*
Δ Average teacher salary	0.088	0.048*	0.097	0.049**
Net effect of finance reform	–0.487	0.843	–0.384	0.825
Summary statistic				
N (schools, districts)	2,464 (417)		2,464 (417)	
R^2	0.513		0.523	

Source: See table 8-3.

*$p < .10$, **$p < .05$, ***$p < .01$.

a. The scales of all outcomes have been transformed from 0–1 to 0–100.

Table 8-12. *Change in Latino-White Exposure, Difference-in-Difference Estimates of Segregation*[a]

Variable	*Count*		*Median*	
	Coef.	*SE*	*Coef.*	*SE*
Intercept	–2.072		–2.026	
Charter school presence				
Zero charters	...	...	...	...
One charter	–0.626	0.510	...	...
Multiple charters	–0.950	1.091	...	...
Charter share of public enrollment				
Zero charters	...	...	...	...
Less than median (6.6 percent)	...	...	0.069	0.653
Median or greater	...	...	–2.502	0.811**
1990–2000 changes in residential population of school districts				
Δ Residential population enrolled in school	–0.354	0.172**	–0.390	0.166**
Δ Percent residents enrolled in private schools	0.124	0.242	0.026	0.221
Δ Percent white residents enrolled in private schools	–0.158	0.242	–0.077	0.218
Δ Percent black	–1.059	0.123***	–1.029	0.122***
Δ Percent Latino	–0.851	0.118***	–0.832	0.112***
Δ Percent housing units in urban areas	0.013	0.008	0.016	0.009*
Δ Percent poor	0.073	0.053	0.068	0.053
Δ Percent homeowners	0.010	0.018	0.009	0.018
Δ Percent residents with some college or higher	0.111	0.052**	0.108	0.051**
1990–2000 changes in characteristics of schools and districts				
Δ Number of traditional public schools in district	–0.199	0.063**	–0.240	0.059***
Δ Average student-teacher ratio	–0.133	0.081	–0.154	0.080*
Δ Percent students scoring satisfactory				
Satisfactory in math, 4th-grade students	0.034	0.025	0.038	0.024
Satisfactory in reading, 4th-grade students	–0.005	0.031	–0.012	0.032
Δ Average teacher salary	0.028	0.040	0.038	0.040
Net effect of finance reform	–0.128	0.761	–0.040	0.758
Summary statistic				
N (schools, districts)	2,543 (445)		2,636 (484)	
R^2	0.656		0.730	

Source: See table 8-3.

*$p < .10$, **$p < .05$, ***$p < .01$.

a. The scales of all outcomes have been transformed from 0–1 to 0–100.

Table 8-13. *Change in White-Black Exposure, Difference-in-Difference Estimates of Segregation*[a]

Variable	Count Coef.	Count SE	Median Coef.	Median SE
Intercept	0.426		0.515	
Charter school presence				
Zero charters	...	...	...	...
One charter	0.231	0.293	...	...
Multiple charters	0.867	0.752	...	...
Charter share of public enrollment				
Zero charters	...	...	...	...
Less than median (6.6 percent)	...	...	0.392	0.464
Median or greater	...	...	0.674	0.669
1990–2000 changes in residential population of school districts				
Δ Residential population enrolled in school	–0.013	0.101	–0.014	0.111
Δ Percent residents enrolled in private schools	–0.088	0.159	–0.102	0.154
Δ Percent white residents enrolled in private schools	0.082	0.165	0.098	0.158
Δ Percent black	1.050	0.109***	1.047	0.111***
Δ Percent Latino	0.100	0.084	0.098	0.083
Δ Percent housing units in urban areas	0.002	0.003	0.002	0.003
Δ Percent poor	–0.084	0.048*	–0.088	0.048*
Δ Percent homeowners	–0.011	0.009	–0.011	0.009
Δ Percent residents with some college or higher	–0.023	0.033	–0.031	0.032
1990–2000 changes in characteristics of schools and districts				
Δ Number of traditional public schools in district	0.025	0.043	0.038	0.044
Δ Average student-teacher ratio	0.024	0.048	0.028	0.046
Δ Percent students scoring satisfactory				
Satisfactory in math, 4th-grade students	–0.002	0.015	–0.002	0.016
Satisfactory in reading, 4th-grade students	–0.011	0.016	–0.013	0.017
Δ Average teacher salary	0.018	0.033	0.019	0.033
Net effect of finance reform	0.473	0.468	0.439	0.465
Summary statistic				
N (schools, districts)	2,636 (484)		2,636 (484)	
R^2	0.731		0.730	

Source: See table 8-3.

*$p < .10$, **$p < .05$, ***$p < .01$.

a. The scales of all outcomes have been transformed from 0–1 to 0–100.

Table 8-14. *Change in Black Isolation, Difference-in-Difference Estimates of Segregation*[a]

Variable	*Count*		*Median*	
	Coef.	*SE*	*Coef.*	*SE*
Intercept	0.497		0.490	
Charter school presence				
Zero charters	...	...	...	...
One charter	–0.317	0.565	...	...
Multiple charters	0.001	1.112	...	...
Charter share of public enrollment				
Zero charters	...	...	...	...
Less than median (6.6 percent)	...	...	–0.696	0.666
Median or greater	...	...	0.881	0.794
1990–2000 changes in residential population of school districts				
Δ Residential population enrolled in school	0.472	0.303	0.491	0.301
Δ Percent residents enrolled in private schools	–0.302	0.185	–0.247	0.184
Δ Percent white residents enrolled in private schools	0.236	0.182	0.193	0.178
Δ Percent black	0.935	0.128***	0.916	0.129***
Δ Percent Latino	0.112	0.080	0.099	0.078
Δ Percent housing units in urban areas	0.000	0.013	–0.002	0.013
Δ Percent poor	0.043	0.064	0.046	0.062
Δ Percent homeowners	–0.015	0.013	–0.015	0.013
Δ Percent residents with some college or higher	–0.016	0.063	–0.016	0.063
1990–2000 changes in characteristics of schools and districts				
Δ Number of traditional public schools in district	–0.095	0.077	–0.068	0.075
Δ Average student-teacher ratio	0.106	0.072	0.120	0.071*
Δ Percent students scoring satisfactory				
Satisfactory in math, 4th-grade students	0.029	0.026	0.026	0.028
Satisfactory in reading, 4th-grade students	–0.050	0.025*	–0.045	0.029
Δ Average teacher salary	–0.080	0.039**	–0.086	0.041**
Net effect of finance reform	1.281	0.625**	1.220	0.611**
Summary statistic				
N (schools, districts)	2,464 (417)		2,464 (417)	
R^2	0.539		0.546	

Source: See table 8-3.

*$p < .10$, **$p < .05$, ***$p < .01$.

a. The scales of all outcomes have been transformed from 0–1 to 0–100.

Table 8-15. *Change in Latino Isolation, Difference-in-Difference Estimates of Segregation*[a]

	Count		Median	
Variable	*Coef.*	*SE*	*Coef.*	*SE*
Intercept	–0.603		–0.579	
Charter school presence				
Zero charters	...	...	...	...
One charter	–0.187	0.294	...	...
Multiple charters	–0.150	0.501	...	...
Charter share of public enrollment				
Zero charters	...	...	...	...
Less than median (6.6 percent)	...	...	–0.029	0.271
Median or greater	...	...	–0.484	0.580
1990–2000 changes in residential population of school districts				
Δ Residential population enrolled in school	–0.073	0.085	–0.080	0.082
Δ Percent residents enrolled in private schools	–0.117	0.116	–0.139	0.109
Δ Percent white residents enrolled in private schools	0.145	0.117	0.165	0.111
Δ Percent black	–0.002	0.047	0.003	0.050
Δ Percent Latino	0.700	0.079***	0.703	0.079***
Δ Percent housing units in urban areas	0.000	0.005	0.001	0.005
Δ Percent poor	–0.041	0.030	–0.042	0.028
Δ Percent homeowners	0.001	0.013	0.001	0.013
Δ Percent residents with some college or higher	–0.066	0.031**	–0.068	0.031**
1990–2000 changes in characteristics of schools and districts				
Δ Number of traditional public schools in district	0.436	0.059***	0.430	0.056***
Δ Average student-teacher ratio	0.158	0.051**	0.155	0.051**
Δ Percent students scoring satisfactory				
Satisfactory in math, 4th-grade students	–0.008	0.015	–0.007	0.015
Satisfactory in reading, 4th-grade students	0.015	0.020	0.013	0.019
Δ Average teacher salary	–0.007	0.026	–0.005	0.025
Net effect of finance reform	0.530	0.364	0.542	0.365
Summary statistic				
N (schools, districts)	2,543 (445)		2,543 (445)	
R^2	0.677		0.678	

Source: See table 8-3.

*$p < .10$, **$p < .05$, ***$p < .01$.

a. The scales of all outcomes have been transformed from 0–1 to 0–100.

Table 8-16. *Change in White Isolation, Difference-in-Difference Estimates of Segregation*[a]

Variable	Count		Median	
	Coef.	SE	Coef.	SE
Intercept	–1.926		–2.144	
Charter school presence				
Zero charters	...	...	...	...
One charter	–0.592	0.431	...	...
Multiple charters	–2.121	0.909**	...	...
Charter share of public enrollment				
Zero charters	...	...	...	...
Less than median (6.6 percent)	...	...	–0.983	0.650
Median or greater	...	...	–1.628	0.717**
1990–2000 changes in residential population of school districts				
Δ Residential population enrolled in school	–0.065	0.158	–0.061	0.179
Δ Percent residents enrolled in private schools	0.080	0.162	0.116	0.154
Δ Percent white residents enrolled in private schools	–0.048	0.161	–0.088	0.151
Δ Percent black	–1.113	0.106***	–1.106	0.108***
Δ Percent Latino	–0.632	0.109***	–0.628	0.108***
Δ Percent housing units in urban areas	0.005	0.007	0.005	0.008
Δ Percent poor	0.111	0.050**	0.121	0.051**
Δ Percent homeowners	0.009	0.015	0.010	0.015
Δ Percent residents with some college or higher	0.050	0.046	0.069	0.046
1990–2000 changes in characteristics of schools and districts				
Δ Number of traditional public schools in district	–0.059	0.064	–0.091	0.065
Δ Average student-teacher ratio	–0.065	0.067	–0.075	0.070
Δ Percent students scoring satisfactory				
Satisfactory in math, 4th-grade students	0.019	0.021	0.018	0.023
Satisfactory in reading, 4th-grade students	0.017	0.024	0.021	0.026
Δ Average teacher salary	0.013	0.034	0.011	0.034
Net effect of finance reform	0.240	0.686	0.320	0.680
Summary statistic				
N (schools, districts)	2,636 (484)		2,636 (484)	
R^2	0.674		0.670	

Source: See table 8-3.

*$p < .10$, **$p < .05$, ***$p < .01$.

a. The scales of all outcomes have been transformed from 0–1 to 0–100.

The results are consistent with the findings of the analysis of locational decisions, in that the same dimensions of segregation are sensitive to charter school presence: black-white exposure, Latino-white exposure, and white isolation. However, the additional consideration of charter schools' share of the public population adds much to our understanding of the conditions under which charter schools may affect the larger public school system with respect to segregation. In only one instance does the quantity of charter schools affect segregation (multiple charter schools reduce white isolation); in most cases, districts do not experience significant effects of the charter school movement unless a sizable percentage of their public school students are enrolled in charters (at or above the 1999 median of nearly 7 percent). Under these conditions, black and Latino exposure to white students declined significantly. The average black student was exposed to nearly 2 percent fewer white students, and the average Latino student was exposed to about 3 percent fewer white students. The magnitude of these changes is relatively large, given that the models control for the changing racial composition of districts.

Although charter school presence did not significantly affect black or Latino isolation, districts with multiple charters experienced a significant decline in white isolation, with the effect being the largest in districts where charter schools enroll more than the median percentage of public students. Relative to districts without charter schools, districts with multiple charters and districts with a large share of their public students in charters experienced approximately a 2 point drop in white isolation, and those with a high percentage of students in charters experienced slightly more than a 1.5 point drop.

Aside from the impacts of charter school presence, there are some additional interesting findings with respect to characteristics of public schools and districts. In models examining the impacts of charter enrollment share, increases in student-teacher ratios led to marginally significant declines in black and Latino exposure to whites and increases in black and Latino isolation, although the effects are small. Increases in average teacher salary seemed to influence the segregation of black students, through significant positive impacts on black exposure to whites and negative impacts on black isolation. Improvements in reading achievement also benefited black students with respect to segregation, although these effects were small. Aspects of Latino segregation seemed more sensitive to the educational attainment of district residents; increases in the percentage of residents with some college or higher led to significant increases in Latino exposure to white students and declines in Latino isolation.

In contrast to these more complex results for black and Latino segregation, changes in segregation for whites were affected by only two factors: the racial and the economic composition of the district's residential population. Increases in poverty led to increased white isolation and reduced exposure to black students. Further, these models of changing segregation experienced by whites explained a substantial proportion of the variance in these changes: 67 percent of the change in white exposure to blacks and 73 percent of the change in white isolation. These models also explain a great deal of the variance in changes in Latino isolation and Latino exposure to whites (68 and 73 percent, respectively), yet the models for dimensions of black segregation did not accomplish as much, explaining only slightly more than half of the variation.

In sum, these results describe complex relationships between racial segregation and public schooling that cannot easily be explained by a single model. Most important, they show that where charter schools have enrolled a sizable proportion of the public school population, black and Latino students have become more isolated from white students in traditional public schools. Under these conditions white isolation also declined, which is consistent with charter schools drawing relatively higher proportions of white students in these districts. This would lead to fewer white students in traditional public schools, which would lower white isolation as well as lower exposure to whites for black and Latino students remaining in these schools. However, this is merely a possible explanation, and the processes involved require further investigation.

Another important complexity is the differences in factors relevant to segregation for different racial groups. Segregation for black students is strongly influenced by the characteristics of public schools, but segregation for Latinos seems more sensitive to the characteristics of the residential population. These results suggest a need for analyses using measures of mutual segregation among several racial and ethnic groups, which may succeed in better illuminating these complex relationships.

Conclusion

The main goal of this study is to understand the racial context of the charter school movement in Michigan. The results discussed above indicate that, although at first glance charter schools appear to be serving distinct populations, the racial composition of charter schools is not dramatically different from traditional public schools located in their vicinity. However, charter schools are significantly more likely to locate in districts where black and

Latino students are more isolated from white students in traditional public schools. Even though this trend can be seen in a positive light in that the supply of charter schools is responding to a desire for greater educational options on the part of black and Latino families, there is also a downside: in districts with high proportions of students in charter schools, several forms of public school segregation have been exacerbated. The precise mechanism by which this has occurred has not been clearly defined by these analyses and certainly requires further investigation.

Limitations

Forms of choice—whether of residence or school attendance—are complex social phenomena that defy simple explanation. Therefore there is often the possibility that a researcher has failed to take into account a relevant factor in explaining the consequences of individual choices. In this case, there may be many political and ecological factors that influence the locational decisions of charter schools; further work is clearly needed to more fully understand the supply responses of choice schools. In addition, we know relatively little about how charter schools change the sorting mechanisms within districts: are charters disproportionately drawing students of one racial or ethnic group from local schools? Are they primarily drawing students from private schools or from traditional public schools? These questions are certainly worthy of further investigation.

Segregation is also a multifaceted phenomenon, and dichotomous measures such as those used here are incapable of telling the full story of the racial dynamics of school districts. Further work with more complex measures of mutual segregation may shed more light on the relationship between race and the charter school movement.

Policy Implications

Most of the controversy surrounding charter schools focuses on their ability to improve academic achievement, but their potential effects on segregation remain critical to today's policy debate. The implications of the results presented here are both positive and negative, in that good intentions seem to be having some unintended negative consequences. The fact that charter schools are aiming to serve more disadvantaged districts is important, given that some feared that they would target more affluent or white populations. However, in order to reach their target populations, in many cases these schools must locate in more highly segregated school districts. One cannot fault them for trends that have likely been operating for decades before their arrival; however, the results presented here show that, when they enroll a large share of the public school population, they are significantly increasing several dimensions of segregation.

From a policy standpoint, these results do not point to a simple solution. Some states have racial balance provisions in their charter school legislation, such as requiring that the racial composition of charter schools reflect that of the district in which they are located; these results, however, suggest that such provisions would not be effective in Michigan. As we see, Michigan's charter schools closely resemble nearby traditional public schools with respect to race, and the trends in segregation in their districts certainly predate their arrival. Given that the main effects occur when charter schools serve large proportions of the public school population, it is possible that a more appropriate policy instrument for managing segregation levels may be a cap on the percentage of a district that charter schools may serve. In sum, while Michigan prides itself on having one of the most liberal charter school laws in the country, some retooling may be needed to address the increasing segregation for students remaining in traditional public schools.

Appendix: Exposure and Isolation by Race and Ethnicity: Equations

—Exposure of blacks or Latinos to whites = $\Sigma[(xi/X)^* \, (yi/ti)]$.
—Exposure of whites to blacks = $\Sigma[(yi/Y)^* \, (xi/ti)]$.
—Isolation of blacks or Latinos from whites = $\Sigma[(xi/X)^* \, (xi/ti)]$.
—Isolation of whites = $\Sigma[(yi/Y)^*(yi/ti)]$.

Where

xi = black or Latino population of school i,
X = black or Latino population of district,
yi = white population of school i,
Y = white population of district, and
ti = total population of school i.

Notes

1. For a review of the literature, see Brian P. Gill and others, *Rhetoric versus Reality: What We Know and What We Need to Know about Vouchers and Charter Schools* (Santa Monica, Calif.: RAND, 2001).

2. While much research shows that a majority of school segregation lies between districts rather than within, I have chosen to focus on within-district segregation as a first

step in beginning to understand how the charter school movement may be altering how students are sorted across schools. For a focus on the former, see Sean F. Reardon, John T. Yun, and Tamela McNulty Eitle, "The Changing Structure of School Segregation: Measurement and Evidence of Multiracial Metropolitan School Segregation, 1989–1995," *Demography* 37 (2000): 351–64.

3. Michigan reformed its system of school finance in 1994. The legislation, Proposal A, removed local property taxes as a determinant of local public school revenues and replaced them with a block grant from the state in an effort to equalize per pupil spending across districts. For more information see Paul N. Courant and Susanna Loeb, "Centralization of School Finance in Michigan," *Journal of Policy Analysis and Management* 16 (1997): 114–36.

4. Center for Education Reform, "Charter School Highlights and Statistics" (Washington: 2003).

5. David Arsen, David Plank, and Gary Sykes, "School Choice Policies in Michigan: The Rules Matter" (School Choice and School Change, Michigan State University, 2000); Jerry Horn and Gary Miron, "Evaluation of the Michigan Public School Academy Initiative" (Evaluation Center, Western Michigan University, 1999); Jerry Horn and Gary Miron, "An Evaluation of the Michigan Charter School Initiative: Performance, Accountability, and Impact" (Evaluation Center, Western Michigan University, 2000); Public Sector Consultants and Maximus, "Michigan's Charter School Initiative: From Theory to Practice" (Lansing: Michigan Department of Education, 1999).

6. Arsen, Plank, and Sykes, "School Choice Policies in Michigan."

7. Horn and Miron, "Evaluation of the Michigan Public School Academy Initiative."

8. Notable exceptions are Jeffrey R. Henig and Jason A. MacDonald, "Locational Decisions of Charter Schools: Probing the Market Metaphor," *Social Science Quarterly* 83 (2002): 962–80; and Natlie Lacireno-Paquet and others, "Creaming versus Cropping: Charter School Enrollment Practices in Response to Market Incentives," *Educational Evaluation and Policy Analysis* 24 (2002): 145–58.

9. There were 561 districts in 1990 and 555 in 2000.

10. National Center for Education Statistics, *Common Core of Data,* 1989–90 through 1999–2000 (U.S. Department of Education).

11. Each charter school in Michigan is treated as its own district. To accurately locate charter schools within a district, I geocoded the 1999–2000 addresses for each charter school and reassigned them to the district in which they are physically located.

12. Charter schools are excluded from these calculations in order to construct measures that reflect the experiences of the students remaining in traditional public schools.

13. Referred to as the 1990 and 2000 School District Data Book. U.S. Bureau of the Census, *1990 Decennial Census School District Special Tabulation; 2000 Decennial Census School District Special Tabulation.*

14. All financial variables were adjusted for inflation using the consumer price index and are expressed in dollars corresponding to the 1999–2000 school year.

15. National Center for Education Statistics, *Private School Survey, 1999–2000* (U.S. Department of Education).

16. Eric Bettinger developed an instrumental variable based on a school's distance to one of Michigan's public state universities for which Governor Engler appointed the board. However, in my analyses, the instrument failed on two fronts: first, as noted by

Bettinger, it only operates effectively before 1999; and second, it did not accurately predict the differences in the number of charter schools per district. See Bettinger, "The Effect of Charter Schools on Charter Students and Public Schools" (National Center for the Study of Privatization in Education, U.S. Department of Education, 1999).

17. Other researchers note that many Michigan charter schools do not participate in the federal Free and Reduced Price Lunch Program, accounting for the large number of charter schools reporting that none of their students are eligible; see Horn and Miron, "Evaluation of the Michigan Public School Academy Initiative."

18. Zero eligible students were reported by 90 charter schools (53 percent) and 207 traditional public schools (6 percent).

19. Charter presence was first modeled as an ordered logit, but the impact of relevant factors varied considerably in predicting one versus multiple charters.

20. The marginal effects presented here were estimated using the mfx command in Stata and estimate the marginal effects of the independent variables at their respective means.

21. The scale of the measures of segregation have been transformed from 0–1 to 0–100 to make the coefficients easier to interpret. As a result, the means and standard deviations reported in table 8-5 need to be multiplied by 100 in order to obtain the values used in the difference-in-difference analysis.

22. The median is based on districts having at least one charter school in 1999.

9

Understanding the Political Conflict over School Choice

JEFFREY R. HENIG

One of the hallmarks of the school choice debate has been its hair-trigger responsiveness even to proposals for incremental and experimental change. Because the status quo ante was characterized by a rather constrained set of choices, the prevalent manifestation has been the mobilization of so-called antichoice forces whenever there has been discussion of introducing market forces via open enrollment, charter schools, education tax credits, or public vouchers.[1] As various choice schemes have been enacted, the reverse phenomenon, in which prochoice interests rise up to battle even minor increases in regulation and public oversight of choice schools, has become common as well.

This "high reverberation"[2] characteristic of the school choice debate has been puzzling to some. While disagreement may exist about whether the current educational system is in crisis or just in need of improvement,[3] no serious voices are asserting that all is fine and dandy with the way things are today. Americans generally pride themselves as being a pragmatic lot, and a pragmatic response to poor school performance presumably would include deliberate efforts to fine-tune system parameters and even, with cautions and within limits, to try small-scale experiments in which sharper changes are tested and their consequences rigorously scrutinized. Why, then, have proposals to loosen the link between residential location and school assignment been as instantaneously and aggressively resisted as they have? Why do proposals to build stronger regulatory and oversight provisions into choice programs so quickly and certainly prompt fierce and undifferentiated countermobilizations?

Others who have noted this volatile and polarized nature of the school choice debate have written it off as a straightforward manifestation of ideological warfare or interest group politics. There is little doubt that both of these factors do play a role. Some liberal adherents of a view of government as a progressive and democratizing force view any references to the advantages of choice as the advance troops for a privatization assault intended to eviscerate the public sector. Some conservative believers in the beneficence of market forces react to any claim about the need to exercise public oversight as a disingenuous ploy to keep the bureaucratic foxes in control of the henhouse. In addition to the clash of abstract theories about government and markets, baser individual and group interests—pitting teachers' unions against educational management organizations, cosseted suburbanites against sincere proponents of the needs of inner-city poor children, traditional civil rights leaders against emerging aspirants for power within the minority communities, and politician versus politician each seeking a winning issue—add fuel and heat to the already combustible mix.

In this chapter, however, I suggest that something more—and more interesting—than reflexive ideology and self-interest is involved. Lurking just below the surface of the school choice debate are some genuine uncertainties about the nature and dynamic attributes of the public-private continuum, the extent to which incrementalism is hardwired into the American political system, and the relative influence of learning versus power as the driving forces of policy change. Rather than ideologically motivated posturing—or rather than *just* ideological posturing—I suggest that contending theories about the nature of government, politics, and policy change can account for disparate predictions about the likely consequences of privatizing education. Deciding whose fears are legitimate and whose are capricious, in other words, will depend on more than better theories about markets or better studies of existing choice plans. It will also require grappling with some basic conundrums of democratic theory and political thought.

I begin by discussing the distinction between pragmatic and systemic privatization. Pragmatic privatization is selective and involves fine-tuning the allocation of public versus private responsibility in order to maximize the collective good. Pragmatic privatization may involve increasing reliance on market forces along a single dimension, but it does not diminish the core capacity of public institutions. Systemic privatization, on the other hand, involves a concerted and substantial rearrangement of public versus private authority; rather than administrative calibration, it is powered by political, ideological, and institutional forces that, once unleashed, can be mutually reinforcing and may spin out of the orbit of democratic oversight and public control.

In at least one of its common manifestations, the debate over school choice represents a disagreement over whether it is best understood as a pragmatic effort to make the public sector work better or as an opening wedge in a broader effort to supplant public and democratically responsive forums with decision arenas centered on market forces and individual choice.

I then attempt to explain why the anxiety that some choice skeptics express about privatizing delivery may reasonably seem overdrawn to choice proponents. Given that we already have a public policy system that mixes public and private elements, a cultural bias toward pragmatic and incremental change, and a political decisionmaking system that makes it relatively easy to block or water down risky initiatives, it can be difficult to understand why nerve ends seem so exposed on the school choice issue. But the fact that sensitivity about the risks of seemingly minor choice initiatives can be difficult to understand does not mean that such sensitivity is shortsighted, wrongheaded, or insincere. I go on to explain how there could be a credible basis for the concern that initially incremental steps to privatize education delivery might spark a spiraling set of reactions that could indeed lead to the systemic weakening of public sector capacity and democratic control.

In exploring these issues, I adopt as basic premises several conclusions that emerged from the deliberations of the Brookings National Working Commission on Choice in K–12 Education.[4] First, it is important to pay attention to *different types of choice regimes*. Second, *context matters*. Third, a good choice system is *unlikely to reduce expenditures* significantly and could even require additional funding support. Fourth, and most important, the ultimate consequences of school choice *will not be determined by policy design and initial intent*, most certainly not by those alone. What will matter in the end is how choice policies, and the broader institutional regimes in which they are embedded, are adjusted, enforced, supplemented, supplanted, exploited, and evaded in an ongoing process in which policy, context, economic forces, and political pressures intersect.

This complicated brew ensures that the consequences of school choice will be impossible to control or predict with any degree of precision. But acknowledging that need not induce either fatalism or fear of change. While it is not possible to predict precise and certain outcomes, it is possible to make sensible and informed assessments of likely benefits and risks. And while it is not possible to assert control or dictate outcomes, it is possible to inform political judgment and policy measures in ways that nudge and steer matters in one direction or another. Accordingly, I conclude with a discussion of some conditions under which it might be possible to find common ground—a real and not simply superficial scenario for putting the benefits of privatized delivery systems at the service of a public interest that is democratically responsible and sufficiently muscular to attain its higher ends.

The Four Dimensions of Education Provision

Government and market-based provision of education can be seen as incorporating at least four dimensions: delivery, financing, regulation, and decisionmaking.[5] Each dimension is anchored by collective values associated with public institutions at one end and market-oriented, individual preferences and processes at the other (see figure 9-1). A hypothetical pure public system would see all students educated in publicly funded and operated schools, with curriculum and standards defined through collective institutions and enforced by public officials responsible to the citizenry. A hypothetical purely privatized system would see all students educated in private schools funded by the tuition their parents are able and willing to pay, with the quality and type of education provided ensured through the contracted arrangement between consumer and provider and enforced primarily through families' power to take their business elsewhere.

In principle, it should be possible to privatize the delivery of education without undermining support for a continued strong public sector role in investment. One way to think of this is in terms of distinct and sequenced decisions. First, public officials held responsible through institutions of democratic control would make an assessment about the level and distribution of funding that should be collectively raised (via taxation) and publicly disbursed in order to take into account the public goods aspect of education.[6] Second, based on community values, traditions, and evidence about what works in practice, they would make decisions about how to distribute those resources, including the best mix of public and private delivery systems.

This vision of funding and delivery as distinct decisions—one unaffected by the other—is central to Milton Friedman's classic presentation of the case for school vouchers.[7] Specifically, Friedman argues that the choice between government and markets involves both a question about the delivery of services and a question about the financing of services. While the collective good attributes of education might make it desirable to include public funding

Figure 9-1. *Four Dimensions of Education Provision*

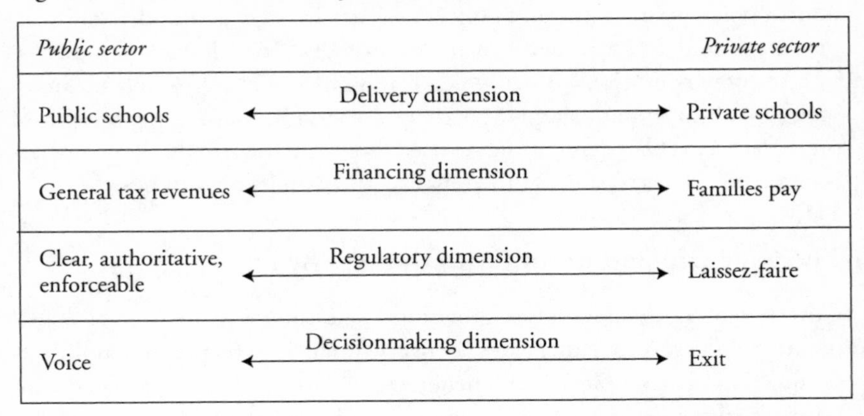

(since reliance on private financing alone would lead to underinvestment from the standpoint of the societal interest), this should not be generalized into an argument in favor of public delivery. If, as he believed, private providers would be more innovative, responsive, and efficient, the best solution would be to retain elements of public funding but channel that funding through private delivery mechanisms. Thus school vouchers.

Most contemporary proponents of school choice hold to Friedman's two-dimensional model. They believe, or at least assert, that decisions about delivery and decisions about financing are entirely autonomous; typically, they do not address the regulatory and decisionmaking dimensions, but to the extent that they do so they see these as largely distinct and autonomous as well.[8] This belief that the dimensions are autonomous is central to the notion of pragmatic privatization. It holds out the prospect that movement along one dimension—say delivery—could be accompanied by a compensatory shift in another dimension, say regulation. In more concrete form, that means for example that a policy of increasing reliance on a semiprivate provider such as charter schools could be linked to a policy of expanding public sector oversight and accountability to collectively articulated values via mandated testing, for example, or insistence on admission by lottery.

But it is uncertainty about whether these dimensions are distinct in practice that accounts for much of the wariness toward privatizing delivery. Those who resist even incremental shifts toward market-based provision fear that in the real world of politics and practice the two may be yoked together in ways that make privatization of delivery a likely precursor to reduced public funding support. In other words, they believe that shifts along one dimension may tend to generate complementary shifts along the other dimensions, whether those shifts are initially intentioned or not.

It is one thing to argue that the several public-private dimensions are analytically distinct and quite another to argue that they are empirically independent. Friedman argues the former point and implies the latter. But he does not offer a fully developed case. A substantial part of the debate over school choice turns on competing theories about the extent to which increasing reliance on private delivery of education will in fact lead to increased reliance on private financing, pro forma regulation, and attenuated democratic control. Although they do not typically express it in these terms, many school choice skeptics are convinced that formalistic efforts to separate delivery from finance will prove difficult to maintain politically. They believe that the constituency for substantial public investment in education is fragile and under attack and that a serious step in the direction of private delivery risks pulling a thread on a loosely woven fabric of political support.

The Case against Concern about Privatizing Education Delivery

The high-anxiety, high-stakes-intensity character of the school choice debate appears paradoxical for at least three reasons. First, while the debate over school choice tends to be framed as a battle between pure government and pure market models, the reality is that the American educational system—like most aspects of American public policy—comprises both public and private financing and delivery, responsive both to consumer exit and political voice. Second, the American political system is noted for its structural inhospitality to radical change; fragmented power, multiple veto points, and a two-party system oriented toward the median voter all conspire to make incremental policy change the norm. Third, while political discourse about privatization in the United States sometimes evokes the same stark images and dramatic rhetoric as has accompanied large-scale, systemic privatization initiatives in other parts of the world, actual practice in this country tends to take the form of pragmatic privatization, involving modest, selective, and conditional introduction of market forces rather than wholesale unraveling of the welfare state.

A Mixed System

Proponents of school choice often portray the existing system as a pure monopoly marked by mandatory assignment to government-run schools based on place of residence. This is seen to have multiple consequences, all bad. Because families have no choice, they cannot exercise power via exit or the threat of exit, as consumers are free to do when they are dissatisfied with a provider in a competitive market arena.[9] Because the system is supported by imposed taxation, school officials have little incentive to eliminate waste or explore cost-saving innovations. Because broad policies are shaped by majoritarian political processes, schools and teachers are constrained by a net of regulations intended to ensure that the will of the majority is not subverted at the implementation stage.[10] Because professionalism tends to promote a conventional wisdom and because bureaucracies tend to favor standardized routines, schools offer a one-size-fits-all curriculum that is insensitive to individual learning styles and divergent values.

But even leaving aside the roughly 6 million (10 percent) of children who attend private schools,[11] the American educational system offers considerably more choice and diversity than this image implies. John Witte, back in 1990, demonstrated many ways in which the educational landscape was in fact "extremely diversified" and decentralized, and the subsequent expansion of school choice options has made that even more the case today.[12] Magnet schools, alternative schools, open-enrollment policies, homeschooling, and charter schools provide many students with alternatives to their local attendance zone public school, allowing them to exercise at least some elements of consumer pressure and matching between particular interests and school curriculum. Analysis by the National Center for Education Statistics suggests that, in 1999, 14 percent of public school students attended schools their families selected, up from 11 percent in 1993.[13] Of the public choice options, charter schools go the furthest in the direction of private delivery. Although their core funding and approval to operate derives from government, charter schools themselves are private organizations. Most charter schools are formally nonprofit, but a growing proportion is run by, or in close association with, for-profit educational management organizations. The first charter school law was passed by Minnesota in 1991; just six years later there were 428 schools in operation, and by the 2003–04 school year there were just under 3,000 charter schools operating in forty-one states.[14] In light of the continued growth of charter schools, the 1999 estimate of 14 percent for schools of choice is almost certainly too low.

Also pointing to the mixed nature of the American education system is the extensive and apparently growing importance of private funding for public schools. "While public schools and districts have always attracted private support, anecdotal reports and a limited body of documented research suggest they are pursuing private support with increased sophistication and aggressiveness."[15] Private contributions to public schools can be channeled through various forms of nonprofit organizations, including family foundations, local education foundations, alumni groups, booster clubs, and parent-teacher associations. While the full extent of the phenomenon is not well understood, it is clear that the amounts involved can be quite substantial. Elite public schools, like Boston Latin and Brookline High School in Massachusetts, or Brooklyn Tech and Bronx High School of Science in New York, conduct multimillion-dollar fundraising campaigns.[16] Large foundations, such as Annenberg, inject millions of dollars into what they see as promising efforts. In addition, several states have recently begun to experiment with very aggressive tuition tax credit programs providing individuals (Arizona) or corporations (Florida, Pennsylvania) hefty deductions for contributions to scholarship funds; for tactical political as well as constitutional reasons, these typically include components covering certain expenditures for public schools. To the extent that public schools come to rely upon private giving, if even just for the kinds of extras that make the difference between capacity to innovate and austere survival, they, like private businesses, must pay attention to the interests and desires of the givers.

Against this backdrop, a movement toward greater reliance on markets, choice, and private delivery of education services would not appear to represent a revolutionary step. Indeed, one might credibly argue that this would simply constitute an extension of a trend reaching back at least to the 1960s.[17]

Incrementalism and Pragmatism

In addition to that fact that we already operate in a mixed public-private system, the general tendency of American politics to stall, strangle, or shave down innovative policies and nonincremental changes makes the sensitivity of some choice skeptics appear overly hysterical. While the debate is animated by hopes and concerns about dramatic changes in the basic form of schooling and school policy, the reality is that the American educational system—again, like most aspects of American public policy—unfolds in a political and social context that nearly always constrains policy to incremental and tentative forms.

Political scientists have long observed this tendency toward incrementalism, which they ascribe to several distinct attributes of our political structures and processes. Some emphasize the role of a formal system of governance to deliberately build in checks and balances by dividing power both horizontally (across the branches of government, across different policy specialties, between general purpose governments, and between special districts) and vertically (up and down the ladder of federalism). Others put more weight on our relatively open interest group system, which tends to find a settling point at some equilibrium roughly balancing the many legitimate but conflicting interests the citizenry holds. Still others put greater weight on ideology and political culture, suggesting that Americans—more so than their hot-blooded and highly politicized counterparts in other parts of the world—favor a cautious pragmatism both in their personal lives and, even more emphatically, within the public realm (which they regard with some diffidence). Overall, political science as a discipline emphasizes the ways in which these various factors combine to generate "veto points," "subgovernments," "iron triangles," and policy "subsystems" defended by elite-managed problem definitions.[18]

Regardless of the particular weighting one puts on the structural, procedural, or cultural elements, the combined result is a system that, on a day-to-day basis, makes it easier to block or co-opt change than to carry out major reforms. Against that backdrop, fears that small steps in the direction of privatization of education delivery will snowball into a radical threat to the existing system of public education seem overdrawn. The status quo appears sufficiently privileged to ensure that brakes will be effectively applied.

Americans have long been known as a pragmatic lot, less taken with the seduction of grand and abstract theory than with a more straightforward and concrete determination of what works. Among the hallmarks of pragmatism are a toolbox orientation to public policy, a willingness to experiment, and a preference for reversible commitments. Just as a successful handyman carries multiple kinds and sizes of screwdrivers, drill bits, saws, nails, and screws so as to be able to select the best one to work in a specific task, a toolbox orientation toward policy means having multiple options for pursuing social goals and recognizing that what works best in one time and place might not be the best alternative in other contexts. Experimentation refers here not to formal adherence to the dictates of random assignment and scientific design but to a tendency to base decisions about policy selection more on *giving it a try* and less on theories about *what should work*. A preference for reversible choices follows from the baseline assumptions that context matters and that knowledge is usually incomplete; in order to facilitate social learning and allow for open feedback chains, it is important that changes in policy be undoable if the expected results do not materialize or if unintended negative consequences emerge.

This pragmatic culture may help to explain why Americans adopted and ultimately still favor institutional arrangements that promote incrementalism, such as divided power, veto points, and pluralistic processes as discussed above. But the culture also operates within that institutional context to further mute the appeal that grand programs of reform otherwise might hold for mass voters vaguely dissatisfied with the status quo.

Such general policy pragmatism has been reflected in the particular way that privatization has unfolded in the United States. Compared to privatization efforts elsewhere, privatization in the United States often has been limited, selective, and harnessed to plans to make government work better rather than not at all.[19] Pragmatic privatization initiatives frequently are introduced as technical solutions to meet an immediate social problem. The key actors perceive privatization simply as one among several alternative tools through which recognized priorities of the society might be furthered. In deciding whether and when to privatize, they focus on the specific characteristics of the problem and its context, giving little thought to ideological consistency or political consequences.[20]

Indeed, within the United States, a strong case can be made that by far the bulk of the efforts to privatize—through contracting out, imposition of users' fees, deregulation, and vouchers—has emerged as *pragmatic efforts to make government work better at fulfilling its broad range of public responsibilities* and not as efforts to scale back those responsibilities.[21] Such is the case, for example, when state and local governments, in the new computer age, responded to the need to upgrade internal data and management systems by contracting with private corporations that possessed the needed technical expertise. Such is the case, too, when a state or local government privatizes a peripheral function like janitorial service in order to reallocate scarce budgetary resources to meet other public needs.

Selectively and conditionally providing public funds to private education providers falls within the bounds of existing norms and practices of public policy in a range of policy arenas and is not even revolutionary in American education. When a local government contracts with a private firm to spray insecticides when there is a near-term threat of disease transmission through mosquitoes and it would be too costly to buy planes and hire pilots directly, that is a case of pragmatic privatization. When public school districts are responsible for students with unusual and severe needs that can be better met—or less disruptively or less expensively met—by private schools specializing in that disability, that can be an example of pragmatic privatization as well. These need not, and typically do not, represent contractions of the public sphere or government responsibility.

In terms of educational choice as expressed in figure 9-1, pragmatic privatization would consist of movements along the delivery dimension, with compensatory shifts along the dimensions of finance, regulation, and decisionmaking. A compensatory shift in finance, for example, would occur if a substantial proportion of the funding to start and operate charter or voucher schools represented net new investments. A compensatory shift in regulation would occur if increased reliance on nongovernment employees as providers was linked to an increased government capacity to monitor charter and voucher schools' policies and practices in admissions, curriculum, personnel, discipline, and educational results. A compensatory shift in the decisionmaking dimension would occur if the movement to private delivery provided voters with more abundant and accurate information and more transparent procedures for defining public priorities and exercising accountability.

The Case for Concern about Privatizing Education Delivery

Against this backdrop—in which U.S. governments have historically and on a wide scale turned to markets and private providers to pragmatically maintain or extend their reach and effectiveness; in which political institutions, processes, and the reigning culture make radical change less likely—further privatization on the delivery dimension of public education might be expected to raise eyebrows but not an urgent hue and cry. Given the background of a mixed system, incrementalism, and pragmatic privatization, is concern that privatized delivery will spark a much more massive deconstruction of public education reasonable?

Expressed simply as an undifferentiated reaction against anything that smacks of markets, it is not reasonable. But embedded within a broader theory about the political dynamics of privatization and systemic change, it is. The background factors that moderate the prospects for dramatic change—mixed systems, incrementalism due to institutional fragmentation and pluralistic equilibriums, and traditions of pragmatism—are not immutable forces of nature but are themselves the outcomes of political interests, institutions, and ideas. And while these political factors typically align in ways that make it unlikely that the new policy initiatives will do more than nudge the weighty structure of our educational system a few degrees to one side or another, there are definable conditions under which they can converge to generate sharper, nonincremental changes—what are sometimes referred to as "punctuations" in the equilibrium state that normally obtains.[22] Such punctuations are not necessarily undesirable; they can be a bracing liberation from stultifying norms or practices that have been held in place for the convenience of the powerful rather than by virtue of established worth. But when there is a prospect that the resulting changes may erode, in ways that are not readily reversible, the basic capacity of public institutions to take the measure of and effectively act upon the public interest, there are good reasons to take note and take care.

Systemic Privatization

Within the U.S. education community, debate and research about school choice can sometimes be quite specific and concrete, focusing on the "devil in the details" of particular school choice plans. But in the wider arenas of politics and policy, the school choice issue is irretrievably interwoven with broader conflicts about privatization on a massive scale. There, the goal is not limited to making government work better; rather, there is a higher stakes battle about where the boundary between public and personal responsibility ought to be drawn. In this arena, compromise often is seen as capitulation; accommodation, when it occurs, is often tactical in nature; so interest in technical detail can be diversionary and insincere.

This is the arena of systemic, rather than pragmatic, privatization, where the goal is a wholesale shrinking of the realm of public authority and a fundamental deconstruction of the taxing, regulatory, and service delivery apparatus of the welfare state. Sometime during the 1980s, a major international political movement was born as scores of nations began selling publicly owned enterprises and otherwise exploring ways to shift functions and responsibilities from government to markets.[23] While the most noteworthy early plans involved industrialized nations in Western Europe and Japan, privatization rapidly caught on worldwide. Less developed countries, prodded by international lending agencies, began experimenting seriously with asset sales. By the early 1990s, former bastions of state ownership—Russia, Poland, Czechoslovakia, and Hungary—not only had joined the privatization parade but were embarking on some of the most aggressive efforts in the world. According to some, this movement amounts to nothing less than a revolution.[24] While some such claims of advocates were hyperbolic and inflated, more than rhetoric was at work. During the last two decades of the previous century, privatization "worldwide reduced state-owned enterprises' share of global GDP from over 10 percent . . . to less than 6 percent."[25]

In this broader debate, the ideological, political, and material stakes are perceived to be very high indeed. Opponents of systemic privatization believe that conservative ideologues seek nothing short of the wholesale unraveling of the welfare state and a return to a form of social Darwinism in which the rich—particularly those whose wagons are hitched to the horses of global capitalism—get richer while the rest are forced further down the side streets of dependence and subsistence living. Proponents, for their part, see every assertion about the limits of markets and the legitimate role of government in protecting social values as part of a cynical effort by those who feed from the government trough to mask their privileged position behind a false front of nice-sounding words. Because the two major political parties have aligned themselves at different points of the market-government continuum, there are huge partisan stakes in the current battle as well. Republicans position themselves on the privatization issue as the party of the future and seek to portray Democrats as defenders of a failed and obsolete set of institutions and practices. Lurking behind some of the highly ideological and partisan battles is a more straightforward competition for the goodies that are at stake; while privatization advocates are accurate when they note that some interests oppose them out of fear they will lose access to valuable patronage, contracts, favorable regulations, and direct benefits, it is equally true that there are corporate and other interests anticipating that *they* will prosper financially from a movement toward a privatization regime.

The high-stakes, winner-take-all character of the politics of systemic privatization accounts for much of the skittishness and hyper-reactivity of school choice debaters. Those who believe in the legitimate exercise of public authority and see it as necessary to the pursuit of social justice regard the arguments about school choice as freighted with connotations that go well beyond the particulars of the subject at hand. They fear that initially small changes undertaken in the name of market efficiency may—either by intention or not (but they suspect the former)—spiral into a much broader set of consequences. And their fears are not without basis.

Along with Harvey Feigenbaum and Chris Hamnett, I argue elsewhere that systemic privatization, which unlike pragmatic privatization *does* entail a substantial and self-reinforcing shrinkage of government scope and responsibility, may come about via any or all of three mechanisms.[26]

A *power shift* involves a "nontransient change in the capacity of already mobilized interests to pursue their agendas as currently conceived."[27] In the case of education, a power shift would occur if an increased reliance on private modes of delivery weakened interest groups that currently provide important support for public investment in schools or strengthened groups that currently oppose such investment and the taxes that support it.

A *perceptual shift* involves a "nontransient change in the values, culture, and expectations of the active public, resulting in a broadening of the sphere of activities regarded as personal and private and a shrinking of the sphere of activities considered to constitute legitimate areas for public scrutiny and intervention."[28] In the case of education, a perceptual shift would occur if an increased reliance on private modes of delivery led to a broad devaluation of the collective goods aspects of education, undermining existing beliefs in the connection between public education and collective economic, social, and civic well-being.

Finally, an *institutional shift* involves "nontransient restructuring of the institutional arrangements of the society (legal, political, economic) in such a way that the array of incentives presented to individuals and groups encourages a greater reliance on private and market oriented solutions."[29] In the case of education, an institutional shift would occur if an increased reliance on private modes of delivery systematically reduced the capacity of government to carry out core functions relating to public schooling, stimulating a spiral of decline and exit. Let us consider these in a little more depth.

A Shift in Power

In relatively open, pluralistic systems, such as is found in the United States, policy positions on reasonably visible issues tend to reflect a rough balance of power among competing interest groups. Barring sharp external disruptions (wars, depressions, crises of other sorts), these constellations of interest group alignment tend to be relatively stable. Groups favoring change in one direction (let us say, toward a stronger market orientation) may win some battles due to clever tactics, more intense focus, and short-term "windows of opportunity."[30] But this will typically spark a countermobilization by those on the other side (let us say, those favoring a stronger public sector role), with the result that policy will be pulled back and forth, with neither group gaining a permanent advantage. In this pluralistic model of American politics, most political activity is centered on a relatively small number of organized interest groups, with the bulk of the public presumed to be generally disengaged and content.

Although it is something of an oversimplification, we can think of the core elements of the promarket side of the school choice debate as being represented largely by a coalition comprising Republican politicians, conservative foundations, libertarian organizations, many sectarian private schools, and various corporate and financial groups that see a potential for profiting from a more privatized environment. The competing coalition at its active core comprises teachers' unions, liberal Democrats, and many civil rights organizations. Suburbanites play an important sotto voce role; ideologically, many are responsive to privatization appeals and calls for restrained taxes and government, but generally content with their public schools and somewhat wary of choice policies that might force them to accommodate students from surrounding jurisdictions. They frequently throw their considerable political weight to the antivoucher side when specific proposals are being considered. The broad American public is somewhat but not intensely aware of the school choice issues, generally responsive to the idea that parents should be free to make choices for their children, but highly loyal to the ideal of public education.[31]

This configuration of counterbalancing interests and a relatively disengaged majority has helped to account for the constrained politics of school choice witnessed to date. Despite the reports, media pieces, and political speeches underscoring the educational crisis and need for systemic reform, change continues to come in small doses. Public voucher referendums fail. And when states have made fairly dramatic movements in the direction of charter schools, there have often been subsequent pressures to impose caps, tighten oversight, and otherwise engage in what market choice proponents consider reregulation and general backsliding.

Would privatization on the delivery dimension destabilize this balance of competing interests in a way that might give proponents of more systemic privatization a decided new advantage? In particular, would it weaken an already shaky alliance of forces supporting the investment of public revenues in public schools? It might. Privatizing the delivery dimension of education could undermine support for public finance if it substantially reduced the current constituency for public investment and taxes that support it or substantially strengthened the current constituency against public investment and taxes that support it.

There are at least three reasonable scenarios that suggest that privatizing school delivery could peel off or neutralize important elements of the conventional public system coalition:

—Exacerbating fissures in minority communities that traditionally support candidates who favor public spending;

—Weaning from this coalition conservative Jewish groups interested in saving Jewish private schools; and

—Weakening support for public school spending among homeowners by weakening the link between schools and property value.

African Americans have been a large and loyal component of the Democratic electoral coalition and on public opinion polls reveal that they are among the strongest believers in a strong government role for meeting social needs.[32] For both tactical and symbolic reasons, the prospect that they might respond to political appeals for vouchers is rightfully regarded as a threat to Democratic candidates.[33] Public opinion polls suggest strong support for vouchers within the African American community, particularly those in the younger generation, and a handful of prochoice African American individuals and organizations have been highly visible.[34] Much attention has focused on the poll results, but the still-dominant elite voices and organized civil rights organizations continue to speak forcefully against vouchers, and these leaders have been able to rally their supporters when critical showdowns emerge.

Less is known about the position of the Latino community, but there are reasons to believe that it may be more willing than the African American community to part with the traditional Democratic stance on the issue of schools. A 2002 survey by the Joint Center for Political and Economic Studies, for example, found that 60.8 percent of Hispanics supported vouchers, versus 57.4 percent of blacks and 51.4 percent of non-Hispanic whites.[35] Perhaps more important in terms of interest group politics, the major organizations and leaders within the Hispanic community have less invested in the current structure of public education delivery. Legal and political battles during the heyday of the civil rights movement helped African Americans gain control of public school districts in many urban centers, and the jobs and contracts this provides gives the existing leadership a strong material interest in defending the status quo.[36] In cities where their populations are growing, however, Latino leaders sometimes see this privileged status as an obstacle to their own aspirations and the families they represent. They are more open, as a result, to allying with reform efforts that have the potential to shake things up, even if these are framed in a corporate, promarket language that is otherwise at odds with their political agenda.[37]

Privatizing education delivery could easily exacerbate the generational cleavages within both the black and Latino communities and highlight the divergent material interests between an African American population heavily invested in existing institutions and a Latino population still on the outside looking in. The threat that this will also mean a weakening of support for public investment is real *even if* minorities do not defect to Republicans in large numbers and *even if* those minorities who do favor vouchers also favor maintaining (or even expanding) public investment in education (that is, favor large vouchers and do not favor funding them out of revenues currently channeled to conventional public schools).

Even if the cross-pressures experienced by the minority communities do no more than put a damper on their turnout or force Democratic candidates to spend more time and resources shoring up their core support, the consequence would be advantageous for Republican (and, generally, for fiscally more conservative) candidates. The fact that African Americans and Latino supporters of vouchers might strongly wish vouchers to be large and progressive and funded fully out of "new" revenues is not sufficient to ensure those results. It is important to distinguish between electoral and governance regimes. Sowing division within the minority communities will weaken the Democrats' electoral regime; it is unlikely to mean that defecting or ambivalent minorities will gain access to a Republican governance regime. And it is at the governance stage that key issues about taxation and funding are likely to be made. Despite their own values and desires, minority splinter groups that help elect Republicans because of their support for privatizing delivery are, in other words, unlikely to have the leverage to win the subsequent battles over the form that privatization takes.

The lever of power shift could drive a wedge into a smaller but also critically important component of the core coalition supporting public investment in education: the Jewish community. Although the number of Jewish families in the United States is relatively small, their strategic importance for both national politics and school politics is disproportionately large. Nationally, the Jewish vote is important because of their high rates of voter turnout, strong liberal and Democratic identities, and concentration in the metropolitan areas of key states in the electoral college.[38] In the specific arena of education politics, "public schools rely more heavily on Jewish support than the numbers would suggest, in part because Jewish organizations, fearful of any breakdown of the wall between Church and State, have traditionally lobbied hard against school vouchers and other government aid to private schools."[39]

There is a growing and highly mobilized segment within the Jewish community, however, that has begun reassessing its traditional resistance to vouchers.[40] The proportion of Jews who sent their children to public schools "declined from more than 90 percent in 1962 to about 65 percent [in 1999],"[41] with about 200,000 of these attending full-time private Jewish schools. Despite this growth in student population, the sector of private Jewish schools is struggling financially,[42] and vouchers look to some like the answer they need. While most non-Orthodox Jewish groups still reject school choice, a number are revisiting the issue and some groups have emphatically made up their minds. The executive vice president for government and public affairs of Agudath Israel of America writes: "Well, all right, we'll admit it (though we've never pretended otherwise): The organization I represent . . . supports vouchers primarily because we think they will help Jewish schools and Jewish families. We also think they will help other segments of the American population, especially the inner-city poor who desperately seek but are unable to afford an alternative to the failing public schools to which their children are consigned. But, to be perfectly frank, that consideration is only of secondary significance in our admittedly self-interested calculation."[43]

The privatization of delivery will also alter homeowners' calculations of their stake in supporting strong public schools. Viewed from the realm of narrow self-interest, it initially seems hard to explain why policies to support public education through general taxation are politically viable. After all, fewer than one-third (32.8 percent) of American households contain children under the age of eighteen, and roughly one in ten of these send their children to a private school.[44] Most Americans, in other words, lack the kind of direct stake in the public schools that would seem sufficient to lead them to abide the heavy tax burden that supporting the public system requires. Noneconomists account for the fact that majoritarian institutions nonetheless *do* typically produce support for education budgets by referencing the collective good aspects of education or by noting the ties of family and community bonds that may lead some to support spending not because their own children benefit but because others they care about do. Many economists find such indirect and collective explanations suspect and, instead, zero in on the fact that some voters may enjoy direct and material payoffs from strong public schools despite the fact they do not have children in school. The key linkage, in this instance, is property value.

A number of studies have found evidence that property values go up when the community invests in its public schools. W. E. Oates, in a classic early analysis, found that this increase in value exceeded the added cost of the tax payments the homeowners bear.[45] This suggests that it can be rational, even on narrow terms, for homeowners without children to support increases in taxes that get invested in their local schools. But that linkage depends upon the relatively tight geographical nexus between the taxation and the investment. School choice programs attenuate and potentially sever that connection. R. Reback, for instance, found that Minnesota's interdistrict open-enrollment plan, which allows students to transfer into public schools in districts other than the one in which their family resides, decreased the demand for property in districts that had the most attractive schools. He speculates that this might generate opposition to choice proposals in suburban districts that have a reputation for good schools, since it "seems reasonable that a homeowner would vote against a school choice proposal that would reduce the value of her home."[46] E. Brunner and colleagues' analysis of Los Angeles County's precinct-level voting returns in California's 1993 voucher referendum (Proposition 174) found evidence that this may indeed translate into political behavior: voters in precincts where public schools were already good were more likely to vote against the voucher initiative; indeed, such suburban voters were a major factor in the initiative's lopsided defeat.[47]

In addition to weakening the conventional public school coalition, a power shift might entail a structural enhancement of the political power of the coalition that favors systemic privatization of education, including increased reliance on private funding. One way this might take place is if privatizing delivery adds muscle to existing members of that coalition. Another would involve the creation of *new* interest groups or the enlistment of powerful and previously ambivalent third parties.

Privatization on the delivery side will increase the number of families in private schools, and to the extent that numbers translate into power in our democratic system, will thereby add leverage to the organized interests already speaking on behalf of private deliverers of educational services. Currently, about 10 percent of the nation's schoolchildren attend private schools, mostly Catholic schools—although diversity in the sector is increasing. At this point, the primary responsibility for articulating and pursuing the interest of this sector rests more on the Catholic Church than on the aggregated voices of the parents. The church can call on substantial moral and symbolic power when communicating directly with political leaders. When there is a need to add political muscle to such moral suasion, church leaders' presumed ability to mobilize Catholic voters overall probably carries more weight than does a tabulation of the number of students attending their schools. Even though the total number of Catholic schools and students enrolled in Catholic schools has been declining in recent decades, one would be hard-pressed to make the case that their clout has declined as a result—and certainly not proportionally. Nonetheless, a substantial increase in the overall size of the private school sector, especially if politicians and governments increasingly *count on* private providers to absorb excess student loads, could make the private provider community a more powerful force.

Winning the battle to privatize education delivery might also add to the luster and resources of other members of the general privatization coalition. Political scientists have recognized that one's reputation for power often gets converted into genuine power, as potential opponents think twice about taking you on and others find you more attractive as a potential ally in battles of their own.[48] So, too, in the competitive world of fundraising, money often follows success; conservative foundations and conservative politicians who have been battling on this issue may find it easier to attract new donors when they have clear policy victories to tout.

But perhaps most likely to tip the equilibrium, because it has the potential to more dramatically shift the balance of power, is the addition of new allies, either by the creation of new interests or by the mobilization of powerful interests that previously were uninvolved. Privatizing delivery of education creates new interests: organizations that were fledglings or did not exist before but that have the potential to become major sources of pressure within an interest group arena. Two prominent examples are educational management organizations and state-based charter school coalitions.

Educational management organizations are major emerging actors in the realm of privatized education delivery. They come in different shapes and sizes: some are for-profit, some are legally constituted as nonprofits; some operate with a national scope, others are regional or limited to only one or two states; some open and run their own network of charter schools, some contract with existing charter schools to provide a range of educational services, and some manage traditional public schools under contract with local or state boards of education. Although the ultimate economic viability of the industry is still a subject of debate,[49] the evidence shows that they are making inroads.[50] For the most part, both proponents and opponents of these management organizations have framed their arguments within the paradigm of microeconomics, with debate centering on such matters as whether there are sufficient economies of scale to enable the organizations to make sufficient profit and whether greater reliance on technology and teacher aides can reduce the labor costs substantially below what is typical in public education.

But educational management organizations are not limited to market actions; they are free to pursue their interests as political actors as well. In interviewing politicians and advocacy groups in four states, I and my colleagues have found evidence not only that these organizations are active lobbyists but also that in at least some cases conservative proponents of vouchers and less regulated charter school regimes have deliberately cultivated these organizations in order to add muscle and legitimacy to their agenda.[51] And a study of the dynamics of charter laws across the fifty states finds some evidence that the presence of such organizations in a state may increase the likelihood the state will change its charter laws in ways that make them more in line with the parameters favored by promarket advocates.[52] Moreover, as they begin to extend credit and develop relationships with charter school providers, elements within the politically muscular financial community are likely to be drawn into the interest group battles, lending their support to measures they believe will reduce the risks and raise the levels of public support.

A Shift in Perception

Although interest group politics provides the spectator sports element of our decisionmaking system—the source of day-to-day drama that fills newspapers and serves as grist for commentators—political scientists know that the real exercise of power often operates less visibly.[53] The pushing and tugging among interest groups may be less likely to lead to sharp institutional shifts than would a broad shift in the way the public defines problems.[54]

Normally, policy is held within bounds by elites within a subsystem buffered from challenge not only by its superior resources but also by institutional position and ideology. In the case of public education, critics of the current system argue that there is a powerful "public school ideology"[55] operating to keep Americans from recognizing the ways in which current education delivery arrangements fail to deliver on their promises of accountability, democracy, and equity. According to Terry Moe, "Many Americans simply like the idea of a public school system. They see it as an expression of local democracy and a pillar of the local community, they admire the egalitarian principles on which it is based, they think it deserves our commitment and support, and they tend to regard as subversive any notion that private schools should play a larger role in educating the nation's children."[56]

Whether one thinks that the public's loyalty to the ideal of public education is grounded on ideology or reasoned assessment may depend on one's own ideological home base, but Moe is almost certainly correct that a set of premises, norms, ideas, and expectations plays a powerful role in priming the American public to defend the existing public school system and to regard as somehow risky and undemocratic proposals to abandon that system for one constructed more centrally around market processes.

Deeply engrained political ideas and issues definitions are not easy to challenge, especially if one tries to battle them head-on.[57] But from the standpoint of those favoring sharp change, winning this battle over perceptions could be a huge victory. And the way to do it would be to promote a new vision of what public education looks like rather than to propose that public education be pushed aside. In particular, rather than championing vouchers as a private, market-based alternative to public education, it would be strategically adroit to reshape the public's vision of vouchers and private schools in such a way that they are seen as constituting *a different type* of public education rather than an *alternative to* public education.

Privatizing the delivery of public education has already begun to play an important role in setting the stage for such a reconceptualization. In an effort to control the vocabulary with which market-oriented proposals are discussed, proponents have downplayed the terms "privatization" and "vouchers" in favor of labels that salute public purpose, such as "the GI bill for children" and "opportunity scholarships." Charter schools, which combine elements of public accountability with private organizational form, have led some to argue that we should redefine public schooling to refer to whether a public purpose is being served, regardless of whether government is involved.[58]

While Americans' commitment to the idea of public education is based at least in part on attachment to an *idea*—a vision of the common school nurturing the skills and values of good citizenship—it is likely that it is the concrete manifestation of public education—the way they encounter it in the form of real buildings, real teachers, and the way these affect children in their own communities—that is the more reliable forging ground for the loyalty that makes Americans willing to foot the bill. M. Lipsky makes the point that citizens' ideas about government are greatly shaped by their experiences at the "street level"; it is the teacher in the classroom, the policeman on the corner; the bureaucrat in the vehicle registration office who defines for most Americans what government really represents.[59] That experience can cut either way. Bad experiences with officious, indifferent, or inept street-level bureaucrats have almost certainly played a role in souring many Americans on the idea of government and made them more receptive to the antigovernment message of the broad privatization movement.

Despite the widespread sense that American schools are underperforming, however, public opinion surveys continue to show that most Americans have very positive attitudes toward the teachers their children have had and the community schools their children attend. Asked generally about public schools in the nation, only 24 percent of respondents to the 2002 Phi Delta Kappa/Gallup Poll gave them a grade of A or B. But 47 percent gave an A or B to schools in their own community, and 71 percent gave these grades to the school their own (older) child attended.[60] This suggests the possibility that it is felt experience with public schools that may account for the generalized "public school ideology" that Moe finds so paradoxical. In that case, privatized delivery of publicly funded education—by displacing the concrete emissary of government—might seriously attenuate the bonds of loyalty that emanate from people's street-level experience of schools to their more generalized support for public education that determines the political context. When families feel good about the schooling their children receive in a private school, will the fact that the price tag was borne by the public sector be enough to entice them to think of government as a source of bounty, or will the experience further erode any sense they might have that government plays a role in the betterment of their lives?

Adding to the risk that privatizing delivery could fuel a self-reinforcing disillusionment with government is the fact that citizens are often confused about whether service providers are part of the public or the nonprofit sector. Analyzing data on citizen satisfaction with social services, David Van Slyke and Christine Roch find that citizens frequently misidentify whether the providers they use are nonprofits and, more important, that there is a systematic bias in this misidentification process: "Citizens who are dissatisfied with services actually being provided by nonprofits are more likely to believe that the entity providing the service is a government agency."[61] In the complicated arena of contemporary public policy, where privatization efforts increasingly have blurred and muddied the boundaries among government, nonprofits, and corporate providers, even when holding performance constant the public sector is more likely to be blamed if the service is poor.

In addition to attenuating Americans' appreciation for the concept of public education, it is possible that privatizing delivery will further enhance the notion that education is primarily a private good, the cost of which families should be expected (and possibly required) to bear. Most existing school choice programs maintain the full public funding feature of conventional public education; that is to say, in charter schools and existing voucher programs participating schools must accept the government funding as payment in full; they cannot set a higher tuition that parents must pay out of their own pocket. From the standpoint of equity and public support for educational spending, this is an absolutely critical provision. If choice laws allow providers to charge tuition above and beyond the amount covered by public funding, schools will be free to use cost as a screen to ward off lower income families and thereby make it easier to maintain high test scores and sustain an air of exclusivity. Families with the capacity to pay will have less incentive to support per pupil levels of public funding, since their ability to maintain such enclave schools will depend on the gap between those levels and market rates at the better schools.

Some choice proponents are deeply committed to maintaining the full-funding feature, but that is not universally the case. Some, like Milton Friedman, oppose on principle and explicitly any limitation on families' right to invest as much as they wish in their education of their children. Others tactically accept such provisions because they are seen as politically necessary compromises to assuage concerns about equity that otherwise might undermine support for the choice plans they favor. It is an open question whether prohibitions on parental add-ons will prove sustainable—legally and politically. In a more privatized delivery environment, it is at least as likely that the norms and expectations associated with contemporary private schools (parents should be free to spend more if they like; schools should be free to charge more) will come to dominate the framing of the voucher issue as is the contrasting scenario: that the public ethos of full funding through general tax revenues will be carried over to schools that accept vouchers.

A Shift in the Institutional Environment

Privatization of education delivery could make the institutional environment less supportive of public authority in either of two ways. First, it could alter the principal-agent relationship between public officials charged with pursuing democratically defined collective interests and the private and semiprivate entities that deliver schooling. Second, it could move key decisions about education into arenas in which groups that favor a strong public system are fundamentally disadvantaged.

Policymakers always must depend on the behavior of others to ensure that their directives are carried out, but the nature of the principal-agent relationship is more problematic in some situations than others. Federal systems, for example, increase the number of decision points between policy and implementation, making it more likely that centrally generated objectives will be watered down, co-opted, or simply ignored.[62] Informational imbalances can allow agents to pursue their own interests, especially when service is delivered in multiple and relatively inaccessible sites and when the service recipients are somehow limited in their ability to evaluate quality or articulate concerns.

Compared to most other public policies, education has long been regarded to be especially loosely coupled due to traditions of localism and the technical challenges of monitoring what goes on behind thousands of closed classroom doors.[63] Moreover, compared to other functions—like paving roads, providing data services, and recycling—education is a service in which we hope to maximize multiple, somewhat vaguely defined, and not easily reconciled values, such as learning basic facts, honing critical facilities, nurturing confidence and self-esteem, learning to deal with others, and so on. Doing the "right thing" in education necessarily requires the exercise of judgment in concrete instances. Bureaucratic regulations, hierarchical authority, training and socialization of workers, and the like are tools that legislatures can use to increase the probabilities that the laws they enact will be carried out according to their vision. As J. D. Donahue notes, the argument in favor of relying on employees as distinct from contracted agents strengthens the more a task is uncertain, hard to measure, and difficult to change in midstream.[64]

The privatization of delivery is not necessarily incompatible with democratic accountability; when contract performance can be readily monitored and multiple providers exist, it is conceivable that private agents might be held more directly accountable than public employees protected by civil service or union provisions. But the loosely coupled nature of education, combined with the complexity of the values at stake and the vulnerabilities of children, make it perhaps the least readily adapted to a contracting regime.[65]

Nonincremental change in policy sometimes occurs when interest groups are able to shift decisionmaking from one institutional arena to another.[66] Different decisionmaking venues—for example, cities as opposed to states, courts as opposed to legislatures—have their own distinct sets of norms, processes, and structures affecting the probability of success. By redefining issues, groups sometimes succeed in shifting the decisionmaking responsibility to an agency or a level of government that is more favorable to them. Privatizing education delivery could shift decisionmaking into venues where decisional criteria disadvantage those favoring a high level of public investment in human capital and a strong pursuit of racial and socioeconomic equality while avoiding the complications arising from intermingling church and state.

For various historical reasons, large urban centers tend to be more responsive politically to the interests of groups—teachers' unions, civil rights organizations, Democrats—generally more likely to support high spending and public control over schools. Proposals to privatize education delivery often entail a simultaneous shift of decisionmaking and resource allocation from local jurisdictions to the state.[67] Without actually changing the array of interest groups engaged in the issue, a shift to a statewide decisionmaking arena may have the consequence of weakening the influence of these city-centered groups.[68]

Privatizing education delivery could also push a wider range of decisions into the courts, where precedent allocates very different rights and responsibilities to parties involved in private market exchanges than to those involved in relations between citizen and government. It is difficult to predict whether the courts will regard educational agents that mix elements of public and private—such as charter schools or private schools with large voucher enrollments—as analogous to public entities, private entities, or something in between. But to the extent the market analogy prevails, the reigning decisional criteria might be weighted more in favor of those claiming rights of property and privacy and less in favor of those asserting a collective interest exercised through the state. For example, to reduce inequities across schools some school districts have put limits on parent associations' ability to raise money to supplement regular operating budgets within their school; a limit on parents' right to make such donations may be less defensible within a more privatized delivery system. To reduce the risk that choice schools will select students with the most advantaged backgrounds and turn others away, most charter school laws currently require these schools to use a lottery to allocate scarce seats. The laws are typically less clear about the procedures charter school may use to weed out students after they have been in the schools; if families feel that their children have been thrown out of school or harshly disciplined for illegitimate reasons relating to bias or to a desire to improve school test scores, it is not yet clear whether courts will subject such practices to the same level of scrutiny that they apply to conventional public schools or will accord them the greater discretion that private schools enjoy.[69]

A Case for Cautious Optimism about Pragmatic Privatization in Education Delivery

There are powerful forces constraining change in the American system of public education, but these are not sufficient to ensure that incremental steps toward privatization will not ripple and spiral in ways that corrode basic institutions of democratic responsibility and government capacity to pursue the collective good. Those who see school choice as a pragmatic tool for making public education better serve public interests see the restraining factors as very powerful and the associated risks as highly speculative and easy to inoculate against. Those who see school choice as a wedge issue in a broader battle over the boundaries of public and private see the risks as huge and believe that those sincerely committed to a strong public education system have alternative options available, ones that place democratic mobilization, civic capacity, and efficacious government and not the market metaphor on center stage. Does looking at the issue in this manner simply etch the conflict in sharper terms? Or are there conditions under which we may look at the issue in a way that leads us toward productive common ground?

Most of those who have tried to stake out moderate positions on the choice issue emphasize the importance of program design. The devil is in the details, they observe, and go on to specify particular program provisions (such as prohibitions on "hate" teaching, maintenance of full funding, prohibitions against tuition add-ons, admission by lottery, required standardized testing, parent information centers). The analysis presented here takes a different tack. Program details as debated and even as legislated are important only to the degree that political processes are likely to hold them in place and ensure they are enforced. That, in turn, depends on the nature of political constituencies—mobilized and potentially mobilizable—and the institutional capacity of government to do what it sets out to do.

Figure 9-2 illustrates the competing theories about policy change that lie beneath the surface of much of the public debate. The distinctions rest on different notions of the source of policy change (does policy change in response to learning or to shifts in power?) and on the degree of change (incremental versus systemic) that the system typically allows. Proponents of pragmatic privatization argue that change tends to be incremental and can be fine-tuned as knowledge is accumulated. If policy tends to be incremental and steered by social learning, experimenting with privatized delivery is a low-risk enterprise with likely positive consequences. Although they disagree on many points of emphasis, members of the National Working Commission on Choice in K–12 Education generally agree on the desirability and viability of such a pragmatic, learning-based approach. Some expect that trials with choice will accumulate evidence of its advantages, which may eventually lead to much broader, systemic change. Others believe that the benefits will prove modest and restricted to particular situations, with costs in terms of equity and democratic control that will make large-scale adoption problematic. But all agree that we remain low on the social learning curve—there is much about school choice and its consequences that is not yet known—and all agree that it would be better to base policy on better information rather than ideological purity or political muscle alone.

But is pragmatic privatization (cell I in figure 9-2) a viable stopping point in the real world of politics, where the commitment to better information sometimes takes second place to the advancement of strategic interests? The volatility of the choice debate reflects the fact that advocates toward both extremes lack confidence that this is the case. Many committed proponents of systemic privatization believe that only large-scale interventions will make

Figure 9-2. *Alternative Models of Policy Change*

Source of change	Degree of change: *Incremental change*	Degree of change: *Systemic change*
Learning	I Pragmatic privatization	II Market superiority revealed
Power	III Pluralistic equilibrium; iron triangles	IV Public institutions undermined

a difference but that, once put into place, markets will be revealed to be consistently and dramatically superior to public bureaucracies in meeting human needs (cell II). They fear that their opponents will use the language of pragmatic privatization to whittle choice down to insignificance, with the ultimate goal being to protect a position in which public employee unions and other powerful interests in favor of public spending can reassert the status quo (cell III). Committed critics of privatization efforts also believe that power—not learning—is the real driver of change; they suspect that their opponents are using the language of pragmatic privatization to mask their real intentions and disarm critics. They worry that modest steps in that direction will shift power, ideas, and institutions in ways that will leave favored elite interests well equipped to thrive in marketized arenas but at the cost of systematically weakening public institutions and the nonmarket values they are depended upon to protect (cell IV).

It is relatively easy to pose pragmatic incrementalism as a normative model and to caricature those who favor other positions as ideologues, cynics, or dupes. But is the gradual, knowledge-based experimentation represented in cell I an accurate portrayal of how politics, policy, and change are likely to play out in the American context? Some who might prefer a pragmatic approach may nonetheless reject it as empirically naive. The belief that power will trump pragmatism may make a whole lot of sense if any of the following conditions apply:

—If public policy is generally driven by mobilized elites with a strong stake in one approach over another.

—If mass publics engage only episodically and then prove highly responsive to simple and universalistic claims ("markets are better than bureaucracies" or "democracy is better than profiteering").

—If our existing mixed system reflects a fragile set of compromises rather than a grounded solution with strong support of its own.

A critical question is whether a substantial and controlling constituency exists—or can be constructed—in support of pragmatic privatization. It makes a difference, in other words, whether the messy and incremental nature of our current system is simply a by-product of ongoing battles between evenly matched opponents or a center of gravity with coherence of its own. Can citizens and public officials be counted upon to rally affirmatively in support of so bland and unexciting a platform as mixed systems, selective and contingent experimentation, weighing the (always tentative) evidence, and balancing among values in tension? If so, it seems plausible that efforts to selectively expand and learn from privatization of school delivery could keep proponents of choice and proponents of a strong public sector working toward common interests instead of thrusting and parrying for competitive advantage. But let us be clear. Building, maintaining, and mobilizing coalitions of the reasonable is tough work. It is easier to rally small and intense groups with simple messages and ideologically laced appeals. In a context of public indifference, distraction, or lassitude, it is unlikely that a politics of pragmatism will hold sway. Thus the anxieties that fuel the volatile politics of school choice are likely to remain raw, and neither side in the polarized school choice battles is likely to cede ground in pursuit of common ground.

Notes

1. The American system was never as devoid of parental choice options as some analysts claim. Choice via residential location and private schools has always been available, and even within public systems selective options to move to alternative schools or to request a transfer based on particular family needs have existed in many districts for many decades; magnet schools began spreading widely and rapidly about three decades ago.

2. Clarence Stone and others, *Building Civic Capacity: Toward a New Politics of Urban School Reform* (University Press of Kansas, 2001).

3. David C. Berliner and Bruce J. Biddle, *The Manufactured Crisis* (New York: Longman, 1995); M. Lieberman, *Public Education: An Autopsy* (Harvard University Press, 1993); R. Rothstein, *The Way We Were?* (New York: Century Foundation, 1998).

4. National Working Commission on Choice in K–12 Education, *School Choice: Doing It the Right Way Makes a Difference* (Brown Center on Education Policy, Brookings, 2003).

5. Harvey Feigenbaum, Jeffrey R. Henig, and Chris Hamnett, *Shrinking the State: The Political Underpinnings of Privatization* (Cambridge University Press, 1998); Jeffrey R. Henig and others, "Privatization, Politics, and Urban Services: The Political Behavior of Charter Schools," *Journal of Urban Affairs* 25, no. 1 (2003): 37–54.

6. This public goods aspect derives from the fact that citizens who do not currently have school-age children nonetheless share in the benefits of having a more educated citizenry. Those spillover benefits may comprise such things as lower crime rates, a more educated and competitive national labor force, and a more discerning and involved electorate. Because of the free rider problem, a community of rational and self-interested individuals will tend to discount these public goods when assessing how much to voluntarily invest in education, since their own families will reap the benefits of others' expenditures whether or not they ante up themselves. All but the most extreme libertarians accept the need for mandatory taxation to address this dilemma. As Milton Friedman writes: "A stable and democratic society is impossible without a minimum degree of literacy and knowledge on the part of most citizens and without widespread acceptance of some common values. Education can contribute to both. In consequence, the gains from the education of a child accrue not only to the child but also to other members of society. The education of my child contributes to your welfare by promoting a stable and democratic society. It is not feasible to identify the particular individuals (or families) benefited and so to charge for the services rendered. There is therefore a significant 'neighborhood effect.'" See *Capitalism and Freedom* (University of Chicago Press, 1962), p. 82. Friedman does not argue that public funding levels should be determined solely by considerations of efficiency in providing public goods. He suggests that other values beyond efficiency—such as democratically defined commitments to certain levels of equity—might also legitimately come into play.

7. Ibid.

8. While typically favoring a light regulatory hand, they suggest that privatized delivery is compatible with a wide range of reasonable regulations that citizens might wish to impose. They expect privatization of delivery to lead to greater reliance on exit as a form of influence but typically see this as coming at the cost of bureaucratic rigidity, not democratic control.

9. Albert O. Hirschman, *Exit, Voice, and Loyalty: Responses to Decline in Firms, Organizations, and States* (Harvard University Press, 1970).

10. John E. Chubb and Terry M. Moe, *Politics, Markets, and America's Schools* (Brookings, 1990).

11. National Center for Education Statistics, *Mini-Digest of Educational Statistics, 2002* (U.S. Department of Education, 2003).

12. John F. Witte, "Choice and Control: An Analytical Overview," in *Choice and Control in American Education,* vol. 1, edited by W. H. Clune and John F. Witte (New York: Falmer, 1990).

13. Stacey Bielick and Christopher Chapman, *Trends in the Use of School Choice: 1993 to 1999* (Washington: National Center for Education Statistics, 2003). Notably, the most noticeable trend toward public school choice was among the lowest income families. Between 1993 and 1999 the percentage of students attending public assigned schools among households earning $10,000 or less declined from 83 to 74, and the percentage attending public chosen schools rose from 14 to 22.

14. RPP International, *The State of Charter Schools 2000: Fourth-Year Report* (Office of Education Research and Improvement, U.S. Department of Education, 2000); "Charter Schools Laws across the States: Ranking and Scorecard," 8th ed. (Washington: Center for Education Reform, 2004), available at www.edreform.com/_upload/charter_school_laws.pdf.

15. Ron C. Zimmer and others, *Private Giving to Public Schools and Districts in Los Angeles County: A Pilot Study* (Santa Monica, Calif.: RAND, 2001).

16. Jacques Steinberg, "Alumni to Give Brooklyn Tech Huge Donation," *New York Times,* March 20, 1998, p. A1; Patricia Troppe, "Private Funding for Public Education: A Local Response to State Actions?" (Public Policy Program, George Washington University).

17. The 1960s witnessed a movement toward alternative schools. During the 1970s and early 1980s, magnet schools came into fashion. The mid- to late-1980s saw the launching of additional public school choice options, such as cross-district open enrollment. Charter schools, as noted above, began spreading early in the 1990s.

18. Michael T. Hayes, *Incrementalism and Public Policy* (New York: Longman, 1992); Charles E. Lindblom and Edward J. Woodhouse, *The Policy-Making Process* (Upper Saddle River, N.J.: Prentice-Hall, 1993).

19. John D. Donahue, *The Privatization Phenomenon* (New York: Basic Books, 1989); Donald F. Kettl, *Sharing Power: Public Governance and Private Markets* (Brookings, 1993); Feigenbaum, Henig, and Hamnett, *Shrinking the State.*

20. Feigenbaum, Henig, and Hamnett, *Shrinking the State.*

21. Jeffrey R. Henig, "Privatization in the United States: Theory and Practice," *Political Science Quarterly* 104, no. 4 (1998–99): 649–70.

22. Frank R. Baumgartner and Bryan D. Jones, *Agendas and Instability in American Politics* (University of Chicago Press, 1993).

23. Feigenbaum, Henig, and Hamnett, *Shrinking the State.*

24. Peter Young, "Privatization around the World," in *Prospects for Privatization,* edited by Steve H. Hanke (New York: Academy of Political Science, 1987).

25. M. Victoria Murillo, "Political Bias in Policy Convergence: Privatization Choices in Latin America," *World Politics* (2002): 462.

26. Feigenbaum, Henig, and Hamnett, *Shrinking the State.*

27. Ibid., 51.

28. Ibid., 51.

29. Ibid., 52.

30. John W. Kingdon, *Agendas, Alternatives, and Public Policies* (Boston: Little, Brown, 1995).

31. Terry M. Moe, *Schools, Vouchers, and the American Public* (Brookings, 2001); Lowell C. Rose and Alec M. Gallup, "The 34th Annual Phi Delta Kappa/Gallup Poll of the Public's Attitudes toward the Public Schools," *Phi Delta Kappan,* September 2002, pp. 41–56.

32. Donald Kinder and Lynn Sanders, *Divided by Color: Racial Politics and Democratic Ideals* (University of Chicago Press, 1996).

33. The symbolism emanates from the history of school segregation and the role that school choice played as part of white efforts to evade or delay integration in the wake of the *Brown* decision; see Jeffrey R. Henig and others, *The Color of School Reform* (Princeton University Press, 1999). Lingering concerns that vouchers and choice might contribute to

resegregation have dogged the prochoice efforts, so signs that African Americans might themselves favor choice are taken by many to indicate that this framing of the issue is obsolete.

34. For the polls, see Moe, *Schools, Vouchers, and the American Public;* David A. Bositis, *2002 National Opinion Poll: Education* (Washington: Joint Center for Political and Economic Studies, 2002). Among supporting individuals are Polly Williams, Floyd Flake, and Howard Fuller; a notable supporting organization is the Black Alliance for Educational Opportunity.

35. Bositis, *2002 National Opinion Poll,* table 5.

36. Henig and others, *The Color of School Reform.*

37. On the stance of Chicago Latinos in relation to Mayor Daley's various school initiatives, see for example Dorothy Shipps, "Chicago: The National 'Model' Reexamined," in *Mayors in the Middle: Politics, Race, and Mayoral Control of Urban Schools,* edited by Jeffrey R. Henig and Wilbur C. Rich (Princeton University Press, 2004).

38. Alan M. Fisher, "Realignment of the Jewish Vote?" *Political Science Quarterly* 94, no. 1 (1998): 97–116; Geoffrey B. Levey, "Review Article: The Liberalism of American Jews: Has It Been Explained?" *British Journal of Political Science* 26 (1996): 369–401.

39. Peter Beinart, "The Rise of Jewish Schools," *Atlantic Monthly* 284 (1999): 21–22.

40. Marshall J. Breger and David M. Gordis, eds., *Vouchers for School Choice: Challenge or Opportunity? An American Jewish Reappraisal* (Brookline, Mass.: Wilstein Institute of Jewish Policy Studies, 1998).

41. Beinart, "The Rise of Jewish Schools."

42. "The reality is that many Jewish schools are struggling mightily—sometimes unsuccessfully—to meet skyrocketing budgets. Some of the most outstanding teachers are being driven away because paychecks are skimpy and late. Facilities are often inadequate, basic maintenance and repairs frequently neglected, educational materials in short supply, resource rooms and other special education services few and far between—all for a shortage of funds." David Zweibel, "Let's Stop Pretending," *Jewish Media Resources,* available at www.jewishmediaresources.com/article/300/ (2002).

43. Ibid.

44. U.S. Bureau of the Census, *Profile of General Demographic Characteristics: 2000 Data Set,* DP-1; *Census 2000 Summary File: 100 Percent Data,* SF 1.

45. Warren E. Oates, "The Effects of Property Taxes and Local Public Spending on Property Values: An Empirical Study of Tax Capitalization and the Tiebout Hypothesis," *Journal of Political Economy* 77, no. 6 (1969): 957–71.

46. Randall Reback, "Capitalization under Schools Choice Programs: Are the Winners Really Losers?" Occasional Paper 66 (New York: National Center for the Study of Privatization in Education, 2002), p. 25.

47. Eric Brunner and others, "Capitalization and the Voucher," *Journal of Urban Economics* 50, no. 3 (2001): 517–36. By the same reasoning, a shift from local property taxes to state taxes as the primary vehicle for funding schools could also undermine support for public spending on schools, as William A. Fischel argues did in fact happen in the aftermath of California's *Serrano* decision. *The Homevoter Hypothesis: How Home Values Influence Local Government Taxation, School Finance, and Land-Use Policies* (Harvard University Press, 2001).

48. Peter Bachrach, and Morton Baratz, "The Two Faces of Power," *American Political Science Review* 56 (1962): 947–52; Matthew A. Crenson, *The Unpolitics of Air Pollution* (Johns Hopkins University Press, 1971).

49. Bill Barket, "Is Edison Schools a Rule Breaker?" *Motley Fool,* May 2000, available at: www.fool.com/ portfolios/rulebreaker/2000/ rulebreaker000920.htm; Alex Molnar, "Calculating the Benefits and Costs of For-Profit Education," *Education Policy Analysis Archives* 9, no. 15 (2001).

50. Alex Molnar and others, *Profiles of For-Profit Education Management Companies, 2000–2001* (Milwaukee: Center for Educational Research, Analysis, and Innovation, 2001); Gerald W. Bracey, *The War against America's Public Schools: Privatizing Schools, Commercializing Education* (Boston: Allyn and Bacon, 2002); Katrina Bulkley, "Recentralizing Decentralization? Educational Management Organizations and Charter Schools' Educational Programs," Occasional Paper 60 (New York: National Center for the Study of Privatization in Education, 2002); Gary Miron and Christopher Nelson, *What's Public about Charter Schools? Lessons Learned about Choice and Accountability* (Thousand Oaks, Calif.: Corwin, 2002).

51. This work has not yet been published. As discussed below, the involvement of such organizations will not necessarily be translated into demands for more systemic privatization. The greater likelihood is that educational management organizations will lobby for higher expenditures, not lower ones. On the regulatory front, they are likely to weigh heaviest on the side of deregulation, although some larger organizations may selectively favor regulation as a vehicle to dampen the entry of new competitors.

52. Jeffrey R. Henig and others, "The Political Dynamics of State Charter School Policies," paper prepared for the annual meeting of the American Political Science Association, Boston, 2002.

53. Bachrach and Baratz, "Two Faces of Power"; Crenson, *Unpolitics of Air Pollution.*

54. Baumgartner and Jones, *Agendas and Instability in American Politics.*

55. Moe, *Schools, Vouchers, and the American Public.*

56. Ibid., p. 87.

57. Baumgartner and Jones, *Agendas and Instability in American Politics.*

58. Frederick M. Hess, "What Is a 'Public School'? Principles for a New Century," *Phi Delta Kappan* (February 2004): 433–40.

59. Michael Lipsky, *Street-Level Bureacracy: Dilemmas of the Individual in Public Services* (New York: Russell Sage, 1980).

60. Rose and Gallup, "The 34th Annual Phi Delta Kappa/Gallup Poll."

61. David M. Van Slyke and Christine H. Roch, "What Do They Know, and Whom Do They Hold Accountable? Citizens in the Government-Nonprofit Contracting Arrangement," *Journal of Public Administration Research and Theory* 14, no. 2 (2004): 204.

62. Martha Derthick, *New Towns In-town: Why a Federal Program Failed* (Washington: Urban Institute, 1972); Jeffrey Pressman and Aaron B. Wildavsky, *Implementation* (University of California Press, 1979).

63. Karl E. Weick, "Educational Organizations as Loosely Coupled Systems," *Administrative Science Quarterly* 21 (1976): 1–19. That the direct recipients are children, often regarded as unreliable reporters, exacerbates the problem.

64. Donahue, *Privatization Phenomenon.*

65. Marc Bendick Jr., "Privatizing the Delivery of Social Welfare Services: An Idea to Be Taken Seriously," in *Privatization and the Welfare State,* edited by Sheila Kamerman and Alfred J. Kahn (Princeton University Press, 1989).

66. Baumgartner and Jones, *Agendas and Instability in American Politics.*

67. The causal connections here are difficult to map. It is possible that states take the lead on privatizing delivery because the political constellation within central cities is too inhospitable. But there also is a logical link distinct from practical politics: to the extent that choice plans are based on a strong theoretical claim about the importance of consumer mobility, the market metaphor may encourage a disregard of local jurisdictional boundaries.

68. This observation holds whether the movement toward a stronger state role is instigated in the name of choice, fiscal equity, or standards and accountability. Thanks to Tom Loveless for reminding me to make this point.

69. For a related discussion of this issue as applied to the rights of students with disabilities, see Laura F. Rothstein, "School Choice and Students with Disabilities," in *School Choice and Social Controversy,* edited by Stephen D. Sugarman and Frank R. Kemerer (Brookings, 1999).

10

School Choice and Civic Values

Patrick J. Wolf

For centuries scholars and policymakers have debated the question of whether assigned government-run public schools have a comparative advantage over public schools of choice and private schools in steeping their charges in the civic values necessary for democratic citizenship. The theoretical argument in favor of such an advantage is both intuitive and popular. Political philosophers from Benjamin Rush to John Dewey, as well as the more contemporary Benjamin Barber, Amy Guttman, Eamonn Callan, and Stephen Macedo, argue that neighborhood public schools are ideally if not uniquely situated to inculcate civic values in American students.[1] As free government schools, open to all on equal terms, public schools make an important statement about equality, a fundamental democratic value. Because all students in a particular community traditionally are assigned to a specific school, public schools are "common schools," where children from diverse backgrounds gather to learn about social cooperation and the toleration of differences. Finally, public schools are, well, public, and the government operation and political control of them ensures that society's interests in promoting civic values are advanced. The former education secretary Richard Riley aptly captures this argument when he says that civic values are "conveyed not only through what is taught in the classroom, but by the very experience of attending [a public] school with a diverse mix of students."[2]

Supporters of school choice and of the option of private schooling are not persuaded by these arguments. They draw upon the theories of Thomas Paine, Alexis de Tocqueville, and John Stuart Mill in claiming that parentally chosen public schools and even private schools are laboratories of democracy as much as, and perhaps even more than, traditional public schools.[3] Charles Glenn argues that neighborhood public schools are not actually open to all and that the common school vision is largely a myth.[4] The geographic boundaries that determine public school assignment transform neighborhoods into walled communities, where entry into quality public schools comes at the cost of a residence in the neighborhood—a cost that is often prohibitive for families of modest means. Jay Greene and Nicole Mellow argue that the walled communities created by neighborhood assignment to public schools results in the exact opposite of what public school advocates seek: traditional public schools are less likely to contain a diverse mix of students than are schools of choice, and within schools, students of different racial backgrounds are more likely to segregate themselves by race if they have been assigned to their school.[5] As communitarians such as Anthony Bryk and libertarians such as Stephen Gilles argue, schools of choice are more likely than assigned schools to be communities of equality and social cooperation because they are freely chosen.[6] Their writings provoke the question, How could having the government tell students where they can and cannot go to school possibly be the first step in preparing them for autonomous citizenship in a democracy?

This theoretical argument remains largely unresolved at least partly because neither side has had recourse to much empirical evidence to support their claims. As Macedo states, "The comparative success of different types of schools at teaching civic values is not much studied."[7] That probably was true at the time of his writing. However, since that time a number of rigorous empirical studies of the effects of school choice on civic values have been published as articles or research reports. It is time to take stock of the evidentiary record surrounding the question of whether or not assigned public schooling better prepares students for their responsibilities as democratic citizens. That is my purpose here.

Empirical Studies of the Effects of Choice on Civic Values

For this review, I examine the results of twenty quantitative studies regarding the effects of school choice on seven civic values that relate to the capacity of individuals to perform as effective citizens in our representative democracy. The values, in order from the most studied to the least studied, are

—Political tolerance: the willingness to extend the full slate of civil liberties even to people and groups that one dislikes,

—Voluntarism: the contribution of one's time, without material compensation, to support the activities of a charity or community organization,

—Political knowledge: a basic understanding of the U.S. political system and an awareness of current events and political leaders,

—Social capital: a close connection with one's community via social networks, group norms, and "cooperation for mutual benefit,"[8]

—Political participation: the exercise of a number of citizenship responsibilities, including voting, attending public meetings, and contacting government representatives,

—Civic skills: experience in and confidence with activities such as public speaking and letter writing that can be used to influence the political process, and

—Patriotism: a visceral positive connection to one's country and respect for its national symbols and rituals.

The figures in this chapter summarize the distribution of findings from the twenty empirical studies of the effects of private schooling (most of the studies) or the practice of public school choice on the civic values of the students or parents in private or choice schools relative to those of comparable students or parents in assigned public schools. A complete list of the studies is provided in the chapter appendix, along with summaries of the findings.

A finding is categorized as negative in the figures if the evidence suggests that private schooling or the exercise of choice produced a statistically significant (at the 90 percent confidence level or better) reduction in the realization of the particular civic value regardless of the type of school chosen. A finding is classified as contingently negative if a particular class of choice school, but not other classes, generates the significant negative effect. Studies that find no significant effect of private schooling or choice on a particular civic value are classified as neutral. Studies that identify a statistically significant positive effect of school choice—but only of a specific type of choice school—on a civic value are categorized as contingently positive. Finally, studies that find choice to enhance a civic value, regardless of the type of school chosen, are listed as positive.

Each finding summarized in the figures is taken from a large-sample statistical analysis of the effect of school choice or private schooling on one or more civic values. Nevertheless, not all studies reviewed here are equally rigorous in their design and execution. In education studies perhaps the greatest threat to the validity of an analysis is selection bias. Relatively advantaged parents tend to place their children in more effective educational environments. Often, though by no means exclusively, those environments are private schools. If one merely compares the civic values of parents or students in public versus private schools, one might improperly attribute to private schooling influences that actually are the result of more fundamental familial advantages. To be considered in this review, a study had to employ some acceptable technique to rule out familial advantage as a cause of the civic values effects that were uncovered.

Four different techniques were employed in the studies reviewed here to address problems of selection bias. One was to randomly assign participants to the treatment group (for example, "offered private school scholarship") or the control group ("not offered scholarship") before assessing impacts. Such randomized field trials are often considered the gold standard of educational research, since the randomization process ensures that the two comparison groups are similar, on average, in all respects except for the application of the treatment of private schooling.[9] For randomized field trials to live up to their reputation, however, several conditions must be in place:

—A large number of subjects must participate in the study,

—High percentages of the treatment group must actually avail themselves of the treatment,

—Low percentages (ideally, none) of the control group must obtain the treatment on their own, and

—A large and representative sample of the treatment and control group must return for evaluation.

The randomized field trials reviewed here vary somewhat in the extent to which these conditions obtained.

Absent experimental designs, some research summarized here employed a matching technique, an instrumental variable technique, or both techniques to control for possible selection bias. Under the matching approach, the school districts or schools whose populations are to be compared are first matched on important characteristics, such as race and income demographics, before data are collected. Instrumental variable analysis, in contrast, is a technique employed after data collection to purge data of possible selection bias by statistically modeling the selection process that is suspected of producing the bias. To be successful in properly correcting for selection bias, the instrumental variable used must be highly correlated with the biased condition (such as private schooling) but uncorrelated with the outcome in the analysis (such as a particular civic value). Thus the studies that employ this strategy and a matching strategy to control for selection bias were evaluated based upon the effectiveness of the instruments and matching criteria that were used.

In the figures in this chapter, findings that were produced via studies that used random assignment, matching, or instrumental variable analysis are distinguished by darker shading in the bars. This is to distinguish them from findings drawn from observational studies that used the most common and straightforward method to control for possible selection bias: including control variables in multivariate regression models. Certain factors, such as race, income, parental education, and urban residence, are likely associated with both private schooling and levels of civic values. These factors are prime candidates to produce selection bias in any analysis of the effects of private schooling on civic outcomes unless their effects are captured in the analysis. Studies that rely upon control variables to avoid selection bias were evaluated on the extent to which the particular set of controls encompassed all of the likely factors that otherwise might bias the results. Still, these studies as a group are distinguished from the experimental, matching, and instrumental variables studies in the figures because control variables, by their very nature, are only able to control for sources of bias that are observable and have been measured.

Most of the studies that met the methodological standards for inclusion in the analysis focus on students in private schools. Only three of the twenty studies present results for students in charter or magnet schools. This circumstance is somewhat surprising, as magnet schools are often justified as instruments for promoting greater cohesion among students of various racial backgrounds in a given community, and empirical studies of magnet schools tend to focus upon the effects on minority group isolation and student test scores.[10] Aside from David Campbell's study of the National Household Education Survey (included in this analysis), I am not aware of any other study that takes the additional step of determining if the intermediate effects of magnet schools on integration and achievement translate into higher levels of civic values for their students. Charter schools are sufficiently new to the educational scene that large *N* studies of their effects on civic values have yet to establish a significant presence in the literature. Therefore, the results described below primarily map out the effects of private schooling on civic values.

Figure 10-1 presents the distribution of findings regarding the effects of school choice on all seven civic values. The forty-eight results of the twenty studies suggest that the general effect of private schooling or school choice on civic values trends neutral-to-positive. Only three negative findings are

Figure 10-1. *Distribution of Findings on All Civic Values*

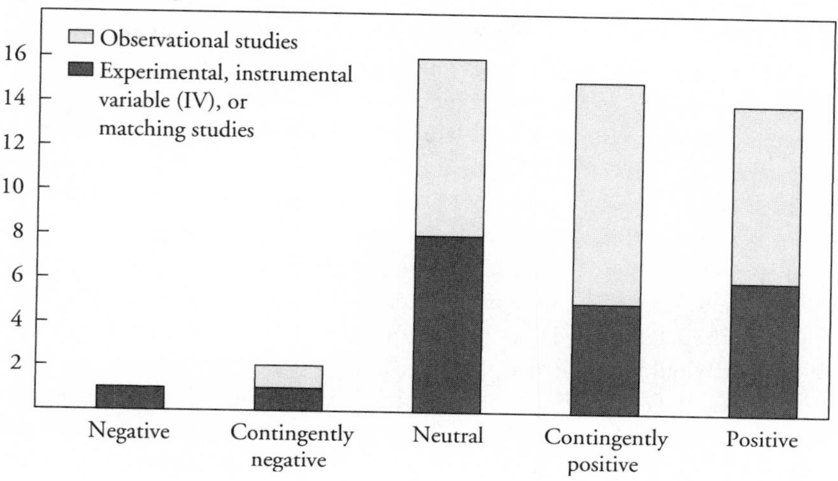

reported in the studies, and two of those are from merely observational studies. Sixteen neutral results appear in the studies, indicating that school choice neither increased nor decreased the civic values of students. Half of the neutral findings are from studies that went beyond observational research methods to mitigate possible selection bias problems. Fifteen findings are contingently positive, suggesting that specific types of choice schools outperform assigned public schools in promoting civic values or that particular groups experience increases in civic values when they exercise school choice. Ten of the fifteen contingently positive findings are from merely observational studies. Finally, fourteen findings indicate generally positive effects of school choice or private schooling on civic values. Six of the fourteen generally positive results are from studies that employed an analytic technique to address selection bias problems. As a whole, these forty-eight findings suggest that the effects of school choice on civic values tend, in almost all cases, to be either positive or nil.

What specific civic values appear to be most affected by school choice programs? How rigorous are the studies that produced this surprising distribution of findings regarding school choice and civic values? We now consider these important questions in the context of a critical methodological review of these provocative findings.

Studies of Political Tolerance

Of the important civic values considered here, the effect of school choice on the willingness of people to extend constitutional rights to disliked political groups has been studied the most. The popularity of studying political tolerance is partly due to its importance as a civic value and partly because researchers have developed a reliable protocol for measuring a person's political tolerance.[11] Respondents are first asked to either think of their least-liked political group or select one from a list (which tends to include the Ku Klux Klan, Nazis, Communists, prolife groups, prochoice groups, civil rights groups, and the religious Right). Respondents then are asked if they agree or disagree (and how strongly) with a series of questions about extending legal rights to their least-liked group. The questions generally ask whether the respondent would permit members of the disliked group to exercise constitutional rights such as making a public speech, running for political office, and teaching in the public schools. Responses are aggregated into a tolerance scale, which becomes the dependent variable for the exploration of what factors explain variation in political tolerance.

With one exception, the eighteen findings regarding the effect of school choice on political tolerance are confined to the neutral-to-positive range (figure 10-2). Five empirical studies conclude that private schooling has a positive effect on political tolerance, regardless of the type of private school attended. Jay Greene, Joseph Giammo, and Nicole Mellow studied the effects of private schooling on the political tolerance specifically of Latinos.[12] The authors drew upon the Latino National Political Survey, a nationally representative sample of over 3,400 ethnic Latinos who were interviewed in 1989 regarding a number of factors, including their willingness to tolerate disliked political groups. Specifically, they were asked to choose their least-liked group from a standard list and then were asked if they would permit members of that group to stage a public rally, hold public office, or teach in the public schools.

Respondents also were asked how many years of their education occurred in private schools in the United States. Controlling for country of origin, parental education, gender, age, years of residence in the United States, income, and the respondent's education, the authors find that Latinos who received more of their education in U.S. private schools tend to display slightly higher levels of political tolerance. The independent effect of twelve years of private schooling on political tolerance is estimated to be 0.2 of a standard deviation, a modest effect, which is statistically significant beyond

Figure 10-2. *Distribution of Findings on Political Tolerance*

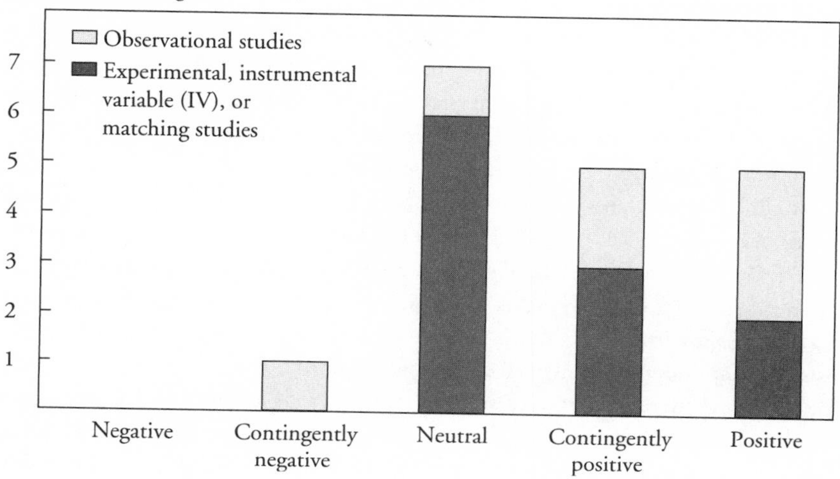

the 95 percent confidence interval. Two possible shortcomings in this analysis are that a few potential confounding factors, such as political ideology, are omitted from the analytic models and that the models themselves explain only 2 percent of the variation in the political tolerance scale scores. Also, missing data limit the analysis to fewer than 2,000 of the respondents in the sample.

Patrick Wolf, Paul Peterson, and Martin West used an abridged version of the political tolerance scale to study the effect of switching to a private school on the tolerance of low-income middle school students in Washington, D.C.[13] They surveyed students regarding whether they definitely would permit people whose views they opposed to, one, give a speech in their community; two, live in their neighborhood; and three, run for president. The students in the private school treatment group are more likely to give the tolerant response to all three questions than are members of the public school control group. The size of the differences ranges from 16 percent for giving a speech to 20 percent for living in their community, and all are statistically significant at least at the 90 percent confidence level. The strength of this study is that the students were randomly assigned to treatment and control groups two years earlier. Thus there was no need to control for potentially confounding factors in the analysis. The shortcomings of this study include the sample size, which was only around 350 respondents for each question, the abbreviated version of the tolerance protocol employed, and the fact that only 47 percent of the treatment group actually attended private schools and only 50 percent of the original study participants attended the second-year data collection sessions.

David Campbell confirms the results of the Wolf, Peterson, and West experiment in his reanalysis of data collected for an earlier evaluation of the Children's Scholarship Fund's national, privately funded, school voucher program.[14] Campbell is able to include some observations that had been excluded from the original analysis and to thereby obtain clearer results. Vouchers were awarded to participants by lottery, permitting evaluators to conduct a randomized field trial of their effects. The same three-point political scale used in the Wolf, Peterson, and West experiment was employed here; however, the survey was administered by phone instead of in a more controlled environment. In his examination of the evidence from 461 to 474 survey respondents, Campbell finds that, after one year, students who used a voucher to switch to private schools score 0.8 of a point to 1.0 full point higher on the tolerance scale than do comparable students who remained in public schools. This represents a political tolerance gain of 27–33 percent, which is statistically significant beyond the 95 percent confidence level. Campbell's analysis shares most of the strengths and weaknesses of the Wolf, Peterson, and West randomized field trial of vouchers in Washington. The strengths of the Campbell study are the random assignment of students to treatment and control groups and the national scope of the study. Its shortcomings include a low rate of treatment use (29 percent) and only a moderate rate of survey response (46 percent).

Wolf and other colleagues surveyed college students in Texas regarding their educational backgrounds and levels of political tolerance.[15] Nearly one thousand students at six Texas colleges and universities completed the survey, which used the complete protocol to gauge their levels of political tolerance. Controlling for over twenty factors that otherwise might confound the analysis, including the respondents' political ideology and the extent to which they felt threatened by their least-liked group, the authors find that more private schooling is associated with higher levels of political tolerance, all else being equal. Although the positive effect of private schooling on tolerance appears to be strongest for students who had attended secular private schools, even the students who had received all of their K–12 education in religious schools demonstrated higher average tolerance levels than comparable students from public school backgrounds.

The positive effect of receiving all of one's prior education in private secular schools on political tolerance is nearly one-half standard deviation and is statistically significant beyond the 95 percent confidence level. The positive effect of receiving all of one's prior education in private religious schools on political tolerance is nearly one-third standard deviation and is statistically significant beyond the 90 percent confidence level. The strengths of this study include the fact that it used the full political tolerance measurement protocol, employed a sample drawn from a state that is sometimes maligned for having intolerant religious schools, and included a full slate of control variables in the analytic model. The main shortcomings of the study are, one, the limited ability to generalize the results to young adults who do not attend college or to college students in states other than Texas and, two, the fact that self-selection cannot be ruled out entirely as a contributor to the reported private schooling advantage.

Finally, in an analysis of the 1996 National Household Education Survey, Richard Niemi, Mary Hepburn, and Chris Chapman report positive results regarding private schooling and political tolerance.[16] The survey contains the complete results of interviews with a random sample of nearly 4,000 high school students and their parents across the United States. Controlling for an impressive array of background characteristics, including parents' level of political tolerance, these researchers find that high school students in private schools are more likely to respond that their school library collection ought to include "controversial" books than are comparable students in public schools. Attending a private school is only slightly less important in explaining political tolerance than is having tolerant parents. The result is statistically significant beyond the 95 percent confidence level. The main advantages of this analysis are the size and scope of the National Household Education Survey and the solid control variables used. The main disadvantages are that the full tolerance measurement protocol was not employed and that private schooling has no clear effect on student responses to the second tolerance question regarding whether people should be allowed to speak out against religion and churches—a particularly tough tolerance test for students attending religious schools.

A stratified sample of eighth-grade students in New York City and in Dallas–Fort Worth produced two analyses that conclude that certain types of private school have a positive effect on political tolerance. Public, private religious, and private secular schools in both cities were matched on the racial characteristics of their student populations. Then, all eighth graders in the matched schools were surveyed regarding their demographic backgrounds and attitudes toward politically controversial groups. The complete standard tolerance measurement protocol was used. In an examination of the results from over 900 students surveyed in New York City, Wolf and his colleagues find that students in private secular schools scored an average of one-quarter standard deviation higher in tolerance than students in public schools, a difference that is statistically significant beyond the 99 percent confidence level.[17] They find no significant difference between the tolerance levels of students in private religious schools and the students in public schools. The analysis controlled for gender, race, academic performance, the extent to which students discussed politics at home, and the extent to which they felt threatened by their least-liked group. In a further analysis, the researchers find that schools in all of the sectors that encourage student government and organized community events at the school tend to produce students who are more politically tolerant, suggesting that the school-based modeling of democratic processes enhances civic values like tolerance. The main shortcoming of the study is the absence of a control variable for family income.

R. Kenneth Godwin, Carrie Ausbrooks, and Valerie Martinez further analyzed the complete set of over 2,000 eighth-grade respondents in both New York City and Dallas–Fort Worth.[18] They find that students at private secular and nonevangelical religious private schools indicate significantly greater support than public school students for democratic norms in the abstract, whereas students in evangelical private schools demonstrate a level of support for democratic norms that is indistinguishable from the level for public school students. When asked to apply democratic values to the case of tolerating their least-liked groups, the average responses of students in all four types of school (public, private secular, private evangelical, and private nonevangelical) are similar. The researchers also note that students in evangelical private schools (all in Texas) are much less likely to choose a racist group as their least-liked political group than are students in the other types of school. The strengths of this study are that it draws upon data from two very different locales and employs instrumental variable analysis to adjust for possible selection bias in the samples. The shortcoming of this study is that the instrumental factors used in the correction are quite weak, meaning that they may merely introduce noise into the analysis, blurring real distinctions between the outcomes in the various school sectors.

Following the lead of Niemi and his colleagues, Campbell drew upon the 1996 National Household Education Survey to study the effects of various types of private school on political tolerance.[19] Campbell's analysis controlled for about thirty possible confounding factors regarding the student, the student's family, and the school attended. He concludes that private secular and Catholic schools engender somewhat higher levels of political tolerance than do public schools. The advantage of private secular schools in this regard is particularly strong and statistically significant beyond the 99 percent confidence level. However, non-Catholic religious schools (such as evangelical Christian schools) actually appeared to be significantly (beyond the 95 percent confidence level) worse than public schools in inculcating political tolerance in their students. The strengths of this study are the size and national scope of the sample, the opportunity (because of size) to disaggregate private school students into meaningful subcategories, and the extensive set of control variables employed. By disaggregating the private school variable, Campbell was able to uncover why Niemi and colleagues' earlier results are ambiguous regarding the "free speech against religion" measure of tolerance. The answer is that the opposition to such a principle engendered by evangelical Christian schools partially cancels out support for it by the Catholic and private secular educational experience.

Campbell also collected original data on the civic attitudes of students in traditional public, public charter, private secular, and Catholic junior high and high schools in Massachusetts.[20] His stratified sampling method was designed to include a significant number of responses from students in high-performing, average-performing, and low-performing traditional public schools to compare with the results from three types of choice school (public charter, private secular, and Catholic). Since both schools and students ultimately self-selected into the sample, there is a strong likelihood that his sample is not representative of all such students in Massachusetts, a point that Campbell admits. The selectivity of the sample is particularly high for the traditional public school students in his sample, since they represent less than 12 percent of their respective student bodies. The response rates for the students at public charter, private secular, and Catholic schools are far higher: 41 percent, 45 percent, and 42 percent, respectively. Thus the selection bias in Campbell's sample likely biases comparisons in favor of traditional public schools, which selected only their most cooperative students to participate in the study.

In spite of those conditions, Campbell uncovers results from his analysis of 1,606 survey respondents suggesting a contingent school choice tolerance advantage. Controlling for parental voluntarism, parental education, student's age, student's ethnicity (that is, whether or not Hispanic), student's grades, and frequency of church attendance, Campbell finds that students at secular private schools are significantly more politically tolerant than are the students in traditional public schools. All things equal, the students in public charter and Catholic schools do not differ significantly from the traditional public school students in political tolerance levels. High-, average-, and low-performing public schools do not differ from each other in the average levels of tolerance of their students. As with the previous studies that drew upon the National Household Education Survey, a significantly abridged version of the tolerance protocol was used, focused exclusively on controversial library books and speech critical of religion.

Jay Greene, Nicole Mellow, and Joseph Giammo examined the results of a 1997 survey of the political tolerance of adults in Texas.[21] The poll of a randomly selected sample of 1,000 Texans is administered annually by the University of Texas and relies upon an abbreviated version of the political tolerance index described above. The researchers controlled for demographic factors such as gender, age, race, residential location (urban or nonurban), residential mobility, religion, and income. They also controlled for the degree to which respondents disliked their least-liked group and the extent to which they felt threatened by it. Greene and his colleagues found the only positive effect of private schooling on tolerance (an increase of nearly one-quarter standard deviation) among the group of respondents who had attended both public and private schools. Texans who had received their entire education in private schools were no more (or less) politically tolerant than Texans who had received their entire education in public schools. The strengths of this study are the fact that respondents were selected randomly and that a rather extensive set of appropriate control variables was employed. The weaknesses are the difficulty in generalizing beyond Texas and the fact that the treatment of private schooling had its greatest effect when tempered by some public schooling, a curious but not inexplicable result.

Finally, the evaluations of three additional randomized field trials of school vouchers include an abridged version of the tolerance index in their surveys of middle school students (grades four through nine). Like the studies of Washington voucher students after two years and the national Children's Scholarship Fund participants described above, the programs that were studied all assigned vouchers to a low-income population of students at random, allowing some to switch from public to private schools. Unlike the second-year Washington evaluation and Campbell's reanalysis of the scholarship fund data, which both find higher levels of tolerance among voucher users, the evaluations of the Washington program after three years, a Dayton program after two years, and a San Francisco program after two years uncover no significant differences in the level of political tolerance between voucher users and the randomly generated control group.[22] The random assignment of participants to the private and public school conditions is a clear strength of

Figure 10-3. *Distribution of Findings on Voluntarism*

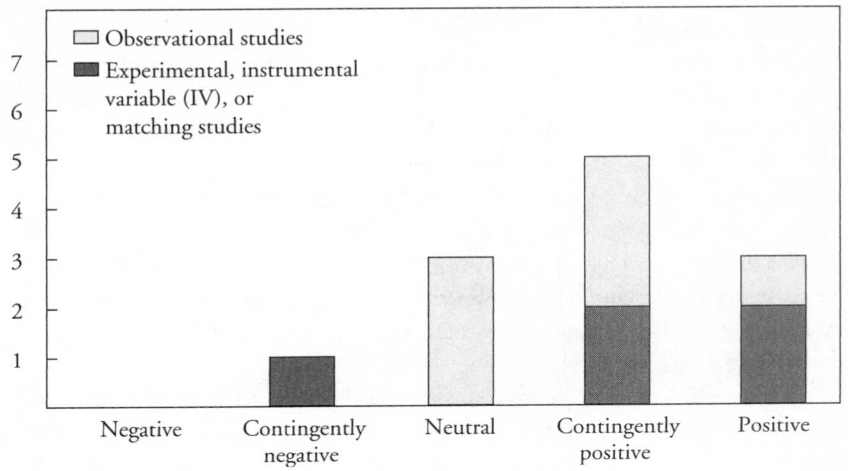

these studies. However, the sample sizes in each individual study were relatively small (200–900), and the students surveyed may have been too young to produce a reliable assessment of political tolerance. Combined with modest voucher usage rates and study response rates that hovered around 50 percent, the resulting noise in the data may explain why no significant differences in tolerance levels are identified in these experiments.

Studies of Voluntarism

Eight empirical studies generate twelve results regarding the extent to which private schooling or school choice affects the likelihood that students or parents will volunteer their time in community enterprises (figure 10-3). As with the distribution of political tolerance results, with one exception, the school choice effects on voluntarism range from neutral to positive. Jay Greene examined the information about voluntary activity among twelfth-grade students in public and private schools collected by the U.S. Department of Education via the 1992 National Education Longitudinal Study.[23] Controlling for students' socioeconomic status, race, and the racial composition of their classroom, Greene finds that students in private schools are 20 percent more likely to have volunteered their services in the past two years than are students in public schools, a difference statistically significant beyond the 99 percent confidence level. He finds a similarly large positive effect of private schooling on the percentage of students who say they volunteer every week and a somewhat smaller (but still statistically significant) positive impact on student opinions that it is very important to volunteer in one's community.

The National Education Longitudinal Study is a highly regarded survey, and its national scope is a clear strength of the Greene study. However, since the survey provides information about private and public schools as they existed in 1992, the data may be somewhat outdated. The importance of service learning has been stressed in public schools recently, raising the possibility that newer surveys might reveal a shrinking or even elimination of the private school advantage in promoting voluntarism present in the 1992 data. Also, relatively few control variables were used in the analysis, raising the possibility that confounding factors (such as urban residence) might be biasing the results.

R. Kenneth Godwin and Frank Kemerer report the results of a successful attempt to replicate Greene's voluntarism findings, using the sample of 2,000 eighth graders in New York City and Dallas–Fort Worth mentioned previously.[24] Employing a dual strategy of matching schools on student demographics and instrumental variable estimation to correct for possible selection bias, they find that private school students are 21 percent more likely to volunteer in their community than are comparable public school students, virtually identical to the private school advantage that Greene uncovered. They further discovered that private school students report volunteering an average of 50 percent more hours a week than their public school peers. Again, the main shortcoming of this study is the absence of a family income control variable.

Mark Schneider and his colleagues studied the effects of school choice on the likelihood of parents volunteering in New York City and the New Jersey suburbs.[25] The researchers matched New York's District 4, a hotbed of public school choice options, with the demographically similar District 1, which does not allow school choice. They also compared a sample of parents in Montclair, N.J., which actually requires all parents to choose their child's public school, with a sample from Morristown, N.J., which they argue is similar in all relevant respects except that it does not permit school choice. In their sample of 1,200 respondents they find that parents in school choice districts are about 6 percent more likely to volunteer than are comparable parents in nonchoice districts. The difference is statistically significant at the 95 percent confidence level using the less stringent one-tailed test. To correct for selection bias not controlled for by the matching, the researchers used instrumental variable analysis. However, their instrumental variables—

parental opinions about whether or not their child's school is diverse or espouses certain values—are questionable, since they are likely associated with the outcome (volunteering) that they are explaining. Nevertheless, this study was published in the flagship political science journal, *American Political Science Review*.

Employing a matching protocol similar to that of Schneider and colleagues as well as individual-level demographic control variables, Wolf and his colleagues find that private schooling promotes voluntary activity among eighth-grade students in New York City but only if they attend religious private schools.[26] In the most complete analytic model that they estimate, students in private secular schools are nearly 17 percent *less* likely to volunteer than are their public school peers, a difference statistically significant beyond the 95 percent confidence level. However, students in private religious schools are 23 percent *more* likely to volunteer than are their public school counterparts, an effect significant beyond the 99 percent confidence level. As with the study of political tolerance among eighth-grade students in New York, their analysis finds that schools in all sectors that encourage student participation in decisionmaking significantly enhance voluntarism among their student bodies. The primary weaknesses in this study are the imprecise nature of the matching protocol, which matched schools within the various sectors that fall within a racial demographic range, and limitation in the ability to generalize the results beyond New York City.

In their analysis of the 1996 National Household Education Survey, Niemi, Hepburn, and Chapman partially confirm the results reported in Wolf and others.[27] Controlling for nine variables, including whether or not the student's parents volunteer, they find that high school students in private religious schools are much more likely to volunteer than are comparable students in public schools. The only variable more closely associated with voluntarism than religious schooling is whether or not the school arranges voluntary activities for its students. Unlike Wolf and others, they uncover no significant differences in the rates of volunteering for students in private secular schools compared with their public school peers. Campbell confirms Niemi, Hepburn, and Chapman's results in his follow-up analysis of the 1996 survey.[28] The main advantage of these two analyses is the fact that the survey is a large, nationally representative survey.

Campbell further suggests that charter schools in Massachusetts promote voluntarism largely by making it mandatory.[29] Controlling for parental voluntarism, parent's education, student's age, student's ethnicity (whether or not Hispanic), and student's grades, he finds that students in the charter schools in his sample are more likely to volunteer than are students in high-performing public schools, even though the demographics of the charter population would predict a voluntarism rate 13 percent less than the high-performing public school average. As mentioned above, Campbell's original data for this study are not necessarily representative of the student population in Massachusetts, and thus the conclusions drawn from them should be treated as suggestive.

Christian Smith and David Sikkink analyzed an even larger data set, the 9,393 parental responses to the 1996 National Household Education Survey.[30] Controlling for income, education, age, race, family structure, region, and weekly work hours, the authors find that parents of students in religious private schools or who homeschool their children are significantly more likely to volunteer in their communities. Of the many subgroups examined in this particularly rich database, only the parents of students in secular private schools fail to demonstrate a voluntarism advantage relative to public school parents. The researchers do not specify the levels of statistical significance obtained by their subgroup differences and may not have included all relevant control variables. Still, the size and scope of their analysis is impressive.

Studies of Political Knowledge

For democracy to work effectively, citizens must be reasonably well informed about the issues and choices that exist in the political realm.[31] Five studies produce six findings regarding the effect of school choice on political knowledge (figure 10-4). Godwin and Kemerer discuss the results of an unpublished study of the effects of private schooling on the political knowledge of over 2,000 eighth-grade students in New York City and Dallas–Fort Worth.[32] Using race, parent education, family size, self-esteem, and several interactions of these factors as instruments to control for selection bias, Godwin and his colleagues determine that private schooling overall modestly improves student levels of political knowledge.[33] Controlling for seven important background factors, they find that attending a private school increases a student's performance on a six-question civics quiz by an average of 0.3, statistically significant beyond the 99 percent confidence level. In a separate estimation on the responses only of the Dallas–Fort Worth students, Godwin and colleagues conclude that evangelical Christian schooling specifically exerts a powerful positive effect on political knowledge, increasing the quiz score by an average of 1.8 points, all else being equal. The main strength of this study is the use of both matching and instrumental variable techniques to control for selection bias. The primary weaknesses are the limited set of control variables in the regressions and the challenges to generalizing beyond the two arguably unique metropolitan areas studied.

Figure 10-4. *Distribution of Findings on Political Knowledge*

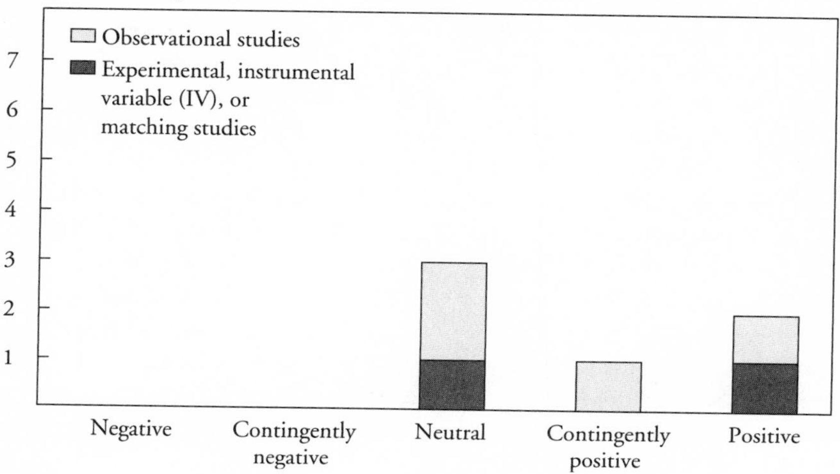

Niemi, Hepburn, and Chapman include an estimation of the causes of political knowledge in their analysis of the 1996 National Household Education Survey described above.[34] In a regression that includes seventeen important explanatory variables, they find that high school students in private schools score somewhat higher then their public school peers on a five-question civics quiz. Although substantively modest, the private schooling effect is statistically significant.

Campbell, in his analysis of the 1996 National Household Education Survey, finds that students who attend Catholic schools score significantly higher on an index of political knowledge than do comparable students in assigned public schools.[35] The Catholic school advantage in conveying political knowledge to students is statistically significant beyond the 99 percent confidence level. Campbell uncovers no significant difference in political knowledge levels between students in assigned public schools and comparable students in chosen public schools or non-Catholic private schools.

In the randomized field trial evaluation of the Children's Scholarship Fund program, Paul Peterson and David Campbell find no significant differences in average political knowledge levels between the users of the fund's vouchers and comparable students in public schools. Analyzing the U.S. Department of Education's High School and Beyond data set, James Coleman and Thomas Hoffer similarly uncover no significant difference between public school and Catholic school students on their levels of political knowledge.[36]

Studies of Social Capital

Work by the Harvard political scientist Robert Putnam has revived interest in the concept of social capital.[37] Putnam describes social capital as "features of social organizations such as networks, norms, and social trust that facilitate coordination and cooperation for mutual benefit." In that sense, social capital might be considered a means to certain positive civic ends and not an end in itself. Nevertheless, it is worth considering whether school choice and private schooling contribute to the social capital of those who avail themselves of it.

Four studies generate four findings regarding the effect of school choice on social capital (figure 10-5). Schneider and his colleagues examined the effects of choice in New York City and suburban New Jersey on parental self-reports of social capital.[38] They find that parents with school choices are 10–13 percent more likely to join a parent-teacher association, talk to other parents about school matters, and trust their child's teachers. Most of these effects are statistically significant beyond the 99 percent confidence level. Again, the major limitation of this study is the debatable quality of the techniques used to control for selection bias.

Greene, Giammo, and Mellow operationalized the concept of social capital by asking respondents to the Latino National Political Survey how many civic organizations they belonged to.[39] Controlling for socioeconomic status, age, gender, and country of origin, they find that Latinos who spent nine years in private school tend to belong to one more civic organization than do comparable Latinos who were educated exclusively in public schools. The positive effect of private schooling on this measure of social capital is statistically significant beyond the 95 percent confidence level, though it could be a product of one or more confounding factors that are not included in the analysis.

Coleman and Hoffer are the first researchers to examine whether private schooling enhanced social capital. James Coleman is credited with coining the phrase "social capital." In an assessment of the High School and Beyond survey, Coleman and Hoffer find that students who attended Catholic schools evidence higher levels of social capital, all else equal.[40] They include in their analysis the standard set of control variables for family background and individual demographics.

Peterson and Campbell sought to confirm Coleman and Hoffer's results in their randomized field trial of the national Children's Scholarship Fund private voucher program.[41] Although the parents of scholarship winners communicated more frequently with teachers than did the parents of students in the control group, there are no other significant differences in the social capital of parents in the randomly determined treatment versus control group.

Figure 10-5. *Distribution of Findings on Social Capital*

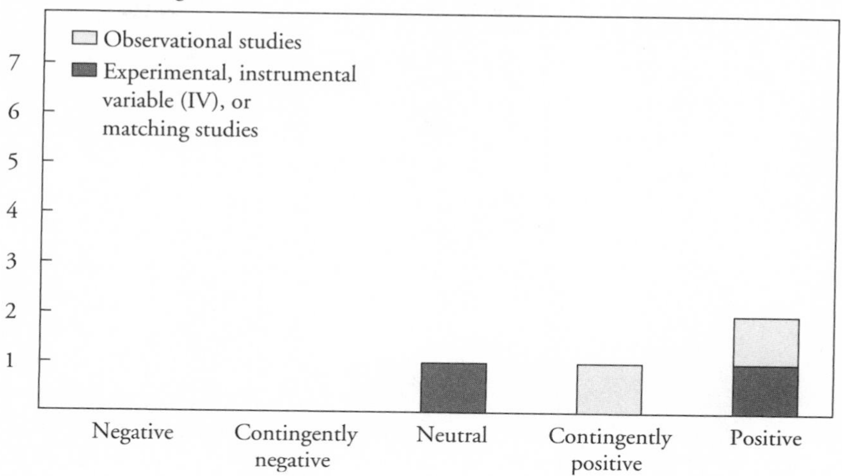

Studies of Political Participation

Another seldom studied question is the extent to which private schooling encourages political participation, with three studies producing four results regarding that question (figure 10-6). Greene, Giammo, and Mellow find that Latinos who received all of their K–12 education in private schools are 16 percent more likely to say that they voted in the last presidential election than are comparable Latinos who were educated exclusively in public schools.[42] The private school advantage for Latino political participation is statistically significant beyond the 99 percent confidence level. Again, the strength of this study is its national scope and automatic control for ethnicity. The weakness of the study is the possibility of uncontrolled selection bias and limits in the ability to generalize the results to adults of non-Latino ethnicity. Greene, Mellow, and Giammo also report a positive effect of private schooling on the political participation of Texas adults, regardless of their ethnicity.[43] They find that some exposure to private schooling increases the likelihood of voting by 9 percent, all else equal. Curiously, they find that Texans who received all of their education in private schools are no more likely to vote than their public school peers.

Smith and Sikkink also examined the relationship between private schools and homeschooling and parental political participation, using data from the

Figure 10-6. *Distribution of Findings on Political Participation*

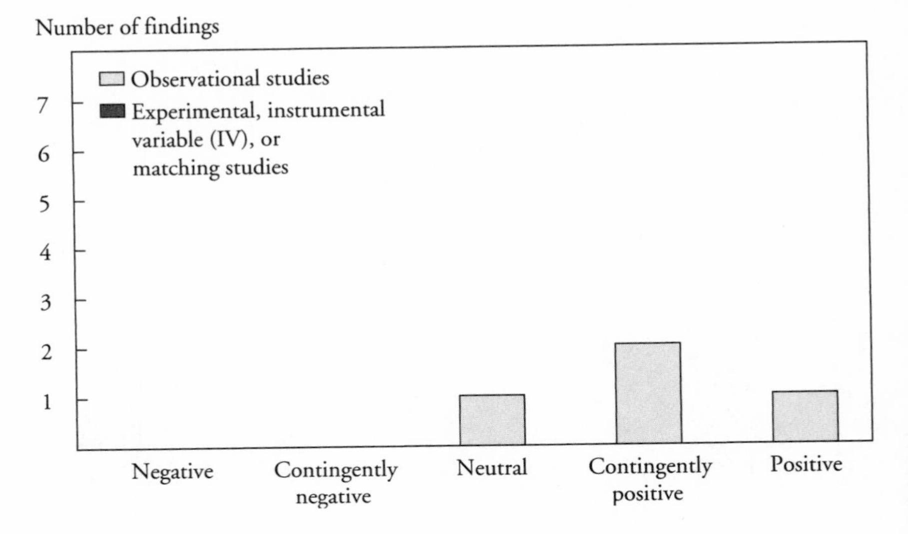

1996 National Household Education Survey.[44] Their results mirror those for voluntarism reported above. Parents who enroll their children in private religious schools or who homeschool them are more politically active than are otherwise comparable parents who enroll their children in public schools. Parents of students in private secular schools do not differ significantly from public school parents in their rates of political participation.

Studies of Civic Skills

Civic skills are the final element of democratic citizenship analyzed by Niemi, Hepburn, and Chapman and by Campbell in their studies of the 1996 National Household Education Survey. These two studies generated three diverse findings regarding the effect of school choice on civic skills (figure 10-7). The survey asked students, During this school year, have you done any of the following things in any class at your school:

—Written a letter to someone you did not know?

—Given a speech or an oral report?

—Taken part in a debate or discussion in which you had to persuade others about your point of view?[45]

Niemi, Hepburn, and Chapman report that students in private high schools are more likely to have engaged in these three activities, which are

Figure 10-7. *Distribution of Findings on Civic Skills*

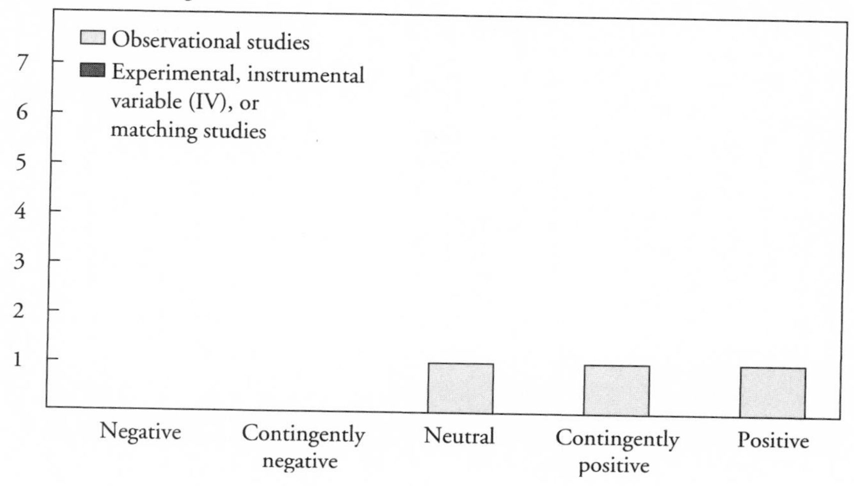

central to political efficacy, than are comparable students in public high schools.[46] The effects of private schooling on the probability of having given a speech or taken part in a debate are statistically significant; however, the effect on having written a letter appears to fall just short of statistical significance at conventional levels.

Campbell finds that students in Catholic schools score slightly higher (1.69) on an index of these three civic skills than do comparable students in assigned public schools (1.56).[47] Although substantively small, the difference is statistically significant beyond the 95 percent confidence level. No significant differences in civic skills were uncovered between students in assigned public schools and comparable students in non-Catholic private schools. However, Campbell does find that students in all three types of private school (Catholic, non-Catholic religious, and secular) indicate greater "confidence" in using their civic skills.

Studies of Patriotism

Finally, Wolf and his colleagues examined the average scores of the eighth-grade students in various types of New York City schools on an index of patriotism.[48] This represents the only known empirical study of the effect of school choice on patriotism and produced the lonely result displayed in figure 10-8.

Figure 10-8. *Distribution of Findings on Patriotism*

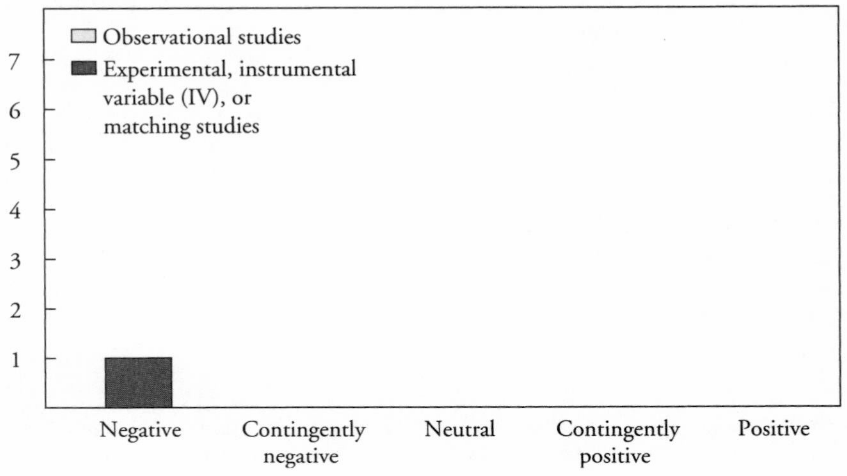

The patriotism index includes five questions about students' visceral attachment to their country and its symbols (such as the flag and the Pledge of Allegiance). The study reports that students in private schools score somewhat lower on patriotism, on average, than do comparable students in public schools. The size of the negative private school effect on patriotism is about one-quarter standard deviation and is statistically significant beyond the 99 percent confidence level. The report does not separate out religious from nonreligious private schools. However, being Catholic was a control variable in the analysis, and Catholicism displays a strong positive relationship to patriotism. The weaknesses of this analysis are its limitation to New York City schools and the fact that the patriotism scale employed (a scale well established in the psychology literature) could be interpreted as a measure not of true patriotism but of national chauvinism or jingoism.

The Catholic Schooling Effect

A close consideration of the studies reviewed above might lead one to surmise that Catholic schooling may be largely responsible for the generally positive school choice effects on civic values. A majority of students educated in private schools are in Catholic schools. Among the subset of religious private schools, Catholic schools dominate the field. Students who switched from public to private schools in the randomized field trials reviewed for this study primarily chose Catholic schools.[49] Privately schooled Latinos, who demonstrate significant advantages vis-à-vis publicly schooled Latinos in their levels of several civic values, are predominantly educated in Catholic schools. Thus the generally positive school choice effects on civic values outlined in figure 10-1 might be more properly characterized specifically as Catholic schooling effects. Several prominent scholars have made such claims in the past.[50]

If it is true that Catholic schools are the only schools of choice that outperform traditional public schools in promoting civic values, then the change in levels of citizenship preparation wrought by future expansions of school choice could be nil or even negative, should proportionately fewer new choosers select Catholic schools. Although highly speculative (recent expansions of school choice in urban settings have generated a veritable stampede to Catholic schools) this possibility is worth examining. What might happen if Catholic schools (and the Latinos who strongly prefer them) were entirely excluded from a program to expand school choice? Would the likely effects of choice on political tolerance, voluntarism, and other democratic values disappear or turn negative with Catholic schools out of the picture?

Figure 10-9 provides the findings from figure 10-1 excluding all results based on comparisons between public school populations and any private school population that includes Catholic schools or focuses exclusively on the experiences of Latinos. Only about half of the findings from figure 10-1 remain in figure 10-9, so figure 10-9 provides a sketchier portrait of the effects of school choice on civic values, since it deliberately excludes the most commonly studied school choice option. Nevertheless, we are still left with an approximately normally distributed set of results, which clusters in the neutral-to-positive range. Eight generally or contingently positive school choice results remain, suggesting that secular private schooling enhances political tolerance, that charter schooling increases voluntarism and social capital, and that education at an evangelical private school increases political knowledge. Eight findings indicate that school choice has no clear effect, positive or negative, when schools besides Catholic schools are chosen.

The three negative choice findings remain from the earlier figure, suggesting that evangelical Protestant schools reduce political tolerance, that secular private schools decrease voluntarism, and that private schooling of any sort may diminish a particularly passionate form of patriotism. Non-Catholic schools of choice seem to be responsible for the only negative effects of choice on civic values. However, non-Catholic schools of choice also appear to generate many positive outcomes regarding democratic values. These

Figure 10-9. *Distribution of Findings on All Civic Values, Excluding Catholic Schools and Hispanic Students*

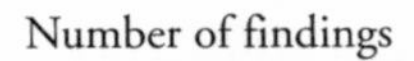

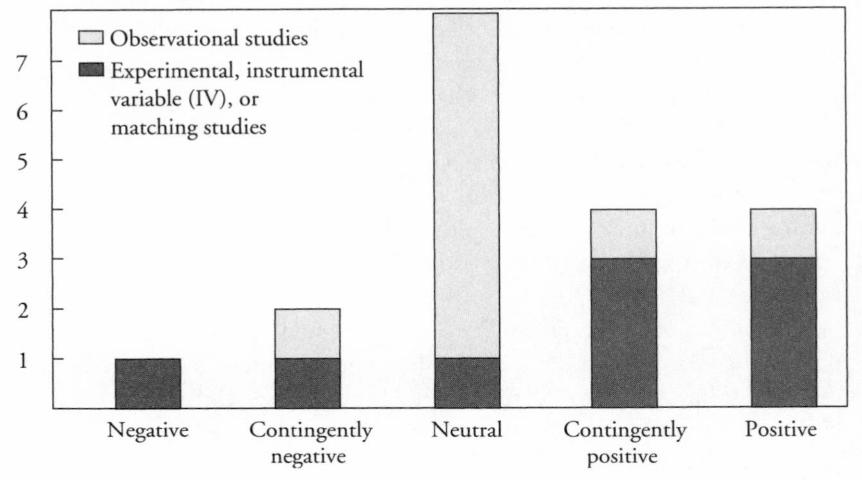

results suggest that the expansion of school choice is more likely to enhance than diminish the civic values of our next generation of citizens, even if *none* of the new choosers end up in communitarian infused Catholic schools.

Summary

The definitive study of the effects of private schooling and school choice on civic values remains to be completed. Although all of the studies reviewed here have a number of methodological strengths, they also all suffer from at least some empirical limitations. Moreover, the studies all draw upon data either about the various school sectors as they existed in the 1980s and 1990s or from modestly sized school voucher experiments. The demographic composition of the various school sectors and the independent effects of private schooling and school choice on the civic values reviewed here would likely change somewhat under a complete or even larger-scale school choice regime. Therefore, one should be cautious in drawing strong conclusions from the empirical record to date on school choice and civic values.

Nevertheless, there is a clear clustering of findings in the neutral-to-positive range, especially if results from Catholic schools and the populations that frequent them are included in the mix. The three negative choice effects uncovered all are based on empirical studies that lack random assignment. None of those three negative results has been replicated but several of the positive private school results have been. A large number (sixteen) of null findings are reported, at least one for six of the seven civic values considered. However, for every civic value studied, except patriotism, at least one empirical study reports that certain types of choice schools actually do a better job than public schools in fostering the skills and attitudes that are important to citizenship. Just as the three negative results reported should give us some pause and inform our deliberations about sound choice regulations, the twenty-nine positive results should inform us about the likely beneficial effects of greater school choice.

What aspects of choice schools generate the modestly positive civic values outcomes featured in this analysis? On that point, both the theoretical and empirical literatures require further development. Coleman and Hoffer, John Brandl, and others theorize that schools of choice foster stronger educational communities typified by regular parental involvement and a concern for the welfare of all members.[51] Schools of choice are voluntary associations where parents, students, and educators come together to pursue a shared enterprise. As Charles Glenn argues, "Schools that truly belong to the parents who send their children provide settings of unparalleled intensity for the development of the habits of responsible activity on the part of adults and children alike."[52] Some empirical evidence exists, outside of their own studies, confirming their claims about school choice and the nature of communities that it fosters. Specifically, a report from a major longitudinal evaluation of school choice indicates that parents become more involved in their child's school if they have selected it.[53] However, the three-city experimental evaluation of school voucher impacts led by Howell and Peterson reports mixed results regarding the effects of choice on parental involvement and social capital.[54] School choice may foster stronger civic values because of greater parental involvement, but it also may boost students' preparation for citizenship even while parental involvement remains unaffected.

If parental involvement and the resulting levels of social capital are not necessarily the cause of the general private schooling advantage regarding civic values, and if family background characteristics are largely eliminated as a cause for the outcomes analyzed in this study, then what else might explain these results? Teachers in private schools may be freer to infuse instruction with moral values.[55] Students who regularly encounter value-based claims and perspectives may become more tolerant of people with value-based positions that differ from their own. They also may feel more motivated to volunteer for activities that seek to bring about social and political change. Research in the Netherlands suggests that exposure to a value-rich educational environment is an important motive for parents to exercise school choice.[56] Belgium even provides government subsidies to "pluralistic" schools of choice that define their mission as producing "an open mind which acknowledges and respects diversity of opinions and attitudes, and which, despite this diversity, emphasizes common values."[57] Such claims remain highly speculative in the United States, however. Although most studies of school choice programs indicate that parents are more satisfied with the teaching of morality in their child's new private school, field-based studies have yet to confirm that the moral content of education in private schools differs markedly from that in public schools or to link any such differences specifically to positive civic values outcomes.[58]

Do schools of choice promote somewhat higher levels of civic values simply because they tend to be more effective schools? A certain level of sophistication may be necessary, particularly for political tolerance, which requires that the person distinguish between opposing a group's views while still allowing it to seek to advance those views in the public arena. Schools of choice may do a better job than assigned public schools in imparting the understandings and self-confidence necessary for a young person to make such a distinction. Again, the evidence is merely circumstantial. Students with strong academic abilities may tend to be more tolerant, and choice programs generally appear to have modest positive effects on students' academic achievement, although such findings remain contentious.

The most novel, and in my opinion most intriguing, explanation for the apparent school choice advantage in promoting civic values is tied to the generally higher levels of order and discipline in schools of choice. Public charter schools and private schools tend to be better ordered educational institutions than neighborhood public schools, especially in urban environments.[59] A well-ordered and nonthreatening educational environment likely contributes to students' feelings of security and confidence. Such feelings might be a necessary precondition for young people to develop a willingness to tolerate potentially disruptive political ideas and political groups and to venture out into the community to promote social causes, an idea suggested by Alan Peshkin in his case study of a Christian fundamentalist school.[60] Conversely, students who are educated in less safe and less predictable environments may develop strong fears of controversial political groups and ideas and hesitate to become involved in their communities or in political activities. By first establishing a safe and ordered educational environment for students, private and charter schools could unwittingly also be laying the foundation for students to become more engaged and tolerant citizens. Moreover, a physically safe and secure environment may be the most effective setting for highlighting value-rich moral discussions, which might be considered too explosive in less secure environments. I am not aware of any rigorous empirical field studies that clearly connect a well-ordered educational environment with stronger civic values. However, there is a clear theoretical justification for the link, and I hope that future studies will explore it.

Finally, the tendency of schools of choice to produce higher levels of civic values could be a consequence of self-selection. Unmeasured factors that lead parents to enroll their students in schools of choice, such as greater attentiveness to the quality of their education, could also be the main factors driving the positive civic values results of school choice. Twenty-one of the forty-eight results reported in the appendix are from studies that use random assignment, instrumental variable analysis, or matching techniques to control for such self-selection bias. Although a focus on only those results would yield a slightly more conservative conclusion regarding the positive effects of school choice on civic values, eleven of the twenty-one findings from the more sophisticated studies still suggest either contingently positive or generally positive choice effects on various civic outcomes. If self-selection bias were the primary cause of the positive results for schools of choice, then we would expect the distribution of results from the studies that attempt to control for such bias to differ more markedly from the results from the observational studies in the review. They do not. Self-selection bias cannot be ruled out conclusively as a factor in producing the results of this analysis. However, in theory, self-selection should be less of a danger regarding analyses of civic values outcomes than it is for studies of test-score impacts, since parental attentiveness to educational concerns is more clearly a cause of academic achievement than it is of citizenship preparation. The evidence largely confirms this view.

The fact that we cannot pinpoint the exact mechanisms that lead schools of choice generally to produce young adults with somewhat higher levels of civic values should not diminish the importance of what has been learned. At a minimum, the results of the empirical studies fail to confirm the fears of many opponents of choice who claim that private schooling inherently and inevitably undermines the fostering of civic values in a democracy. The statistical record thus far suggests that private schooling and school choice rarely harms and often enhances the realization of the civic values that are central to a well-functioning democracy. This seems to be the case particularly among ethnic minorities (such as Latinos), in places with great ethnic diversity (such as New York City and Texas), and when Catholic schools are the school of choice. Choice programs targeted to such constituencies seem to hold the greatest promise of enhancing the civic values of the next generation of American citizens.

Appendix: Effects of Choice on Seven Civic Values, Twenty Studies, Summary of Findings

Following is the list of studies that supported the findings in this chapter. The list is arranged by subject and category reflected in the figures. Those categories with no finding are not listed.

Experimental studies are shown in bold; studies using instrumental variables or matching are shown in italics.

Findings, Including Catholic Schools and Hispanic Students

1. Political tolerance

Contingently negative:
- Campbell (2002)

Neutral:
- **Howell and others (2002)**
- **West and others (2001)**
- **Peterson and others (2001)**
- *Godwin and others (2001)*
- *Campbell (2001a)*
- *Wolf and others (1998)*
- Campbell (2002)

Contingently positive:
- *Campbell (2001a)*
- *Godwin and others (2001)*
- *Wolf and others (1998)*
- Campbell (2002)
- Greene and others (1999b)

Positive:
- **Campbell (2002)**
- **Wolf and others (2001a)**
- Wolf and others (2001b)
- Niemi and others (2000)
- Greene and others (1999a)

2. Voluntarism

Contingently negative:
- *Wolf and others (1998)*

Neutral:
- Campbell (2002)
- Niemi and others (2000)
- Smith and Sikkink (1999)

Contingently positive:
- *Campbell (2001a)*
- *Wolf and others (1998)*
- Campbell (2002)
- Niemi and others (2000)
- Smith and Sikkink (1999)

Positive:
- *Godwin and Kemerer (2002)*
- *Schneider and others (1997)*
- Greene (1998)

3. Political knowledge

Neutral:
- **Peterson and Campbell (2002)**
- Campbell (2001b)
- Coleman and Hoffer (1987)

Contingently positive:
Campbell (2001b)
Positive:
Godwin and others (1999)
Niemi and others (2000)
4. Social capital
Neutral:
Peterson and Campbell (2001)
Contingently positive:
Coleman and Hoffer (1987)
Positive:
Schneider and others (1997)
Greene and others (1999a)
5. Political participation
Neutral:
Smith and Sikkink (1999)
Contingently positive:
Greene and others (1999b)
Smith and Sikkink (1999)
Positive:
Greene and others (1999a)
6. Civic skills
Neutral:
Campbell (2001b)
Contingently positive:
Campbell (2001b)
Positive:
Niemi and others (2000)
7. Patriotism
Negative:
Wolf and others (1998)

Findings, Excluding Catholic Schools and Hispanic Students

1. Political tolerance
Contingently negative:
Campbell (2002)
Neutral:
Campbell (2001a)
Campbell (2002)
Contingently positive:
Campbell (2001a)
Wolf and others (1998)
Campbell (2002)
Positive:
Wolf and others (2001b)
2. Voluntarism
Contingently negative:
Wolf and others (1998)
Neutral:
Campbell (2002)
Niemi and others (2000)
Smith and Sikkink (1999)
Contingently positive:
Campbell (2001a)
Positive:
Schneider and others (1997)
3. Political knowledge
Neutral:
Campbell (2001b)
Positive:
Godwin and others (1999)
4. Social capital
Positive:
Schneider and others (1997)
5. Political participation
Neutral:
Smith and Sikkink (1999)
6. Civic skills
Neutral:
Campbell (2001b)
7. Patriotism
Negative:
Wolf and others (1998)

Studies Cited

Campbell, David E. 2001a. "Making Democratic Education Work." In *Charters, Vouchers, and Public Education*, edited by Paul E. Peterson and David E. Campbell. Brookings.

———. 2001b. "Civic Education: Readying Massachusetts' Next Generation of Citizens." White Paper 17. Boston: Pioneer Institute for Public Policy Research.

———. 2002. "The Civic Side of School Reform: How Do School Vouchers Affect Civic Education?" Working Paper, April 16.

Coleman, James S., and Thomas Hoffer. 1987. *Public and Private High Schools: The Impact of Communities.* New York: Basic Books.

Godwin, R. Kenneth, and others. 1999. "Comparing Tolerance in Public, Private, and Evangelical Schools." Working Paper. Center for the Study of Education Reform, University of North Texas. Available at www.coe.unt.edu/cser.

Godwin, R. Kenneth, Carrie Ausbrooks, and Valerie Martinez. 2001. "Teaching Tolerance in Public and Private Schools." *Phi Delta Kappan* (March): 542–46.

Godwin, R. Kenneth, and Frank R. Kemerer. 2002. *School Choice Tradeoffs: Liberty, Equity, and Diversity.* University of Texas Press.

Greene, Jay P. 1998. "Civic Values in Public and Private Schools." In *Learning from School Choice*, edited by Paul E. Peterson and Bryan C. Hassel. Brookings.

Green, Jay P., Joseph Giammo, and Nicole Mellow. 1999a. "The Effect of Private Education on Political Participation, Social Capital, and Tolerance: An Examination of the Latino National Political Survey." *Georgetown Public Policy Review* 5, no. 1: 53–67.

Greene, Jay P., Nicole Mellow, and Joseph Giammo. 1999b. "Private Schools and the Public Good: The Effect of Private Education on Political Participation and Tolerance in the Texas Poll." *Catholic Education* (June): 429–43.

Howell, William G., and Paul E. Peterson, with Patrick J. Wolf and David E. Campbell. 2002. *The Education Gap: Vouchers and Urban Schools.* Brookings.

Niemi, Richard G., Mary A. Hepburn, and Chris Chapman. 2000. "Community Service by High School Students: A Cure for Civic Ills?" *Political Behavior* 23, no. 1: 45–69.

Peterson, Paul E., and David E. Campbell. 2001. "An Evaluation of the Children's Scholarship Fund." Working Paper 01-03. Program on Education Policy and Governance, Harvard University.

Peterson, Paul E., David E. Campbell, and Martin R. West. 2001. "An Evaluation of the Basic Fund Scholarship." Program on Education Policy and Governance, Harvard University.

Schneider, Mark, and others. 1997. "Institutional Arrangements and the Creation of Social Capital: The Effects of Public School Choice." *American Political Science Review* 91, no. 1: 82–93.

Smith, Christian, and David Sikkink. 1999. "Is Private Schooling Privatizing?" *First Things* 92 (April): 16–20.

West, Martin R., Paul E. Peterson, and David E. Campbell. 2001. "School Choice in Dayton, Ohio, after Two Years: An Evaluation of the Parents Advocating Choice in Education Scholarship Program." Working Paper 01-04. Program on Education Policy and Governance, Harvard University.

Wolf, Patrick J., and others. 1998. "Democratic Values in New York City Schools." Report of the Workshop in Applied Policy Analysis, School of International and Public Affairs, Columbia University.

Wolf, Patrick J., Paul E. Peterson, and Martin R. West. 2001a. "Results of a School Voucher Experiment: The Case of Washington, D.C., after Two Years." Working Paper 01-05. Program on Education Policy and Governance, Harvard University.

Wolf, Patrick J., and others. 2001b. "Private Schooling and Political Tolerance." In *Charters, Vouchers, and Public Education*, edited by Paul E. Peterson and David E. Campbell. Brookings.

Notes

1. See Benjamin Rush, "A Plan for the Establishment of Public Schools and the Diffusion of Knowledge in Pennsylvania; To Which Are Added, Thoughts upon the Mode of Education, Proper in a Republic. Addressed to the Legislature and Citizens of the State," in *Essays on Education in the Early Republic,* edited by Frederick Rudolph (Belknap Press, 1965); John Dewey, *Democracy and Education* (New York: Macmillan, 1963 [1916]); Benjamin Barber, *A Place for Us* (New York: Hill and Wang, 1998); Amy Gutmann, *Democratic Education* (Princeton University Press, 1987); Eamonn Callon, *Creating Citizens: Political Education and Liberal Democracy* (Oxford: Clarendon Press, 1997); and Stephen Macedo, *Diversity and Distrust: Civic Education in a Multicultural Democracy* (Harvard University Press, 2000).

2. Richard W. Riley, "What Really Matters in American Education," white paper prepared for U.S. Secretary of Education Richard W. Riley for speech given at the National Press Club, Washington, September 23 1997 (www.ed.gov/Speeches/09-1997/matters.pdf).

3. See Thomas Paine, "The Rights of Man, Part II," in *Political Writings,* edited by Bruce Kuklick (Cambridge University Press, 1989), p. 145; Alexis de Tocqueville, *Democracy in America,* edited by J. P. Mayer (New York: Harper and Row, 1969); and John Stuart Mill, *Utilitarianism, On Liberty, Essay on Bentham: Together with Selected Writings of Jeremy Bentham and John Austin,* edited by Mary Warnock (New York: New American Library, 1974), pp. 238–41.

4. Charles Leslie Glenn, *The Myth of the Common School* (University of Massachusetts Press, 1988).

5. Jay P. Greene and Nicole Mellow, "Integration Where It Counts," *Texas Education Review* 1, no. 1 (2000) (www.educationreview.homestead.com/integration.html).

6. Anthony S. Bryk, Valerie E. Lee, and Peter Holland, *Catholic Schools and the Common Good* (Harvard University Press, 1993); Stephen Gilles, "On Educating Children: A Parentalist Manifesto," *University of Chicago Law Review* 63 (Summer 1996): 937–1034.

7. Macedo, *Diversity and Distrust,* p. 234.

8. Robert Putnam, quoted in David E. Campbell, "Making Democratic Education Work," in *Charters, Vouchers, and Public Education,* edited by Paul E. Peterson and David E. Campbell (Brookings, 2001), p. 245.

9. William G. Howell and Paul E. Peterson, with Patrick J. Wolf and David E. Campbell, *The Education Gap: Vouchers and Urban Schools* (Brookings, 2002), pp. 39–43.

10. For example see American Institute for Research, "Executive Summary," in *Evaluation of the Magnet Schools Assistance Program, 1998 Grantees: Final Report* (www.ed.gov/print/rschstat/eval/choice/magneteval/finalexecsum.html [August 8, 2004]).

11. See John L. Sullivan, James Pierson, and George E. Marcus, *Political Tolerance and American Democracy* (University of Chicago Press, 1982); and George E. Marcus and others,

With Malice towards Some: How People Make Civil Liberties Judgments (Cambridge University Press, 1995).

12. Jay P. Greene, Joseph Giammo and Nicole Mellow, "The Effect of Private Education on Political Participation, Social Capital, and Tolerance: An Examination of the Latino National Political Survey," *Georgetown Public Policy Review* 5, no. 1 (1999): 53–71.

13. Patrick J. Wolf, Paul E. Peterson, and Martin R. West, "Results of a School Voucher Experiment: The Case of Washington, D.C., after Two Years," Working Paper 01-05 (Program on Education Policy and Governance, Harvard University, 2001).

14. David E. Campbell, "The Civic Side of School Reform: How Do School Vouchers Affect Civic Education?" Working Paper, University of Notre Dame, April 16, 2002.

15. Patrick J. Wolf and others, "Private Schooling and Political Tolerance," in *Charters, Vouchers, and Public Education,* edited by Paul E. Peterson and David E. Campbell (Brookings, 2001).

16. Richard G. Niemi, Mary A. Hepburn, and Chris Chapman, "Community Service by High School Students: A Cure for Civic Ills?" *Political Behavior* 22, no. 1 (2002): 45–69.

17. Patrick J. Wolf and others, "Democratic Values in New York City Schools," Report of the Workshop in Applied Policy Analysis (School of International and Public Affairs, Columbia University 1998).

18. R. Kenneth Godwin, Carrie Ausbrooks, and Valerie Martinez, "Teaching Tolerance in Public and Private Schools," *Phi Delta Kappan* (March 2001), pp. 542–46.

19. Campbell, "The Civic Side of School Reform."

20. David E. Campbell, "Civic Education: Readying Massachusetts' Next Generation of Citizens," White Paper 17 (Boston: Pioneer Institute for Public Policy Research, 2001) (www.pioneer.org).

21. Jay P. Greene, Nicole Mellow, and Joseph Giammo, "Private Schools and the Public Good: The Effect of Private Education on Political Participation and Tolerance in the Texas Poll," *Catholic Education* (June 1999), pp. 429–43.

22. Howell and Peterson, *The Education Gap;* Martin R. West, Paul E. Peterson, and David E. Campbell, "School Choice in Dayton, Ohio, after Two Years: An Evaluation of the Parents Advocating Choice in Education Scholarship Program," Working Paper 01-04 (Program on Education Policy and Governance, Harvard University, 2001); and Paul E. Peterson, David E. Campbell, and Martin R. West, "An Evaluation of the Basic Fund Scholarship Program in the San Francisco Area, California," Working Paper 01-01 (Program on Education Policy and Governance, Harvard University, 2001).

23. Jay P. Greene, "Civic Values in Public and Private Schools," in *Learning from School Choice,* edited by Paul E. Peterson and Bryan C. Hassel (Brookings, 1998).

24. R. Kenneth Godwin and Frank R. Kemerer, *School Choice Tradeoffs: Liberty, Equity, and Diversity* (University of Texas Press, 2002).

25. Mark Schneider and others, "Institutional Arrangements and the Creation of Social Capital: The Effects of Public School Choice," *American Political Science Review* 91, no. 1 (1997): 82–93.

26. Wolf and others, "Democratic Values in New York City Schools."

27. Niemi, Hepburn, and Chapman, "Community Service by High School Students."

28. Campbell, "The Civic Side of School Reform."

29. Campbell, "Civic Education."

30. Christian Smith and David Sikkink, "Is Private Schooling Privatizing?" *First Things* 92 (April 1999): 16–20.

31. Michael Delli Carpini and Scott Keeler, *What Americans Know about Politics and Why It Matters* (Yale University Press, 1996).

32. Godwin and Kemerer, *School Choice Tradeoffs*. The unpublished study that they discuss is R. Kenneth Godwin and others, "Comparing Tolerance in Public, Private, and Evangelical Schools," Working Paper (Center for the Study of Education Reform, University of North Texas, 1999) (www.coe.unt.edu/cser).

33. Godwin and others, "Comparing Tolerance."

34. Niemi, Hepburn, and Chapman, "Community Service by High School Students."

35. Campbell, "Making Democratic Education Work."

36. Paul E. Peterson and David E. Campbell, "An Evaluation of the Children's Scholarship Fund," Working Paper 01-03 (Program on Education Policy and Governance, Harvard University, 2001); James S. Coleman and Thomas Hoffer, *Public and Private High Schools: The Impact of Communities* (New York: Basic Books, 1987).

37. Robert D. Putnam, *Bowling Alone: The Collapse and Revival of American Community* (New York: Simon and Schuster, 2000); Robert D. Putnam, "Bowling Alone: America's Declining Social Capital," *Journal of Democracy*, 1, no. 6 (1995): 65–78; Robert D. Putnam, *Making Democracy Work: Civic Traditions in Modern Italy* (Princeton University Press, 1993).

38. Schneider and others, "Institutional Arrangements and the Creation of Social Capital."

39. Greene, Giammo, and Mellow, "The Effect of Private Education."

40. Coleman and Hoffer, *Public and Private High Schools*.

41. Peterson and Campbell, "An Evaluation of the Children's Scholarship Fund."

42. Greene, Giammo, and Mellow, "The Effect of Private Education."

43. Greene, Mellow, and Giammo, "Private Schools and the Public Good."

44. Smith and Sikkink, "Is Private Schooling Privatizing?"

45. Campbell, "Making Democratic Education Work," p. 251.

46. Niemi, Hepburn, and Chapman, "Community Service by High School Students."

47. Campbell, "Making Democratic Education Work."

48. Wolf and others, "Democratic Values in New York City Schools."

49. Although a mere majority (53 percent) of participants in the Children's Scholarship Fund program switched to Catholic schools, 72 percent of the participants in Washington, 77 percent of the participants in Dayton, and 84 percent of the participants in New York City selected Catholic schools (see Howell and Peterson, *The Education Gap*, p. 37).

50. Coleman and Hoffer, *Public and Private High Schools;* Bryk, Lee, and Holland, *Catholic Schools and the Common Good.*

51. Coleman and Hoffer, *Public and Private High Schools;* John E. Brandl, *Money and Good Intentions Are Not Enough* (Brookings, 1998); Bryk, Lee, and Holland, *Catholic Schools and the Common Good.*

52. Charles Leslie Glenn, "School Choice as a Question of Design," in *Educating Citizens: International Perspectives on Civic Values and School Choice,* edited by Patrick J. Wolf and Stephen Macedo, with David J. Ferrero and Charles E. Venegoni (Brookings, 2004).

53. Stacey Bielick and Christopher Chapman, *Trends in the Use of School Choice, 1993 to 1999: Statistical Analysis Report,* National Center for Education Statistics (no. 2003-031) (Institute for Education Sciences, U.S. Department of Education, 2003), table 7.

54. Howell and Peterson, *The Education Gap,* pp. 114–39.

55. See Lee H. Ehman, "The American School in the Political Socialization Process," *Review of Educational Research* 50 (1980): 99–119; Gutmann, *Democratic Education,* p. 65; Quentin L. Quade, *Financing Education: The Struggle between Governmental Monopoly and Parental Control* (New Brunswick, N.J.: Transaction, 1996).

56. See for example Anne Bert Dijkstra, Jaap Dronkers and Sjoerd Karsten, "Private Schools as Public Provision for Education: School Choice and Marketization in the Netherlands," in *Educating Citizens: International Perspectives on Civic Values and School Choice,* edited by Patrick J. Wolf and Stephen Macedo, with David J. Ferrero and Charles E. Venegoni (Brookings, 2004).

57. Jan De Groof, "Regulating School Choice in Belgium's Flemish Community," in *Educating Citizens: International Perspectives on Civic Values and School Choice,* edited by Patrick J. Wolf and Stephen Macedo, with David J. Ferrero and Charles E. Venegoni (Brookings, 2004), p. 172.

58. For example, see John F. Witte, *The Market Approach to Education* (Princeton University Press, 2000); Howell and Peterson, *The Education Gap,* p. 173.

59. See, for example, Howell and Peterson, *The Education Gap;* and Witte, *The Market Approach to Education.*

60. Alan Peshkin, *God's Choice: The Total World of a Fundamentalist Christian School* (University of Chicago Press, 1986).

Contributors

Julian R. Betts
University of California, San Diego

Brian Gill
RAND

Dan Goldhaber
University of Washington

Kacey Guin
University of Washington

Laura S. Hamilton
RAND

Jeffrey R. Henig
Teachers College
Columbia University

Frederick M. Hess
American Enterprise Institute

Tom Loveless
Brookings Institution

Larry Rosenstock
High Tech High (San Diego)

Karen E. Ross
University of Michigan

Janet A. Weiss
University of Michigan

Patrick J. Wolf
Georgetown University

Index

THE BROOKINGS INSTITUTION

The Brookings Institution is a private nonprofit organization devoted to research, education, and publication on important issues of domestic and foreign policy. Its principal purpose is to bring the highest quality independent research and analysis to bear on current and emerging policy problems. The Institution was founded on December 8, 1927, to merge the activities of the Institute for Government Research, founded in 1916, the Institute of Economics, founded in 1922, and the Robert Brookings Graduate School of Economics and Government, founded in 1924. Interpretations or conclusions in Brookings publications should be understood to be solely those of the authors.